The
Ultimate
Entrepreneur

The
Ultimate
Entrepreneur

The Story of Ken Olsen and Digital Equipment Corporation

Glenn Rifkin and George Harrar

CB

CONTEMPORARY
BOOKS

CHICAGO · NEW YORK

Library of Congress Cataloging-in-Publication Data

Rifkin, Glenn.
    The ultimate entrepreneur : the story of Ken Olsen and Digital
Equipment Corporation / Glenn Rifkin and George Harrar.
       p.   cm.
    Includes index.
    ISBN 0-8092-4559-0
    1. Olsen, Kenneth H.   2. Industrialists—United States—
Biography.   3. Digital Equipment Corporation—History.
4. Computer industry—United States—History.   I. Harrar,
George.   II. Title.
HD9696.C62O487   1988
338.7'61004'0924—dc19
[B]   88-23616
                                             CIP

Material from *The Change Masters* copyright © 1983 by Rosabeth
Moss Kanter reprinted by permission of Simon & Schuster, Inc.

Material from *Organizational Culture and Leadership: A Dynamic
View* copyright © 1985 by Edgar Schein reprinted by permission of
Jossey-Bass Inc., Publishers, San Francisco.

Material from *Culture in Organizations: A Case Study and Analysis*
(Working Paper 1279-82) copyright © 1982 by W. Gibb Dyer
reprinted by permission of M.I.T. Sloan School of Management.

To my father, whose spirit endures; to my mother, sisters, and brother; and to my wife, Deborah, most of all.

—GR

To my father and mother; and to my wife and personal editor, Linda.

—GH

Contents

Acknowledgments

WE GRATEFULLY ACKNOWLEDGE the following people for valuable contributions to this book: Contemporary Books Editor in Chief Bernie Shir-Cliff; our agent at Waterside Productions, Bill Gladstone; *Computerworld* newspaper and its editor, Bill Laberis; David Kluchman, Kelly Shea, Nancy Linde, Amiel Korniel, Jim Bartimo, Lisa Figlioli, and Bill Nussbaum. And a deserved scratch under the chin to Fluffy and Tiffany.

Preface

KEN OLSEN DIDN'T want this book written. He sent a polite, but firm, memo for distribution to all 120,000 employees urging them not to cooperate with us. He said that a book on him and Digital Equipment Corporation would not contribute to the company's goals. DEC, the memo said, would turn away all authors proposing books.

As journalists who have followed Olsen and DEC since 1983, we knew there was more to the lack of cooperation than that. Olsen is a private man despite his public achievement, the rare business leader who avoids, rather than seeks, the spotlight. He feels toward his computer company like a father to his family. Words that question or perhaps disparage DEC's performance hurt him personally.

Three decades of corporate history cannot be written without showing some of the scratches and the scars. Olsen's recollections gloss over the wounds that DEC has suffered along the way to becoming an $11 billion company, and his memory sometimes diminishes the role of those who have chosen to leave him. If he can't write DEC's story as he sees it, then, Olsen believes, the story is better left unwritten.

It was difficult for many working at DEC, especially long-time executives, to refrain from talking to us. And so some did talk. They are proud of their company and of Olsen. They understood that the book would get written with or without DEC's formal cooperation. We had years worth of material—interviews, profiles, facts, and figures—to draw on from our coverage of DEC as editors at *Computerworld* newspaper. We had talked to every key executive, including Olsen, on many occasions.

What we pieced together is a story of an American entrepreneur with no counterpart in style or substance. Olsen shares some characteristics, such as fierce determination and a clear vision of the marketplace, with many successful businesspeople. But he is also an astonishing mix of idiosyncrasies, values, beliefs, and contradictions.

He is infinitely Digital. His story and the story of his company cannot be separated. Therefore, this profile can as yet have no conclusion. Olsen continues to amuse, confound, surprise, shock, and cast an unmistakable mark on American business.

Glenn Rifkin
George Harrar

August 1988
Wayland, Massachusetts

"Success is probably the worst problem for an entrepreneur."

—*Ken Olsen*

The
Ultimate
Entrepreneur

"One company, one strategy, one message."
                                    —Ken Olsen

1
The Entrepreneur

THE WARM SEPTEMBER sun played on the waters of Boston Harbor. Packs of businessmen and women strolled along the concrete pier toward the World Trade Center. The ship stopped them all in midconversation, looming before them like a colossal movie set dreamed up in Hollywood.

Digital Equipment Corporation wanted fanfare, excitement. It was putting on the business event of the year—perhaps of the last five years—and the massive *Queen Elizabeth II* was the perfect symbol. For this one moment, DEC shucked its longtime cloak of anonymity and climbed brazenly into the spotlight.

They called it DECworld, a single company exposition designed to show off the might of the second most powerful company in the computer world. True to its name, it was a world unto itself. Boats, planes, helicopters, buses, and limousines criss-crossed Boston, bringing 50,000 people to the World Trade Center to see DEC's product line and hear DEC's message.

The *QEII* and the *Oceanic*, the world's two largest cruise ships, sat docked amid the $1 million pilings DEC had hastily built to accommodate them. The ships were a glitzy, yet practical, solution to the lack of hotel rooms. Boston had never hosted a conference so big.

The night before the opening, DEC held a kick-off dinner for employees. When Ken Olsen, DEC's founder and president, was introduced, the 3,000 dinner guests rose to their feet and thunderously applauded for ten minutes. Shy and awkward even in small groups, Olsen was taken aback. He let the wave of affection wash over him and then stepped forward and said, "This is for you. You did all this."

The next morning in Anthony's Pier Four restaurant, Olsen strode to the podium to officially open DECworld. A bear of a man, with a broad forehead, deep-set penetrating eyes, and large strong hands, he gripped the sides of the podium and stared out at the packed room. Here were the financial analysts, consultants, and reporters who had written his business obituary just three years earlier. Those were the days of flux and disharmony when the walls were caving in on him—when profits dove and executives fled the company by the dozen.

The press and analysts now waiting for him to speak had wielded the pickaxes and sledgehammers that shook the foundation. Olsen recalled these hard times. "We were in the middle of changing our dream, our mission, and the world wasn't ready to accept it. The world is ready to accept it now." Then he grinned broadly, a smile that stretched toward vindication.

DECworld in 1987 marked the thirtieth anniversary of the day Olsen first opened the doors of his company. The show was the perfect party for a practical man—celebrate but keep selling.

No other American corporation has taken the risk and marshalled the resources to put on such a business extravaganza. DEC spent $30 to $40 million to run the show and expects to earn over time up to $2 billion in orders because of it.

DECworld signaled to the vast computer industry, so long dominated by giant IBM, that for now DEC was the story.

It is in only the second half of this decade that the American business world began to hear the story of Kenneth Harry Olsen and Digital Equipment Corporation. From his headquarters in Maynard, Massachusetts, he has become "America's Most Successful Entrepreneur," according to an October 1986 *Fortune* magazine article. In the cover photograph, his broad face grins out from under an old fishing hat.

For nearly thirty years, Olsen worked in virtual obscurity, quietly building the infrastructure of a computing empire. He emerged in the mid-1980s as a corporate hero, a modern-era Henry Ford, outperforming more famous media personalities such as H. Ross Perot, Sam Walton, and Armand Hammer to earn *Fortune*'s seal as the ultimate entrepreneur.

Olsen and cofounder Harlan Anderson created Digital in 1957. But not until 1985, after surviving a three-year crisis, did the company become the second most powerful force in the highly competitive computer industry.

Just one-sixth the size of IBM, DEC turboed past a startled Big Blue in hundreds of large accounts. VAX computers were the engine of this surge. By 1988, DEC had become an $11 billion company, the thirty-eighth largest industrial in the Fortune 500 and the thirteenth most profitable.

Olsen won't admit that there is vindication in DEC's current performance, but he often refers to those days in 1983 when the media labeled him too old, too insular, too conservative. The call was out for him to resign. He should step aside gracefully, the critics said, let someone else steer the company into the 1990s. It appeared that he had contracted the inevitable entrepreneurial illness, Founder's Disease. The company seemed to be growing too big for him, too out of control for this MIT engineer. By 1983, he had brought his enterprise further than almost any other entrepreneur. But then he hit the wall.

His company was being battered by product failures, administrative ineptitude, and executive defections. The media attacked. But Olsen stood strong when the crisis came in 1983. He had not yet reached sixty years old, and he was not ready to turn over his company. His vision sharpened, his message crystallized: Digital would be one company following one strategy.

Olsen describes himself as the Christian and the scientist, searching for truth and humility in both his personal and business lives. He manages to be simultaneously flexible and unwavering—flexible in the smaller arenas of decision-making, unwavering in setting direction, policy, and tradition. He is the democrat who has given up great personal control of this sprawling organization of 120,000 employees. But he is also the autocrat who has maintained his power as the final word and has never named a clear second-in-command.

Olsen has become the main character in uncounted legends at DEC. Everyone has a favorite "Ken" story to tell you.

There is the time a new employee, startled to see a lumbering man clad in a flannel shirt, old pants, and work boots in DEC's Mill on a Saturday, mistook Olsen for a janitor.

There are "Ken" sightings: sandbagging a DEC facility that was threatened by flood, disappearing into a hole to inspect a broken pipe, buying a toilet seat at Maynard Hardware Supply, browsing through the appliance and tool departments at Lechmere's department store just to see the latest industrial designs.

There are the exaggerations: Olsen chainsawing eight inches off a PDP-10 computer to demonstrate the size of box he wanted. Or wandering inadvertently into an office where two DEC employees were engaged in a furious sexual encounter and immediately ordering that, henceforth, all doors in the Mill would have windows.

There are the facts that mix tantalizingly with fiction: that Olsen came within two weeks of selling his company to AT&T for $5 billion in the early 1980s, withdrawing from the deal when he could not ensure roles for his top executives; that Apple's Steve Jobs visited Maynard, put his boots up on Olsen's desk, and taunted him about DEC's failure in personal computers.

There are the tall tales: Olsen buying one of the first digital watches, hopping into a taxi, and taking the watch apart and putting it back together before he arrived at the airport. Olsen laughs at that one. "I've never been able to put a digital watch back together after taking it apart," he says. "And besides, I never took them apart until they cost $6."

The picture of the man is painted from stories here, observations there—a collage or impressionist work more than a realist's rendering. Consensus comes on a list of adjectives: he is honest, decent, religious, paternal, stubborn, intuitive, commanding, charismatic.

He is the gentle soul, finding pleasure in identifying the wildflowers growing outside the Mill, tending his backyard garden, helping his wife, Aulikki, choose vegetables at a local farmstand, caring for his ninety-year-old mother.

He is the simple man, unadorned by his wealth, estimated in mid-1988 to be $280 million in DEC stock alone. Olsen drives a Ford van, which succeeded his Ford Pinto. He sits on the board of directors of Ford Motor Company, of course, but even before assuming this role he was embarrassed to be seen in his wife's Mercedes. His favorite car: the 1963 Ford Falcon, because of its simplicity and ease of maintenance.

He is the outdoorsman, flying off to the wilds of northern Maine at the controls of his single-engine prop plane for two weeks of canoeing with old pals, and tramping through the woods near his cabin on Governor's Island in New Hampshire, with DEC executives striding to keep up during his regular "Woods meetings."

He is the antagonist, interrupting a young vice president in midsentence during an Operations Committee meeting, handing him his flip charts, and dismissing him with a terse "Don't waste any more of our time."

"Ken has many, many faces," says Gordon Bell, the master architect of Digital's computer lines. "He was different from day to day."

From Olsen's office flows a river of memos, some dictating, some instructing, some complaining about his lack of finding anyone to accept responsibility. Often he sends parables out over DEC's vast electronic network, stories about buying a backhoe or fighting the Civil War or putting together a jigsaw puzzle. And often his employees are left wondering just what Ken means this time.

Olsen, an engineer dressed in the role of a business leader, is disarmingly different from the model of a corporate CEO. He is unexpectedly candid while answering questions at product announcements, often throwing out offhand comments that bring puzzled smiles to the faces of reporters and analysts and grimaces from nearby DEC public relations people. "You know," he told a press gathering not long ago, "I inadvertently told you all about a new product yesterday, but no one noticed. So I'm not going to tell you what it is today." Or when asked why DEC was closing off to third-party developers a once-open protocol, he replied, "I don't remember why we did it differently the first time around. It was stupid."

He can be boring in his public voice, repeating stories about DEC's origins and the roots of interactive computing. His vice presidents sit apparently attentive as he speaks, but they'll tell you they've heard it all before. When Olsen launches into DEC history, one can sense their minds fleeing the room en masse, like schoolchildren let out for recess.

But suddenly comes an offhand remark, a charming image, a touch of unexpected humor. "Did I tell you people about the telephone?" he asked at a recent product introduction. "Well, it used to be pretty simple. You'd pick up the phone and the operator would come on. Now, depending on the hour of the day, she knew who you wanted to talk to. At that time of night, it was your mother. If you made a mistake, the operator would correct it, and you'd talk to your mother. Nowadays, you dial ten digits, but if you get the last one wrong, you don't get your mother. It's unforgiving."

At times he verges on an embarrassing moment but then saves himself: "Now I'd like to introduce Pete Smith to tell you about the new machines. Pete is vice president of . . . of . . . hmmm. Pete Smith is vice president." And the audience laughs with him.

He claims not to read anything written about him, though his public relations people dispute him. When he first appeared on the cover of a national business publication in the mid-1970s, a DEC marketing manager ran into his office with a stack of the magazines. "Look at this. Now you can send one to your third-grade teacher who said you'd never amount to anything."

Olsen replied, "I'm not going to read them."

"You're kidding," the young manager said.

"Two things could happen," Olsen explained. "What if I dislike the article? Should I write a letter to the editor? Or what if I say that is really me? Are you going to like dealing with someone who believes all that?"

Few business associates get close to Ken Olsen. Ever the puritan, he doesn't drink, smoke, or swear. He avoids social gatherings and remains personally distant from even his senior vice presidents.

Though he keeps his distance socially, Olsen is "Ken" to DEC employees around the world. Despite his egalitarian tendencies, the words "Ken wants it" are enough to get something done quickly in any plant or cubicle.

Olsen is the patriarch of his massive corporate family, and he brings both the love and torment of father-child relationships to Digital. He offers little open praise inside DEC to his executives but can scold them before their peers with an acid tongue. In thirty-one years of paternal grace and scorn, he has touched people's lives beyond their careers, taking some to their summit, bringing others to emotional ruin.

Despite and because of him, Olsen's company has taken on a pulsating life of its own. Digital is his story but, at the same time, the story of a company of engineers who created the $30 billion worldwide minicomputer industry.

Olsen planted the rows of seeds—honesty, integrity, profit, quality, doing what is right—the elements of a progressive work environment. DEC regularly ranks high on the annual "best-of" lists as a place to work for all, including minorities and women.

Like its founder, DEC is a body of contradictions. The traditions of hierarchical management that frame much of corporate America are absent here. The bases of power ebb and flow at DEC. Committees flourish for a time and then suddenly die off. Meetings spawn more meetings, which generate even more meetings as managers work each other toward consensus. Nothing gets done at DEC until there is consensus. There is no handholding, no indoctrination in the "DEC way," no road map to internal success. New managers are sent off on their own to find their way through the web of DEC's matrix management structure.

Digital continues to be an environment in search of itself. The famed matrix, which earned praise from the authors of *In Search of Excellence* in 1982, has been tempered by the new philosophy of "One Company, One Strategy, One Message."

While struggling to come to terms with its own enormity, DEC has tried to retain positive ties to the past—when power and responsibility were there for the taking, when risks were more encouraged and idiosyncrasies more readily tolerated. Today Digital is big business and growing bigger, with the heart of a long-distance entrepreneur beating inside it.

"We will make a profit the first year."

—Ken Olsen

2

The Enterprise

IT WOULD TURN out to be a $5 billion decision.

When thirty-one-year-old Ken Olsen stood in front of the senior officers of American Research & Development in the summer of 1957, he needed cash to finance his ambition. It was the onset of the commercial computing age, and Olsen wanted to build computers. But in order to get even $70,000 of capital investment, he was being asked to give ARD a 70 percent interest in his new company.

Olsen and his partner, twenty-eight-year-old Harlan Anderson, were fresh from the electrified environs of MIT's Lincoln Laboratory. Ideas were the currency in this research lab, where the computer age was being soldered and cabled together by hundreds of young engineers. They understood circuits and diodes and the transistors just being invented. But they were ignorant of the accounting, personnel, management, and production skills that could translate ideas into a successful company. They were engineers, not businessmen.

Despite the break-through technology that emerged from building the revolutionary Whirlwind and SAGE computers at

Lincoln Lab, the business world generally scoffed at academic researchers or, worse, ignored them. Olsen bristled at the disregard of his work and saw with Anderson an opportunity to cash in. In that outside commercial world, IBM was putting its million-dollar computers behind glass walls, out of reach of individual users. That notion of computing infuriated Olsen. He believed in the interaction of man and machine—interactive computing.

Nobody cares what I'm doing, he realized. That's what was missing in research. He was happy enough at MIT—after all, he could just about talk his way into getting any money he needed for whatever project he wanted to pursue. But writing papers on interactive computers and even building research computers was no achievement when people were laughing or shrugging. If he was to make a contribution to society, if he wanted to turn his ideas into products people could use, he needed a company.

The thought of starting a business was not new to Olsen. A year earlier, five engineers from inside and outside Lincoln Lab had asked him to join a prospective venture as chief engineer. Anderson was to have been hired as a staff engineer. But the plan was too ambitious: the group was plotting grand buildings before designing the first product. The company never got off the ground. A few months later, Olsen and Anderson together decided to go it on their own.

How to begin? They were engineers: Olsen, MIT, bachelor of science degree, electrical engineering, class of 1950, and master of science, 1952; and Anderson, University of Illinois, bachelor of science in engineering-physics, 1951, and master of science in physics, 1952. The only business principles they knew came from studying management texts at the Lexington town library. From this lunch-time research they formulated a crude business plan and went in search of investors. They found ARD, a pioneering venture capital firm headed by the imposing Frenchman, General Georges Doriot.

In 1957, ARD was quite literally the only venture capital in town. Olsen and Anderson read in an electronics trade publication the short list of risk capital companies—two were in

New York, one was in Boston. Since their first tenet of business was to spend as little money as possible, they ruled out a trip to New York. They chose the local company as their target and penned a simple letter to Doriot. It was the first brush with the man who would counsel and guide Olsen through the next thirty years.

By 1957, Doriot was a teaching legend at the Harvard Business School for a course called simply, *Manufacturing*. A generation of American executives, such as James D. Robinson, III at American Express, William McGowan at MCI, and Philip Caldwell at Shearson Lehman Brothers, cut their business teeth under Doriot. One of his oft-repeated lessons: "Gentleman, if you want to be a success in business, you must love your product." The hard message behind his gentle manner and soft French accent inspired more than 7,000 Harvard students.

Doriot used to tell his students that getting into business is like catching a moving trolley: "You can't jump aboard until you are running alongside." He looked for entrepreneurs who were willing to run long and hard. He ignored no variable in the equation of success, even lecturing on how to pick a wife. He was well known for directing advice to the wives of his young businessmen as well, counseling them on the great commitment and sacrifice they would have to make for their husbands to succeed.

As head of ARD, Doriot never looked for quick profit. Childless during his forty-eight-year marriage, he nurtured his start-ups as if they were his progeny. "When you have a child, you don't ask what return you can expect," he said. "Of course, you have hopes—you hope the child will become president of the United States. But that is not very probable. I want them to do outstandingly well in their field. And if they do, the rewards will come. But if a man is good and loyal and does not achieve a so-called rate of return, I will stay with him." Doriot helped found 150 companies, but none would match the success or fill ARD's pockets like the one proposed by Olsen and Anderson that summer day.

The pair knew nothing of Doriot when they sent him their

proposal to start a computer company. He was intrigued by the simplicity of their notion: that they could build machines more cheaply and easily than IBM. Computers were a curiosity in the investment world, and ARD's board of directors were curious. Should their venture capital be getting in on the ground floor of this new field? Or was the business too risky? ARD staffers were put on the lookout for promising start-ups to back. Olsen and Anderson presented themselves at the perfect time and with perfect credentials—Lincoln Lab was known for the caliber of its engineers. Doriot turned over the letter to staffers William Congleton, Wayne Brobeck, and Dorothy Rowe and told them to make contact.

Olsen and Anderson were advised to submit a formal business proposal. The plan they put together was short, just four pages. Olsen made contact prints off the typewritten original, and they submitted their proposal in reverse—white letters on a black background. "We were very naive," Anderson says.

ARD's staff was a bit young and naive as well, except for Doriot. Venture capitalism itself was a relatively new concept, especially in the nascent computer industry. Congleton asked Olsen and Anderson for more details. So the two went back to the Lexington library. They studied *Moody's Investment Index* and *Standard & Poor's*, concentrating on "respectable" companies. They scoured Paul Samuelson's bestselling textbook, *Economics*. Chapter 5 prescribed how to form a business. It also warned, "Most businesses are here today and gone tomorrow, the average life expectancy of a business being only a half dozen years. Some will terminate in bankruptcy; many more will be voluntarily brought to a close with sighs of regret for dashed hopes and an expensive lesson learned; still others will come to a joyous end when their 'self-employed' owner finally lands a good, steady job or takes up a new line of endeavor."

Olsen and Anderson overlooked this bit of gloom and concentrated on the Appendix, which presented a fictitious business case, the Pepto-Glitter Toothpaste Co. "We studied that model backwards and forwards until we could have started a toothpaste company," Anderson says. But, ARD wondered, could they sell computers?

Olsen and Anderson resubmitted a four-year business plan for the Digital Computer Corporation. And they were invited to stand before ARD's board of directors in their dusky old Boston offices. Congleton and the other ARD staffers worried about the presentation. They had taken a liking to the intense young pair and wanted them to succeed. They offered three pieces of advice:

"First, don't use the word *computer*. *Fortune* magazine says giants like RCA and General Electric are losing money in computers. The board will never believe that two young engineers, barely off campus, can succeed where others more experienced are failing." So Olsen and Anderson said they would make printed circuit modules instead of computers.

"Second, promise more than 5 percent profit. You have to promise a higher return than RCA," Dorothy Rowe told them, "or why would anyone want to invest in you?" So Olsen and Anderson promised 10 percent.

"And last, promise a quick profit." ARD's board, with aging men like Vermont senator Ralph Flanders and MIT treasurer Horace Ford, were not likely to live long enough to enjoy long-term business success. So Olsen and Anderson said, "We will make a profit the first year."

It was not a sophisticated business plan that sold the board, and Olsen knew it. "We didn't have a big volume of spread-sheets and dozens of colored graphs. We did have simple profit and loss statements and simple balance sheets," he says. "When American Research could see that these financial plans were in our head and in our heart, that we made them, understood them, remembered them and they were simple enough to be a model for us to run the company, they committed to invest in us without waiting for a final, beautifully bound proposal." Doriot was investing in the men, not the businessmen.

And they weren't asking for much—just $100,000. ARD offered $70,000 in equity financing and the promise of a $30,000 loan, which they received in the first year. Another $300,000 was set aside several years later as a line of credit for when the new enterprise needed it. Doriot, who was vacation-

ing in France, had little to do with the details. But he had
made it clear that he saw opportunity in Olsen and Anderson—for him to teach and guide, for them to learn and succeed.

Despite their faith in the young engineers, Congleton and
the other staffers were skeptical that any company could
succeed on just $100,000, much less one expecting to sell
computers. They specified that for its risk and money, ARD
should take 70 percent ownership of the company. "Two-
thirds to the venture capitalist and one-third to the entrepreneurs" was ARD's rule of thumb.

Despite what later came to be called in business texts an
"unusual" share of ownership given up for so little capital
invested, Olsen and Anderson didn't argue the terms. They
had no idea how other such deals were structured. And they
were in no position to bargain. They could either take the
percentage of the company offered and $70,000 in capital or
leave with no capital and no company at all. The deal was an
unspoken take it or leave it. Olsen and Anderson took it.
According to *Fortune* magazine's assessment in 1987, Olsen's
decision to deal away so much of the company cost him a $5
billion personal fortune.

Of the 1,000 shares of founding stock, ARD retained 700,
the 70 percent share; Olsen and Anderson received 200 to split
as they wanted; and 100 shares were set aside for an experienced business person who could lend corporate skills to the
pair of engineers. Olsen, the unquestioned leader, took 12
percent of the founders' stock, and Anderson received 8 percent.

The businessman's spot was never filled. One candidate
turned it down, and ARD's suggestions never pleased Olsen.
General Doriot assigned Rowe to serve as the first treasurer of
the new company in order to help train the young entrepreneurs in the complexities of finance. Olsen and Anderson
proved themselves so penny-pinching in the first days of the
venture that ARD did not press the point of bringing in a
businessman. Since the 100 other shares were never issued,
ARD ended up owning not seven-tenths of the new venture

but seven-ninths—77 percent. And because they were forbidden by ARD to build computers initially, Olsen and Anderson changed the name Digital Computer Corporation to Digital Equipment Corporation.

Before he would sign the deal, Doriot insisted on meeting Olsen's wife, Aulikki. He believed that Digital's success depended on a wife's patience and support, her willingness to run the house and raise the family while her husband dove head-first into the new venture. As Dorothy Rowe says, "It took only minutes for Aulikki and the general to establish a rapport that lasted a lifetime." The general blessed the project.

In August 1957, stocked with $70,000 in the bank and the opportunity they had sought, Olsen and Anderson set off to the Assabet Valley and the tiny mill town of Maynard, Massachusetts, to start an electronics company.

"We were cocky. Oh, were we cocky!"

—Ken Olsen

3
Into the Whirlwind

As THE TWO entrepreneurs drove west out of Boston toward their future, their route along the Charles River took them past the rows of stone and concrete buildings that make up the campus of the Massachusetts Institute of Technology. Olsen spent a decade studying and working in this engineering haven and formed a lifetime bond. He still wears the gold MIT ring, with its symbolic beaver sculpted on its face. In his office at Digital he displays a large, stuffed beaver, a gift from his son.

Olsen came of age as an engineer at MIT. It was for him the perfect confluence of time and place. When he left the Navy and enrolled at school in the fall of 1947, the computer era was dawning, and MIT was the Athens of that age. Olsen joined the Whirlwind engineers, Jay Forrester's crack corps designing the computer at the heart of a sophisticated air defense system.

In August 1949, the Soviet Union detonated an atomic bomb, and the Cold War chill settled over both sides of the Atlantic. The threat of communism enveloped America and drove both fear and creation. At MIT, Cold War politics translated into heightened commitment to the technological task at hand—building computers useful to the military. These engineers were a scientific army, bearing slide rules and soldering irons, racing to give the United States an electronic advantage.

Though a vigorous anticommunist, Olsen was no militarist. He was a scientist who could sublimate his ego to the goals of the project. He didn't ask questions or seek excuses; he got the job done. He quickly earned the reputation as a first-class practical engineer.

Whirlwind was born as a computer to power a cockpit flight simulator for the Navy. Forrester, a dynamic and inventive thinker, drove Whirlwind, along with Robert Everett, the engineering brains of the project. In the race to supply the military with computers, Forrester's band was competing against engineering teams at other American campuses. Mathematicians, such as John Von Neumann at Princeton, and engineers, such as Presper Eckert and John Mauchly at the University of Pennsylvania and Howard Aiken at Harvard, were creating break-through computing machines. Eckert and Mauchly's ENIAC debuted on Valentine's Day 1946, in Philadelphia—the first electronic digital general-purpose computer.

Olsen immersed himself in Whirlwind, a completely new approach to computing. ENIAC—the Electronic Numerical Integrator and Computer—was a huge number cruncher, the prototype for the mainframes of the future. Whirlwind, the quickest computing machine of the 1950s, relied on large, awkward vacuum-tube circuits with short word lengths (16 bits) designed to respond quickly. An operator could sit at a keyboard and interact with the computer in a primitive dialogue. Whirlwind's nickname at MIT—the "expensive typewriter"—showed just how familiar to people it was intended to be. For Olsen, the interactive nature of Whirlwind was a revelation. It brought computing power to the individual, made the machine accessible to man.

In 1950, Whirlwind became operational as a computer that far exceeded in sophistication the Navy's original needs for a cockpit simulator. At the same time, the Cold War intensified, and a jittery government sought to utilize to military advantage academia's experiments in building computers. Foremost of their needs was a defense system that could protect the country's suddenly vulnerable borders. The Air Force turned to MIT. Whirlwind became the basis for SAGE, the Semi-Automatic Ground Environment defense system.

Forrester and Everett went looking for "universe-class engineers." Forrester specified that he sought the kind of man who "should have originality and what is often referred to as 'genius.' He should not be bound by the traditional approach." According to *Project Whirlwind*, by Kent Redmond and Thomas Smith, "Forrester was convinced, from his wartime experience, that it was more efficient to pay a higher price for one really good man, then give him his head, than it was to pay less for three average men and have to lead them by the hand."

MIT established Lincoln Laboratory in nearby Lexington as a subsidiary to concentrate on defense needs. Forrester put together a team of 400 engineers to tackle the massive SAGE project. Olsen, embarking on a master's degree in engineering, was among them.

For Whirlwind, Forrester had created the three-dimensional magnetic core memory, a doughnut-shaped device that replaced the temperamental storage tubes generally used. Magnetic core memory would be at the heart of the SAGE air defense system. During a trip to Chicago in 1952 to give the seminal speech on the new memory, Forrester stopped at the University of Illinois to recruit. Only Harlan Anderson signed on to go east to work on SAGE. Anderson, the youngest son of a factory worker from Freeport, Illinois, brought his love of engineering and computers along with a cool, midwestern pragmatism to Lincoln Lab.

Like many components just being designed for the first computers, the core memory was untested—a shaky foundation on which to build an air defense system. Forrester was impatient. He wanted to push ahead with SAGE. He handed the prototype of the magnetic core memory, replete with tubes as big as milk bottles, to Norman Taylor, a trusted lieutenant. Forrester told him, "Build us a memory."

Taylor was a battle-wise engineering veteran who had plied his trade in the military and then for a decade at Western Electric before coming to MIT. He knew reliability was paramount. Pressing ahead with SAGE before fully testing the core memory seemed foolhardy to him. Better to test first than be surprised later.

Taylor told Forrester that a small computer had to be built specifically to test his magnetic core memory. "I didn't really want to build a whole computer," Taylor says, "but I wasn't going to put a memory in SAGE unless it was reliable." Forrester said there was no need, that his design would work; besides, there wasn't time to build another computer. Taylor held fast to his position, and Forrester finally agreed—but he demanded quick results. Taylor picked Olsen for the tough assignment. Of the sixty engineers in his group, Taylor recognized Olsen as "a guy who gets things done." Above all, that's what Taylor needed right then.

Forrester didn't believe a test computer could be built in less than a year, as Taylor was promising. Whirlwind had taken a laboratory full of engineers more than four years to design and wire together. Of course, the test machine was to be a much smaller and simpler computer, but a computer nonetheless; in the early 1950s, computers weren't simple to build.

Taylor was relying on Olsen, a "rat's-nest engineer," to deliver. Olsen's designs verged on reckless, with hundreds of cables, wires, and clipped leads pouring from the back. Taylor told Olsen not to get carried away on the test computer, just keep it simple. And he said one more thing: "I want the test set in nine months." Olsen hardly blinked. He handpicked fifteen engineers to work with him, including Anderson to design the control portion of the computer. Taylor said, "If you do it in nine months, I'll give each guy a bottle of Scotch." To Olsen, a committed nondrinker, Scotch was no motivation. He told Taylor, "I'll see what I can do."

Olsen flourished in the heady atmosphere of Whirlwind and SAGE at MIT. "We were cocky. Oh, were we cocky!" he recalls in *Project Whirlwind*. "We were going to show every-body! And we did. But we had to lose some of the cockiness in the sweat it took to pull it off." Corners were cut in designing the test computer; time was the parameter of every decision. Anderson watched his future partner under the gun during those frantic days and nights of engineering. "There was no particular management style," Anderson says. "It was just personal charisma and leadership, an enthusiasm for every-thing he was doing."

Olsen showed no ego about who contributed which idea to the project. He didn't mind if someone besides himself de-signed the circuit or the logic. "Most of the guys at MIT wanted to become a Von Neumann or a Forrester," Taylor says. "Olsen didn't care about that. He wanted to get the job done."

Olsen and his team built the MTC—Memory Test Com-puter—in nine months. Forrester was astounded. "I felt it was audacious and unlikely that they could actually build a com-puter on such short notice," he says. "But they did it. And that computer served a very useful purpose as a vehicle for testing various kinds of equipment for a long time after magnetic core memory itself had in fact been checked out and transferred to the Whirlwind I computer."

Olsen had established his reputation, and the group got its case of Scotch from Taylor. "The Memory Test Computer," Taylor says, "made Olsen see the need for discipline, the need for a schedule, the need to get rid of the rat's nest." He now understood more than engineering; he knew how to focus a team on a single problem and get it done faster and better than anyone thought possible. He also sensed his own talent emerg-ing: he wasn't just a team engineer anymore; he was a proven leader.

Before tackling the challenge of the Memory Test Com-puter, Olsen interrupted his academic life for a more impor-tant mission. Upon earning his bachelor's degree from MIT in 1950, Olsen received a present from his grandmother of plane tickets to Europe. He set aside his graduate work and partici-pation in the Whirlwind project to make the journey. This trip was for love. He had fallen for Eeva-Liisa Aulikki Valve, a striking blonde from Finland. They had met through Aulikki's roommate in college, who was Olsen's next-door neighbor in Stratford, Connecticut.

Aulikki decided not to finish college in the United States and returned home. Ken used his grandmother's gift to follow her. The young couple reunited in Sweden and became engaged. Olsen took a job in a Swedish ball-bearing factory while he courted Aulikki. But the Cold War sweeping across the world touched Olsen and his bride-to-be. They needed special permission from both the U.S. and Finnish governments to get married. Olsen's sister, Eleanor, contacted a friend in the U.S. State Department, who helped sort through the red tape. And on December 12, 1950, Aulikki's father, a Lutheran minister, married them in Lahti, Finland, her hometown.

Olsen brought his bride back to Massachusetts. As they settled into a $27-per-week campus apartment, Olsen rejoined the SAGE project and his work building the Memory Test Computer. His achievement for Taylor and Forrester led to his next assignment, one technically much easier but intensely more frustrating.

The Air Force had selected Lincoln Lab as consultant and primary contractor for SAGE. Large corporations were jockeying for lucrative subcontracts. The most important prize: manufacturing the main air-defense computer. IBM outmaneuvered Univac, another early entrant in the computer business, for the bid. Though IBM had yet to establish market dominance, it was gaining momentum under Thomas Watson, Jr., as the company to be reckoned with.

For the Lincoln Lab engineers, SAGE was the first step into the business world. The atmosphere they were used to was far from corporate reality. Their budgets, for example, didn't undergo normal military scrutiny, so there was freedom to do whatever was necessary to get a job done. Forrester believed in doing everything first class, regardless of cost.

Taylor, however, wanted Olsen to understand the workings of the commercial world. He told Olsen that only 3 percent to 5 percent of all research engineers ever see their ideas become products. "All the excitement," he said, "is in things that come to production. Production is where the money is."

IBM desperately wanted the prime contract for the project. But Air Force regulations ruled out any one company as a sole source, so IBM grudgingly accepted a subcontract to Lincoln Lab. The contract was signed in October 1952, and within weeks, IBM and Lincoln Lab engineers were shuttling between IBM's Poughkeepsie, New York, site and Hanscom Field in Bedford, Massachusetts—a twice-daily flight on IBM's first corporate aircraft.

By 1953, it became clear to Forrester that he needed a full-time liaison to IBM, someone living in Poughkeepsie and going to the IBM plant daily to mediate between IBM's manufacturing experts and MIT's design engineers. He told Taylor to pick a person who could produce results in this strange mix of research engineers and corporate manufacturers. Taylor chose Olsen.

But Olsen balked. "Why do I want to learn that?" he asked when Taylor suggested he could benefit from exposure to production techniques. "Ken," Taylor replied, "it will be the best experience of your life. You might decide you don't want to play that game. But you've got to go through it to evaluate it. You can't just say you don't want to do production unless you try it. You might find it the most exciting thing you've ever done."

The idea of working on-site at IBM hardly excited Olsen. The relationship between Lincoln Lab and IBM was like fire and ice. The free-wheeling, "just get it done" attitude at Lincoln Lab directly opposed the massive bureaucracy of IBM. Tom Watson, Jr., visited Lincoln Lab early in the project and remarked to Forrester, "How do you achieve so much with so little?" Clearly, IBM couldn't see the value of the creativity Lincoln Lab allowed its people.

IBM assigned 200 engineers, many of them green recruits, to the SAGE contract. The Lincoln Lab engineers had to teach most of them about the intricacies of Whirlwind's interactive computing capabilities. IBM had already embraced the number-crunching mentality. "IBM seemed awful stupid to us,"

Taylor says. "They were still designing circuits like radio and TV circuits. We used special tubes and tolerances, and we had a very special way to evaluate whether a circuit would last a million hours."

Taylor insisted that he approve every circuit designed by an IBMer, which infuriated the Poughkeepsie engineers. To anyone questioning this policy he said, "I am the one who signed the paper with the Air Force saying the circuits will be reliable, and I am going to be damn sure every one of them is."

Olsen moved his wife and infant child into IBM's world in 1953. He rented a small white house in Poughkeepsie, set his jaw, and went to work inside IBM. With nothing but Lincoln Lab as his work experience, Olsen was immediately frustrated. Though the contract prescribed how the two groups should work together, IBM was irritatingly secretive about every piece of the project. "It was like going to a communist state," Olsen says. "They knew nothing about the rest of the world, and the world knew nothing about what went on inside." He was also bothered by what he saw as incredible waste, the levels of managers doing nothing but discussing and recommending. He had to fight even to get furniture for his tiny office. Finally, he just moved some in on his own. That was not IBM's way, and he upset his hosts.

Olsen was joined by other Lincoln Lab engineers, some full time, but most were commuters via IBM's air shuttle. The MIT-IBM connection lasted three years, despite how differently each side viewed engineering. Dinner parties at an IBM manager's house reflected the hierarchy so engrained in the company. Guests were placed around the table by their titles, which worked well enough for IBM. Lincoln Lab engineers laughed at their hosts' attempts to seat them in hierarchical order. Back at the MIT research lab, no such strata existed beyond Forrester and Everett. Titles meant nothing; everyone was an engineer or technician. Certainly the dinner table was the last place such posturing should occur. Olsen hardly socialized anyway. He was content to spend evenings at home with Aulikki and their first child, Glenn.

Taylor stayed over for weeks at a time during Olsen's thirteen months in Poughkeepsie. The two often ate long dinners together, during which Taylor, a veteran of bureaucratic wars, soothed the young engineer's frustration. One cold winter night, late in 1953, Olsen and Taylor stood outside Olsen's tiny house, as Olsen railed once again at IBM. "Norm," he said, "I can beat these guys at their own game." That night, Digital Equipment Corporation was born in Ken Olsen's mind.

"Now I want to do it on my own."

—*Ken Olsen*

4
The Mill

Aₛ DEC TOOK its first breath of life in 1957, IBM passed the $1 billion mark in revenues. This head start did not faze Ken Olsen. Nor did ARD's imposition of a waiting period before DEC could plunge into the business for which he had conceived it in the first place: to build computers.

Doriot, believing that "two young men competing with IBM, Burroughs, and RCA didn't sound quite modest," insisted that a less ambitious plan be followed. So Olsen and Anderson plunged ahead on a slightly different course, building transistorized logic modules for memory testing. Modules were a stepping stone to larger products anyway, and the urge was simply to get the business started. The computers would come later.

Olsen impressed Doriot immediately. "Ken had managed people in the lab. He was extremely perceptive; he realized the relationship between production and distribution," Doriot explained in the book *Computer Establishment*. "He has a full understanding of the market two or three years out, and his ideas are not so advanced that they're dangerous. I think DEC

25

needed less counseling from us than most companies we've been connected with."

In August, with the venture capital secured, the pair set out to find a corporate home. The first place they looked was at Maynard's woolen mill, a massive structure from the Civil War era located only a twenty-minute drive from Lincoln Lab. When Olsen and Anderson initially scouted the Mill, it was 90 percent rented, by such companies as Raytheon, Dennison, and American Can and twenty-one smaller businesses. Floor space could be rented for twenty-five cents a square foot— heat, parking, and watchman's service included. There was no need to look anywhere else. Olsen and Anderson contracted for 8,680 square feet.

Built in 1845, the Mill housed the Assabet Manufacturing Company, which wove blankets and uniforms for the Union Army. As war followed war, the Mill expanded until it encompassed more than one million square feet and covered several acres of downtown Maynard. In 1899, the Mill was purchased by the American Woolen Company, which constructed the largest loom in the world to make blankets. After the boom years of World War II, the company struggled on until 1950 and then closed, leaving many in Maynard without work. Several years later, a development group called Maynard Industries bought the structure and rented space to small businesses. But the few jobs created did little to spur the local economy.

In their excitement to start up, Olsen and Anderson didn't pay much attention to the surrounding community. They rented the second floor of Building 12, the closest one to Main Street. One floor below was Arthur's Discount Furniture. The same building still houses Olsen's office—though he long ago moved downstairs—and remains Digital's world headquarters. Arthur and his discount furniture are long since gone from the Mill.

On the first day of business, Ken's younger brother, Stanley, joined the company. Stan had been a technician at Lincoln Lab and was considering a job at Sylvania when Ken asked him to become Digital's first employee. Stan had grown up in the imposing shadow of his brother, who was older by two years.

The Olsen boys were raised during the Depression in a predominantly European neighborhood in Stratford, Connecticut. They were the middle children of the Olsen family, which included older sister Eleanor and younger brother David. Even in childhood, Ken stood out as the fair-haired boy in the family and in the neighborhood.

Kenneth Harry Olsen was born in Bridgeport, Connecticut, on February 20, 1926, to Oswald and Elizabeth Svea Olsen. Children of Norwegian and Swedish immigrants respectively, Oswald and Elizabeth were born in New York City. Oswald Olsen was an engineer without a college degree. As a machine tool designer, he held several patents—one for a machine that made universal joints for cars. He later worked for Baird Machine Company in Stratford as a machine salesman.

Oswald was a fundamentalist by religion and a disciplinarian by nature. He believed in puritan ethics, applied to both life and work. He was known for advising customers not to buy any machine from him that they didn't really need. He worked until the day he died of heart failure at age sixty-nine.

Oswald raised his family in a modest white house on Soundview Avenue in a working class neighborhood of Norwegian, Polish, and Italian families. He instilled in his three sons a love of mechanical and electrical things, and all three became engineers. He filled his basement with his prized tools, and Ken and Stan spent hours down there, inventing gadgets and repairing their neighbors' broken radios. When Ken was fourteen, he and Stan set up their own radio transmitter, broke in on a local station, and sang a song Stan wrote called "Murphy's Meatballs."

As his father had influenced him, Ken influenced his brother David, ten years his junior. As a Cub Scout, David put together a radio, with schematics courtesy of Ken and Stan. "They gave me a pile of components but then let me do it myself," David says. "I knew how to solder, but it could have been dangerous—the radio was 110 volts."

Though their father was stern, Ken needed little discipline.

As a boyhood friend told a *Fortune* reporter, "Ken was down the path. He didn't do anything that would raise your eyebrows." He was quiet and determined, like his father. Whether it was building a radio or playing center for the Stratford High School football team, he set out to be the best. Nothing less would do.

Upon graduation from high school, Ken joined the Navy, just as World War II was winding down. He was headed for the Far East when Japan surrendered. So it was technical, not combat, experience that marked Olsen from his Navy days. He completed the tough electronics technician training course in less than a year and ran the radio shack on his ship. He began to see electronics as the machine tool of the future. The Navy training was the perfect stepping stone for Olsen into his engineering studies at MIT.

Stan had always tried to follow Ken's footsteps. He also joined the military—the Army—after high school, but then instead of going to MIT, he went to the less prestigious engineering school at nearby Northeastern University. Later, when Ken was a project leader with a top-gun reputation at Lincoln Lab, Stan worked in a supporting role as a technician.

Anderson didn't know why Ken had not asked Stan to be part of the founding team, but Stan himself didn't question the setup. Like Ken, he didn't believe the business world necessarily embraced familial obligations. He was thrilled when Ken asked him to join Digital. "He almost implied that he needed me to start the company," Stan says. "That was very rewarding." Stan has been the only Olsen family member ever to work at DEC. As the company grew, Ken came to believe strongly that nepotism was as bad in business as in politics. David also graduated a few years later from Northeastern as an engineer. He discussed with his brother the possibility of working for DEC, and Ken decided it wasn't a good idea. Digital was his, not the family's, business.

Before the no-family policy became firm in Ken's mind, Stan came on board. He fashioned a twenty-four-year career at DEC and became such a visible player from the beginning that folklore has installed him as a third founder.

As the trio entered the Mill on that late August day, the first task was to construct partitions to create offices out of the one huge room. They made shopping runs to Sears and Roebuck for saws and shop tools and bought cheap benches from a local supply outlet. The floors were greasy, and the walls needed a good scrubbing. When they opened windows for air, pigeons flew in and around the offices.

The dollars were passed out sparingly. "The nice thing about $70,000 is that there are so few of them, you can watch every one," Olsen says. Watch them they did. They bought no furniture. For his office, Ken took a battered old rolltop desk left behind by the previous tenants. Anderson brought in a desk he had constructed in junior high school shop class. ARD loaned a couple of plain steel desks for secretaries—when they finally hired any. Anderson's lawn chairs were good enough for guests.

So frugal was the threesome that they didn't install doors, even on the bathrooms, because doors were so expensive to frame and install. "We were faced with a multitude of tasks, the least of which was to make the facilities great," says Stan. "The most important thing was to design a product and get it built."

ARD advised them to contract with a Boston lawyer and bank, as well as a city accounting firm, Lybrand Ross Bros. and Montgomery. It went against their sensibilities to hire such high-priced advice, but neither Olsen nor Anderson would ignore their majority stockholder's counsel. "We discovered that it cost us more to do the accounting than it did to do the manufacturing," Olsen says.

Everyone pitched in, doing bits of everything, but loosely defined roles evolved. Ken was the unquestioned leader, the president and technical guru. Andy, as Harlan is known, took on the administrative tasks. Stan supervised manufacturing. They hired Alma Pontz, a kindly older woman, to handle the secretarial and bookkeeping chores. It was a symbolic start for women at DEC. They would be relegated to secretarial-clerical chores or assembly-line work until the 1970s, when corporate attitudes toward women and minorities began to change.

"Spend as little as possible" was the motto of the new venture, but still, not every decision saved money. The original plan envisioned using circuits Olsen had worked on at MIT. As he started designing, he heard about the latest version of the transistor, William Shockley's break-through invention of eight years before. Olsen decided to go with it, even though doing so meant designing all new circuitry, essentially starting from scratch. "It was a much better transistor but a terrible gamble, a difficult business decision," he says. "They cost $12.50 each and we bought 1,000 of them. So out of $70,000, $12,500 went into one little box you could hold in your hand. Before we used any of them, the price went down to around $8 and we had a $4,500 inventory loss before we did anything."

Tools were ordered out of the Sears catalog. They built most things themselves, including the printed circuit boards. They did the photography in Olsen's basement, silk screening the boards with real silk on wooden frames, and then went back to the Mill to etch them in an aquarium tank and solder them by hand. A local portrait photographer developed the film. When they etched the circuit boards, chemicals sometimes leaked down through the floor into Arthur's, and they were forced to buy the damaged furniture.

Olsen established an early managerial tenet: Don't ask any employee to do anything that he or his managers could not or would not do themselves. If Digital needed tools, he became the toolmaker, a skill picked up from his father. Aulikki Olsen came in sometimes to sweep the floors. Anderson pasted up the initial sales literature.

They improvised what they did not want to buy. Plastic bottle caps worked as well as expensive, custom-built insulators for the tiny pulse transformers in the logic modules. In another instance, they were making transformers with little ferrite cores that were so sharp they would wear the insulation off the wires, causing the transformer to short circuit. Olsen went to the local Woolworth's, bought a kitchen canister, and filled it with sand. He attached the can to the wheel of a band saw and let it rotate overnight with the cores inside. By morning, the cores were well rounded.

When Norm Taylor stopped by to see how his former charges were doing, he found Anderson sweeping the floors and Ken in a corner making brackets to hold tubes. "What are you doing that for?" he asked incredulously. "If I buy these," Olsen replied, "it will cost me $5 a bracket. But we can build this machine to make them for thirty-five cents each."

The little firm needed employees. Digital ran an ad in the local paper offering to pay minimum wage for assembly people. Not having paid much attention to the Maynard economy, they were surprised by the flood of local workers who turned up to apply. Stan sized up the crowd, singled out one woman because she was nicely dressed, and hired her on the spot to help interview the rest.

DEC needed engineers and technicians if it was to move into the computer business soon. Olsen naturally turned to MIT and Lincoln Lab for talent. He asked Forrester, the inventive, unyielding leader of the SAGE and Whirlwind projects, to join the board of directors. Doriot suggested hiring Norm Taylor, but Olsen balked. He told the General, "Norm was my teacher for ten years; now I want to do it on my own."

The influence of MIT ran deep, but Olsen avoided an academic approach to business. "We were blacksmiths just turning out hardware," Olsen liked to say. "Research," Anderson points out, "is the last thing that Ken would want to be the corporate culture." Olsen brought with him from MIT the thrill of engineering—of taking an idea, designing it, producing it, and watching it work. At Digital, he could go a step further—he could sell it. As he said, "It wasn't really fun unless you affected the outside world."

Olsen learned more from MIT than how to build computers. He remembers the school as "tolerant of mistakes and of people finding that things don't work. Watching that gave us the idea that we could make an organization that would do the same." Olsen wanted to infuse DEC with the essence of MIT: "the openness, honesty, trustfulness and generosity that we'd all felt there," he says. "It was that spirit much more than anything technological that inspired us to start a business." He carried MIT's operations manual along with him and set DEC's policies from it. "We took the same hours, the same vacations; we paid the same holidays," Olsen says. But Massachusetts regulated companies and universities differently and informed Olsen that he could not pay employees for certain holidays. He answered, "MIT does." The state said, "We can't control MIT, but we can control you."

In early 1958, less than a year into existence, DEC shipped its first products—Digital Laboratory Modules and Digital Systems Modules—and hired its first salesman, Ted Johnson. By the end of one year in business, the company sold $94,000 worth of the logic modules for memory testing, mostly to Lincoln Lab, Bell Labs, Cal Tech, and other research facilities. "For a while we had a monopoly," Olsen says. "Not much of a market, but a monopoly." And now the payroll list numbered twelve.

Slowly, the wheels of the new enterprise began to turn. Edgar Schein, the noted organizational management professor and consultant at MIT's Sloan School of Management, saw in Olsen the characteristics of the classic entrepreneur. "I have observed a dozen or more entrepreneurs over the last several decades," he wrote in 1983, "and have consistently found them to be very strong-minded about what to do and how to do it. They typically already have strong assumptions about the nature of the world, the role which their organizations will play in the world, the nature of human nature, truth, relationships, time and space."

Olsen the entrepreneur knew exactly what he wanted to do. He had a clear vision of computing. He just needed Doriot's go-ahead to pursue it. At the close of the first year, Olsen and company showed a profit on the books—small perhaps, but a profit nonetheless. Profit, Olsen believed, was more critical to fulfilling ARD's faith in them than anything else. He took the numbers to Boston and proudly laid the financial statements in front of Doriot. The small, elegant Frenchman looked up and scowled. "I'm sorry to see this," he said. "No one has ever succeeded this soon and survived."

"We had a vision of computing that we knew the world needed."

—*Ken Olsen*

5
Fundamentalist Computers

DESPITE HIS PRONOUNCED fears, Doriot was quietly pleased at DEC's first success. The recession of the late 1950s was troubling many of the three dozen enterprises ARD had invested in. His newest venture—Digital—seemed untouched, and Doriot began to pay more attention to it.

The General believed that a quick profit generally sent founders out to buy "twenty-cylinder Cadillacs, fifty-room mansions, skiing in summer, and swimming in winter," while the enthusiasm for the work itself faded. But he could see that Olsen and Anderson were not men who would be lured away by the trappings of wealth.

After that first year, the General was frequently on the phone with Olsen or visiting with him during Digital's board meetings, which were held in ARD's Boston offices. Though credited with virtually creating the professional venture capital business in America, Doriot was a humble man. He did not force his personal will on DEC, even as a director fourteen years later. But if he was needed, he stood firmly behind Olsen and Anderson; it was the men, not the company, he was investing in.

ARD provided a shoulder for the fledgling operation to lean on. Patrick Liles, who taught a new ventures course at Harvard in 1977, told *Forbes* magazine, "Success in venture investing stems not so much from picking winners as from providing the guidance that helps potentially promising companies avoid the kind of blunder that can prove fatal. You couldn't really say it was ARD that made DEC such a smashing success; but it was ARD's tender, loving care that got it through a difficult childhood. Venture capital, then, is not so much a game of brilliant strokes of insight as it is a game of patience."

Doriot was a very patient man. And he didn't need to worry about DEC running out of control. ARD held a majority position on the board of directors through Bill Congleton, Wayne Brobeck, Harry Hoagland, Dorothy Rowe, and ARD attorney John Barnard sitting beside Olsen and Anderson.

For Olsen, the relationship with Doriot was a lifeline to survival. He and Anderson were learning on the run the business of making computers. "We knew very clearly what we were doing, but we didn't know exactly how to do it," is the way Stan Olsen saw it. Doriot espoused sound and simple business practices—nothing too flashy, nothing too ambitious, nothing too bold. Olsen embraced Doriot's philosophy as his own.

The lack of basic business experience actually helped Olsen and Anderson once. Neither of them knew how to price a product—specifically, their modules. Anderson read in *Electronic News*, an industry trade publication, about a venture capitalist's speech in New York. In pricing an item, this expert advised, you ought to double your manufacturing costs. Olsen and Anderson didn't know their manufacturing cost, so they guessed a figure and doubled it. Then they realized they might have to sell the modules through sales representatives, so they tacked on another 15 percent. "We actually had no idea how much it was going to cost to make these things," says Anderson. "It cost a lot less than we thought; and on top of that, the price of transistors plummeted after we had already priced the modules. So we were making much bigger profits than we anticipated. It was luck."

Despite the unexpectedly higher profit, Olsen remained cautious. He kept expense levels lagging behind sales projections. Extra salesmen weren't hired until the business was already there to require them. He set no growth goals. He bucked the tenet of the day, which said, "Start a company, grow quickly, and then sell out to a larger company for a big profit."

Olsen was in it for the long haul. Let the company grow naturally. Concentrate on profits. "We'd borrowed $70,000 of someone else's money with an understanding that we would try to give a return," Olsen says. "With that simple relationship, most of the people in Digital understood that our obligation was to make a profit." He made a profit in 1958, but he chose to wait another year to start building computers, even though Doriot and ARD gave the go-ahead.

Meanwhile, the infant company was forming a personality. Ideas were gelling, hardening into policies. Olsen took his lessons from MIT seriously. Taylor had instilled the notions of simplicity and discipline—avoiding the rat's nest, that messy, wire-laden, seat-of-the-pants environment that so many engineers worked in. Olsen learned from watching IBM engineers in Poughkeepsie that complexity can lead to frustration. Important things could—and should—be done simply.

It is ironic that Olsen purposely ignored military contracts. The free-flowing money the government had provided Lincoln Labs didn't interest him. He certainly wasn't a pacifist—he had gladly served his Navy stint. But he and Anderson believed that government money corrupted a company that wanted to be a commercial success. Government contracts were too easy to land; and once you got used to them, you lost the hunger to go after commercial business. Most of all, Olsen didn't want his independence constrained by the government's contractural regulations. Digital would sell to the government, but on his terms. "We followed Sears and Roebuck," Stan says. "Here's the catalog, and this is what you get. If you want to buy it, fine; if you don't, go get somebody else to make it."

Olsen and Anderson also decided to go against common practice in another way: they would only sell, not lease, equipment, as IBM did. Leasing, they felt, created a reluctance to allow a product that is still producing revenue to become obsolete, thus slowing technical development.

For the first employees, the atmosphere of freedom and openness was seductive. There was little structure; groups formed around specific projects as they had at Lincoln Lab. For engineers, it was a development paradise. Several of the first hired, such as Dick Best, employee number five, and Jack Smith, number twelve, never left. Others, such as sales chief Ted Johnson, number ten, stayed for more than two decades before losing a role in the new Digital of the 1980s. Badge numbers were assigned based on the order of hire, so a low badge number became a status symbol as DEC grew. Olsen showed his feelings about engineers by reportedly paying his first computer engineer, Ben Gurley, about the same salary as his own, set by ARD, $14,000.

The young engineers coming to DEC found a philosophy they could work with: "He who proposes does." The central management structure was purposely kept lean because, Anderson says, "We didn't want the corporate staff telling people what they ought to be doing, how they ought to be thinking, and the products they ought to be inventing." This philosophy of letting people run with their ideas took many inexperienced employees into new territory.

Smith, now a DEC senior vice president in charge of engineering and manufacturing and one of the most powerful men at Digital, came from a local vocational institute without a college degree. "My wife and I had just had our first child," Smith says, "and when I graduated from school, I was going to take a job at Bell Labs in New Jersey. I wanted to do research and revolutionize the world. But my wife's family is Italian, and when they found out I was going to take their first grandchild to this wilderness called New Jersey, they said, 'No way.' So I went out to this little company in Maynard and took a job."

Smith soon took over DEC's fledgling manufacturing operation. "We knew that if we wanted to build computers, we couldn't keep engineers and technicians tied up stringing wires on circuit boards," Smith says. "Building a computer isn't as complicated as people think. You run wires from A to B and B to C. So we began hiring women for their dexterity. I became involved in manufacturing simply because someone had to be there to supervise these people. I raised my hand and said, 'Hey, I can do that.' And Ken said, 'Fine, if you think you can do it, do it.' "

One of the first women hired, Gloria Porrazzo, started as an assembler and progressed over the next twenty-five years to group manager in manufacturing. "The place was rustic," Porrazzo says. "I thought I was going there to make clocks." She notes that Smith, like most new managers, was "wet behind the ears." Everyone worked together. "It was very informal," she says. "You did what had to be done. Only later did it dawn on me that I was actually working *for* Jack."

With their MIT background, Olsen and Anderson knew how to hire engineers and technicians like themselves. But neither knew much about hiring people for industrial or office environments. One of their first secretaries turned out to be a woman with a drinking problem. In her purse she carried a flask, which she dipped into frequently, according to a co-worker. Hiring was trouble enough—but firing was unknown territory for Olsen and Anderson. They decided to allow the woman to finish the day before letting her go. They didn't want her rummaging through files or typing letters or even answering the phone. So they told her to dust. The task seemed harmless enough. But when Olsen and Anderson sat down in their makeshift conference room to meet with some very early and important customers, the secretary wandered in, a few sips of her favorite liquor in her, and began dusting the table around which they were gathered.

Olsen and Anderson devoted little attention to deciding Digital's employee policies on pay and working conditions at the Mill. They were consumed by selling their products, but now they wanted to do more than build logic modules and memory testers. In 1959, the time was right to get into the business they had targeted in the first place: building computers.

It was not simply a matter of designing the machines. Olsen had already proven his mettle as a computer engineer. But he wanted to commercialize a style of computing unknown outside the MIT campus. It was a gamble. "When we left MIT to start DEC, we had ideas that were so unique we gave up trying to explain them," Olsen says. "We had a vision of computing that we knew the world needed."

The vision is simple to understand now: individuals wanted their own access to the computer. They wanted to interact with the machine via a keyboard and monitor, as Olsen and his colleagues had done at MIT and Lincoln Lab, where the SAGE and Whirlwind computers were, by necessity, interactive. This view was heresy in the world of huge mainframe computers produced by IBM, Univac, and Burroughs. The few companies able to afford these colossal computing machines sent out press releases announcing their purchase as an achievement in itself. Individual users were separated from the mainframes by glass walls and days of waiting. You brought your punch cards to the computer room door and left them with the technician. Several days later, you came back for the results. "And they'd usually be wrong," Olsen says. He realized that maintaining parts and personnel lists or tracking research tests was a mathematically simple task not requiring the power of a million-dollar mainframe. These basic jobs could be handled by a basic machine—a fundamentalist computer. "Our competitors were trying to do the difficult things," Stan says. "You don't have to do the difficult things. There are a lot of things out there that are very important that can be done easily."

Doriot, however, was still concerned about his small venture being on the same playing field with IBM and RCA. The first machine, therefore, was called a Programmed Data Processor, or PDP-1, a direct attempt at masking its true nature. Though it was in fact a solid-state, general-purpose computer, the PDP-1 appeared to the outside world to be just another advance in Digital's line of logic modules. This modest approach allowed DEC to enter what was becoming a high-powered, competitive market out of sight of the giants.

"The usefulness of computers is still limited by a general feeling that they are new and strange."
                                              —*Ken Olsen*

6
Creating an Industry

OLSEN AND ANDERSON weren't simply creating a company, they were creating an industry. In the summer of 1959, they persuaded Ben Gurley, their former SAGE colleague, to join them in Maynard. The job: build the PDP-1, an interactive computer that could be sold at a fraction of the cost of a mainframe and would be easy to install and use. Gurley, a sturdy, handsome man—built like a halfback, according to Norm Taylor—lived just long enough to establish himself as a computer engineer of the first rank, a man with enormous potential in an industry that needed visionary engineers.

"Gurley was one of the best engineers that Ken had," says Taylor. "He had his feet on the ground, an earthy type; he knew what he was doing. If something was wrong, he'd get a soldering iron and fix it." In that regard, he was the model of Olsen's perfect employee: he was willing to stand up and take responsibility.

The PDP-1, with a price tag of $120,000, brought general-purpose computing to a new level of user. These customers, mostly scientists and engineers, did not tax the machine's capabilities. Operating at 100,000 additions per second—still no match for the speed of a giant mainframe—DEC's transistorized digital computer provided more power for the price than users ever expected from a computer.

Olsen knew he was on to something. At MIT, students were lining up even at two in the morning to use Whirlwind's offspring, the interactive TX-0. "They stopped studying, they stopped bathing, they even stopped eating," Olsen says, "as long as they could stay at the machine." One floor below, an IBM 7090 mainframe sat in a glass-enclosed room, virtually ignored by the students. The age of hackers and techno-freaks had begun—two decades before the personal computer revolution swept the world.

The systems modules at the core of the PDP-1 were patterned after circuits used in Lincoln Lab's TX-0 and TX-2 computers. These machines were the first high-speed, high-performance digital computers made with transistors instead of vacuum tubes—machines that Olsen, Anderson, Best, and Gurley helped design at Lincoln Lab after completing the SAGE computer. Taylor was happy to see his MIT boys using Lincoln Lab technology to start a business and make some money. He advised the school's board of directors not to interfere with Olsen. "If he wants to borrow that circuitry, what the hell?" Taylor argued. "He designed half of it."

In December 1959, DEC unveiled the prototype of the PDP-1 at the Eastern Joint Computer Conference at Boston's old Statler Hotel. It was a scramble to get the machine ready for its debut. Olsen, Anderson, and Gurley brought the prototype down to the hotel, switched on the power—and it didn't work. Anderson stayed the night in Boston to nurse the new computer, despite having a newborn child sick at home. "It was a strain," Anderson says, "but it wouldn't have been a crisis if it failed. We had not shot the works on the PDP-1. We had a small, ongoing business already independent of the computer." But Olsen wanted to sell computers, not just modules.

Though possessing just 4K-word memory—hardly enough to start one of today's personal computers—the PDP-1 was the technological marvel of its time. It came with a CRT (cathode-ray tube) integrated into the console, a feature unknown on computers of the day. Through the CRT, users could see what was being entered into and received back from the central processing unit—an instant back and forth. Unlike room-size computers, the PDP-1 was no larger than a refrigerator and did not require a sterilized working environment. Even as the first PDP-1 was sold in November 1960 to Bolt, Beranek, and Newman in Cambridge, Massachusetts, the machine was being refined. Norm Taylor bought the second machine for Itek, a start-up typesetting house not far from Digital. But the machine delivered to him was fiercely unreliable. Gurley was frequently dispatched to get Taylor's PDP-1 up and running.

The DEC-MIT connection flourished. Engineers and technicians flocked from Lincoln Lab to the lablike engineering environment in Maynard. They felt at home with DEC's products, too, which were drawn from Olsen's and their own work at MIT. In June 1960, Chester Gordon Bell left MIT's campus and came to Digital as the company's second computer engineer. It was a fortuitous coupling—the right man with the right company at the right place and time. Bell spent most of the next twenty-three years with DEC, building, guiding, arguing, fidgeting, and creating the computing strategies that would give DEC the foundation to grow into IBM's strongest challenger.

Bell is a computing genius, the Frank Lloyd Wright of computers, as *Datamation* magazine called him. If there were a Digital hall of fame, Bell's portrait would hang just below Olsen's. Bespectacled, with a round choirboy's face and wind-blown hair, Bell is a study in disarray. His mind races far ahead of his tongue into the corners of space and time, into the microcircuits and arithmetic units that make up computers. He rarely finishes a sentence. He'll jump from his chair to make a point, gesturing wildly, head off for a book or paper that will show what he means, then turn around and sit down again, his mind leaping ahead to a new thought, a new insight.

Born in 1934, Bell grew up in Kirksville, Missouri, where his father and uncle owned Bell Electric, an appliance, contracting, and repair shop. He spent the seventh year of his life in bed because of a congenital heart problem. There he wired circuits, ran chemistry experiments, and cut out puzzles with a jigsaw. After recovering, he spent every free hour in the family shop, watching and learning about electrical repair. By the age of twelve, he was a professional electrician, installing the first home dishwashers, fixing motors, and tearing mechanical things apart so he could rebuild them. The idea of quality engineering and the ability to scope out a problem were ingrained in Gordon even as a boy.

As an MIT undergraduate, Bell worked as a co-op student at General Electric and learned to detest mass engineering—dozens or hundreds of engineers working on a single problem. Anything engineered by more than four or five people, he still believes, just won't function as it should.

After earning his master's degree in engineering from MIT in 1956, Bell learned that the University of New South Wales in Australia was getting its first computer, the English Electric Deuce. Bell heard that anyone willing to go to Australia to help set up the machine would be favorably considered for a Fulbright scholarship. He applied, won the scholarship, and then set off for Australia. There he developed and taught the university's first graduate course in computer design. There, too, he met his future wife, Gwen, also a Fulbright scholar and later founder of the Boston Computer Museum.

In late 1958, Bell returned to MIT to pursue a doctorate. While working on speech synthesis on the TX-0, he heard of Digital and went out to Maynard to buy modules. He met Olsen, Anderson, Best, and Gurley and knew immediately that this company was the place for him. Bell recognized that speech synthesis was a twenty-year problem, and he had no interest in spending a lifetime solving a single challenge. "I didn't want to be a researcher. I wanted to be an engineer and build things," Bell says. "Digital looked like exactly the kind of place I wanted to work."

He gave up his doctoral program and accepted a job at the Mill. He maintained a close tie to academia throughout his career and often argued with his engineers about the relative merits of advanced degrees. Bell is an academic elitist, despite his own lack of a Ph.D. He believes fervently that links to universities are critical for technology companies and that DEC's interaction with top schools is what has kept it at the forefront of engineering. "If a computer can't be used by a university, it means it's not good enough," Bell insists. "I'm only interested in building the great computers that everyone follows."

Though it couldn't be classified as a "great" computer, the PDP-1 broke new ground. Each of the first PDP-1s was sold to a different site—Lawrence Livermore Labs; Bolt Beranek and Newman; the Atomic Energy of Canada plant at Chalk River. Each was used for a specialized application, which meant time-consuming and costly customization of the machine by DEC. The PDP-1 faced considerable market resistance: who would believe a company with fewer than 100 employees could produce a reliable, long-life computer?

Like Bell, Olsen believed strongly in academia and thought he could contribute to the progress of computing by giving MIT a machine of his making. He donated a PDP-1 to his alma mater in January 1962. "The usefulness of computers is still limited by a general feeling that they are new and strange," Olsen said at the presentation. "It is essential for modern, high-speed computers to be introduced to engineering students early in their education in a natural and informal way. We hope our gift will make it possible for more undergraduates to sit before a real computer, to communicate with it and to learn exactly what it can do." MIT students quickly embraced the new machine, and the faculty set up a custom network between the TX-0 and the PDP-1 to share programs. For diversion, they programmed the PDP-1 to play mancala, an African counting game.

This early commitment to education openly emulated IBM's policy of giving 60 percent discounts to universities. DEC has donated millions of dollars to MIT and other universities and schools around the world. Students on hundreds of campuses wrote their first programs on DEC machines. A generation of engineers and computer scientists, as well as countless other customers, learned computing on DEC equipment.

In late 1962, DEC won its break-through order. International Telephone and Telegraph bought fifteen PDP-1s to control its message switching systems. This order gave Digital the confidence and financial ability to become a general systems supplier. More important, it established the PDP-1 as a standard DEC computer. "We were very lucky to get that order," Bell says. "If we hadn't, I don't think we would have survived in the computer industry." Though the modules and memory testers were being manufactured in quantity, ITT provided the first multiple order of computers, and it pushed the custom-work mentality off center stage. In this new commercial environment, DEC had to learn how to manufacture a quantity of identical machines as cheaply as possible.

DEC built fifty-three PDP-1s, the last one in 1969. Nearly half were sold to ITT. The initial ITT order gave the board of directors the chance to provide some business common sense to Olsen. ITT's lawyers showed up at DEC with a ten-page contract. Unnoticed by Olsen, a fine-print clause stipulated that if ITT purchased a certain number of machines, it could exercise the option to buy DEC. The board notified Olsen, who refused to sign the contract. He believed the machines were good enough that ITT would buy them anyway, and it did.

In 1962, at the end of its fifth fiscal year, Digital reported sales of $6.5 million and net profits of $807,000. This performance sprang entirely from ARD's base capital of $70,000— DEC had never needed more equity investment, nor would it. Still, Olsen was not satisfied. Though the numbers were impressive, he remained insecure, a neophyte businessman unsure whether he could repeat the performance the next year and the next after that. General Doriot insisted that quick success was actually a threat; long-term viability required constant examination and worry. So Olsen worried. All he had built—and all he wanted to build—could, he feared, come quickly tumbling down. "You need to grow," Olsen knew, "but growing gets you in trouble."

DEC's move into the computer business spurred a rush to hire. New faces entered the Mill constantly. Nick Mazzarese, a Sudbury, Massachusetts, neighbor and friend of Stan Olsen, joined as New England sales manager just as the ITT order came in. At twenty-four, he was named project manager for the PDP-1.

Ted Johnson, a Cal Tech graduate and the company's first Harvard MBA, was already a four-year veteran by 1962. He moved back to Massachusetts from California, where he had been DEC's one-man West Coast sales office, to head up North American sales.

Winston Hindle, a stylish young MIT grad who had spent four years in the university's industrial relations division, was introduced to Olsen by Jay Forrester and came aboard as Olsen's staff assistant.

Jack Shields, a hard-nosed, blue-collar Navy veteran from Lawrence, Massachusetts, arrived in 1961. He compensated for his lack of a college degree with intensity and boldness. He helped install the third PDP-1 at MIT and discovered in the process what perhaps wasn't obvious to trained engineers— customers expect a commercial company to service its machines. The roots of a service organization were already in place, started by Bob Beckman, also a Navy veteran, who hired Shields. Seeing opportunity for the taking, however, Shields built the service organization and steadily rose through the ranks of power to now head sales, service, and marketing.

Today Hindle and Shields, along with Jack Smith, sit together at Digital's second highest level—senior vice president. Olsen created this management rank for them in 1986, raising the three from among nearly forty vice presidents. Olsen himself retains his one and only title—president. At DEC, there is no chief executive officer, no chairman of the board, no executive vice president.

While the PDP-1 was in production, two new machines were being considered. The PDP-2 was slated to be a 24-bit machine and the PDP-3 36-bit. Neither was built. But the next PDP—the 4—did make it from paper to production.

According to *Computer Engineering*, Bell's technical history of Digital computers, the $65,000 PDP-4 was a disappointment. Bell had hoped that a machine offering five-eighths the performance of a PDP-1 for half the price would find a welcome market. Instead, it met with general disinterest and fell short of expectation, selling just fifty-four units.

The cool reception to the PDP-4 portended deeper trouble. DEC's seat-of-the-pants management style worked fine for a start-up, but the company's rapid growth now demanded structure, and Olsen wrestled with just what kind and how much of it suited him and DEC. The research-lab environment that he espoused was degenerating into chaos; the lack of control was haunting him.

The good-humored Ken Olsen of 1957 became a tough man to work for by 1963 in the eyes of those closest to him. Though the venture had grown well out of infancy, there was a sense of being in a speeding car with no steering wheel—or, even worse, no brakes. He was the only one taking responsibility for anything. He had fostered the open environment, and now he could not understand how it was leading to chaos.

Olsen was not trained to know how to change the structure of an organization. His only management experience came from a distinctly different environment. In 1956, he had been asked to manage the Sunday school at the Park Street Church in Boston by its passionate pastor, Harold Ockenga. "It was a very imposing job for a thirty-year-old," Olsen says, "because everybody at the church looked ancient." According to *Fortune* magazine, the school was disorganized and neglected. Olsen pored over management books trying to figure out how to revitalize it. He decided to set up a committee system to foster involvement and market the school to the congregation. He did set the Sunday school right—and he got his first taste of management. "I can tell you all the things I learned then," he says, "but I can't tell you much I've learned since then."

Olsen asked for advice in how to change DEC, but two of the most respected voices in the extended DEC family were already at each other over how best to manage the company. Forrester had left Lincoln Lab to become a professor at MIT's Sloan School of Management in 1956. He began to generate models of business structures based on his own distinctive views of how an organization should be run. And as a director, he began consulting with Digital on management strategies.

Doriot also wielded great influence over Olsen and DEC. Though he wasn't yet a director, his opinions were carried to board meetings by the ARD staff who were. His patient, nurturing style began to clash with Forrester's formalistic, high-tech view of the world. Known as a back-of-the-envelope genius, Forrester customarily sketched out a system for the way things could work while listening to a conversation about a problem. Doriot didn't believe that directors should dictate to Olsen. "Doriot's philosophy," says ARD staffer Congleton, "was that as long as things are going in the right direction, then the board's function is to support management, not control it." And Doriot thought little of MIT's Sloan School—Forrester's home—as a place for management education. It wasn't, he believed, in the same league as his own Harvard Business School.

Stan Olsen, who was involved in sales management by now, tried to make Forrester's ideal models of new businesses work. "I was young enough to believe that once we built the model, it would be perfect, and we'd just follow it," Stan says. "I learned a lot about what modeling won't do for you."

Despite $1.2 million in profit, 1963 was confounding and worrisome for DEC's managers, because the company still hadn't settled on the form—or formlessness—of the corporate structure.

On the engineering side, DEC was trying to overcome its first major defection. Gurley, the company's first engineer, was lured away by the opportunity to become vice president at another Maynard Mill start-up, Information International. Bell stepped in ably as principal computer designer, but Gurley's departure cost DEC one of the industry's brightest minds.

Taylor, who had gone on to become assistant to William Norris, another computer industry pioneer and founder of high-flying Control Data Corporation in Minneapolis, recruited Gurley during the summer of 1963. Taylor had refrained from trying to steal Gurley from DEC but moved quickly after this talented engineer jumped to Information International. CDC struck a verbal agreement with Gurley for him to come to Minnesota, but he never made the move.

Two weeks before John F. Kennedy's assassination, Gurley sat down to a spaghetti dinner in his Concord home with his wife and seven young children. A bullet blasted through the kitchen window and killed him. Five hours later, police arrested Alan Blumenthal.

Blumenthal, a Digital engineer who had been Gurley's coworker at Lincoln Lab in the 1950s, was never brought to trial for the killing. Declared mentally incompetent by a Massachusetts Superior Court judge, he was sent to Bridgewater State Hospital for the Criminally Insane. He died there in the summer of 1987.

Though Blumenthal was never convicted, police are convinced that he was indeed the killer. According to an account of the competency hearings reported by the Concord (Massachusetts) *Journal*, Dr. Ames Robey of Bridgewater State Hospital described Blumenthal as "definitely mentally ill or psychotic of the schizophrenic group with paranoid tendencies." Dr. Robey recounted that in the army in the early 1950s, Blumenthal had climbed a water tower and randomly fired a rifle at the ground below. He was discharged with a section eight.

Though educated only through high school, Blumenthal was hired as a technician at Lincoln Lab, where he became friends with the gregarious Gurley. Blumenthal was wound tight, a perfectionist who couldn't tolerate sloppiness or disarray. Rumors circulated at DEC that Blumenthal had shot another Lincoln Lab engineer several years before—in both arms and legs—for no known reason.

When hired by Digital in 1959, Gurley convinced Blumenthal to join him there. Blumenthal was considered a talented addition to the technical staff, though he was dark and moody much of the time. Despite their friendship, Blumenthal apparently resented Gurley's education and expertise. He himself might have excelled at an engineering school like MIT, but he couldn't afford a college education.

When Gurley resigned from Digital in December 1962, he left Blumenthal behind. Blumenthal felt abandoned; he wanted to be part of Gurley's new company. His young wife died of kidney disease in July 1963, leaving him to care for three small children.

Blumenthal had often been a dinner guest at the Gurley home, the last time just two months before the shooting. He and Gurley argued that night. Blumenthal apparently threatened him and for several weeks parked his car outside the Gurley home, just sitting and watching for movements inside. Gurley and his wife complained to the Concord police but did not ask that Blumenthal be picked up. Gurley did, however, obtain a permit for shotgun ammunition.

Blumenthal steadfastly denied killing Gurley, but police found a twenty-gauge shotgun in his car that night. The shooting terrified DEC employees, who feared that Blumenthal would be released and allowed to return to the Mill.

Gurley's legacy, beyond his work on Whirlwind and the TX-0, was the PDP-1—DEC's first computer. Those who knew and worked with him are convinced that had he lived, his contribution to the computer industry would have been monumental.

"People are starting to think I'm a little dictator."

—*Ken Olsen*

7
The Product Lines

As a young president paddling downstream toward white water, Ken Olsen confronted in 1964 the first in a series of treacherous rapids that threatened to capsize Digital. He sensed his adolescent company was heading for a fall, and this course frustrated him. Failure was unknown to Olsen. Failure scared him.

He grew more dependent on Doriot, and the General provided a seasoned hand to hold throughout the 1960s. His lessons, often taught through parables, were not lost on Olsen. Doriot was, as *Fortune* magazine called him, "a nursemaid to dreams." He preached patience as a businessman and practiced it as an investor. He said, "I don't consider a speculator—in my definition of the word—constructive. I am building men and companies. Your sophisticated stockholders make five points and sell out," he scoffed. "We have our hearts in our companies; we are really doctors of childhood diseases here. When bankers or brokers tell me I should sell an ailing company, I ask them, 'Would you sell a child running a temperature of 104?' "

Olsen listened carefully to the critical business tenets Doriot taught, such as: "The intelligent man doesn't use the 'standard' method of action," and "The smart man knows how to make money on what he has today, but he keeps an eye on the future."

But Doriot, already in his sixties, didn't have the fire that burned within Olsen. ARD had dozens of small start-ups to look after. Doriot had already learned lessons that still awaited his protégé, lessons that could be conveyed only through experience, not words. One such lesson set out the three possibilities of business: success, accepted with humility; failure, which can be constructive if it is decent, honest failure; and mediocrity. Doriot said, "The most accepted, unfortunately, and the most dangerous, is mediocrity."

Seeing the caliber of people coming to DEC, Olsen didn't worry about mediocrity. The best and brightest young engineers in the region saw DEC as the place to work. The influx of such engineers as Edson de Castro, Tom Stockebrand, Henry Burkhardt, and dozens of others, mostly from Lincoln Lab, made Digital a kind of western campus for MIT. Students drove out to the Mill on Friday nights, Saturdays, and even Sundays to handle part-time work and get a chance to be around the new interactive computers, as well as the engineers who made them. But still, even the brilliant fail, Olsen knew. To him, failure at DEC could never be decent or honest. It would just be failure, painful and unacceptable.

In their enthusiasm, DEC engineers often courted failure by overcommitting themselves. They were allowed to overcommit themselves, and in some cases they were encouraged to. If they didn't deliver, Olsen displayed a quick temper in meetings and upbraided the offender. Objecting only made him angrier and louder.

Without a firm structure and knowledgeable managers, such key areas as manufacturing and order processing became logjams. There was no discernible cohesion between the various engineering groups. Product shipments, particularly in the modules business, were often delayed because engineering didn't coordinate with manufacturing. There were too many small, untethered groups doing their own thing.

Olsen began to withdraw into himself. Though he sought out others to blame in public for the lack of controls within Digital, inwardly he was beating on himself. A $10 million company in 1963, DEC went flat, growing to just $11 million in sales for 1964. Worse still, profits dropped from $1.2 million in 1963 to $900,000 the following year. To Olsen, this decline in fortunes was unconscionable. He was in business to make profit. He wanted to prove himself worthy of ARD's faith. He needed answers, and he couldn't get them from his managers. There was trouble in this fluid and perplexing democracy, and no one seemed willing to own up to the problems. Something had to be done.

If things were going wrong, Olsen decided, it must be because he was a weak president. In 1959 he had established the Works Committee, a central advisory body of key managers. Few of them had much business expertise. But, Olsen realized, "They all have ideas about how to spend money. I am the only one to say no. People are starting to think I'm a little dictator."

In the Works Committee meetings, Olsen began to rail at individuals. "We can all see that Joe's head is in the ground on this one!" he would say. Or, "Dave thinks he knows everything. You can't tell him anything anymore because he's making the big salary now, and he's just worried about his office."

"I never had anything but very cordial meetings with the man one-on-one," says a former product-line manager. "But when he wanted to chew on my butt in the group, he seemed to feel free to do it."

As Ken's brother, Stan came under sharp scrutiny. Nick Mazzarese walked into a committee meeting on his first day of work at Digital as New England sales manager and saw Olsen yelling angrily at Stan, the friend who had just hired him. "This is my new boss?" Mazzarese thought, watching from the back of the room as Stan took his brother's anger. What kind of workplace, Mazzarese wondered, have I just gotten myself into?

But it was Harlan Anderson who became the main object of

Olsen's discontent. In the loose organization of the early years, Anderson tried to maintain order on the financial side of the house. Several money managers had been hired through the years, but their efforts to infuse fiscal structure into DEC were ignored. And if Olsen didn't like the score on the bottom line, he didn't hesitate to change the scorekeeper.

There was no detailed budgeting or cash management in the early 1960s. Anderson, an engineer, was out of his element, as were others as well. "People were simply overcommitted," he says. The savvy business leader ARD had wanted as part of the original venture-capital commitment was now greatly missed.

Forrester saw DEC straining to get bigger, and he advised the company not to rush headlong into growth. There were frequent liquidity squeezes because the company was incurring expenses faster than the profit stream could support and selling products faster than Jack Shields could build his field force to service. DEC needed cash in June of 1963 and turned to ARD for a $300,000 loan, payable in three years.

In his president's letter introducing the 1964 annual report—DEC's first financial accounting to the public—Olsen said, "The nature of Digital Equipment Corporation has changed during the last several years. Originally we were builders of rather special laboratory equipment, but now we are tending much more toward being quantity producers of quality products. We now invest much more in research and development and in sales." For fiscal 1964, DEC spent $1.8 million on research and engineering—one-sixth of its revenues.

In his consultant's role, Forrester set up management seminars to instill the idea that growth should be checked and the pricing structure raised. He preached an academician's view that theories, modeling, and discipline would drive success. During SAGE's development, he had shown little patience for Watson's bureaucratic IBM. He hoped Digital could develop solid products on a steady schedule out of a research-oriented environment—his paradigm for business.

"The high-tech companies that started around Boston usually have very good products; the products aren't the problem," Forrester says. "The problem is the policy mixture and the interactions of policies that have to do with pricing, marketing, production, and the stability of resource allocation. A lot of the troubles come from being too flexible and too responsive, moving people back and forth between production and marketing in the early days.

"So there is a production crisis, and they all go to production and neglect the market. Then the orders fall off, and they go back to marketing and neglect production. That is a typical pattern. Most serious is the underpricing of products, which leads to lack of resources and slackening in quality. That's why many Route 128 companies grow to $5 million or $10 million and stagnate."

Anderson sided with Forrester. Olsen did not and took this difference of opinion as a personal affront, an attack on his presidency. Though he wouldn't openly confront Forrester, Olsen was angry at what he perceived as empty advice, especially from someone who had never worked in a nonacademic business environment. "Jay wanted to say how it should be done, but he wasn't there to take responsibility," Stan says. "Ken was looking for doers. He had enough critics around."

Olsen and Doriot began contemplating other alternatives, a more specific management structure that could solve DEC's problems. Frustration pervaded the two floors of the Mill that DEC now occupied. Olsen grew edgy and uncommunicative. "Ken was a more relaxed, easy-going guy when it was a small environment," Anderson says. "But as things started to get out of control, he didn't attribute it to anything he was doing. It was everybody else out of step. He became emotional about the fact that the old style wasn't working, and he was going to become a firmer president. He was pounding the table, and a lot of it was aimed at me."

Hindle, Ken's assistant, pitched in on the financial side until the company hired another business manager, an aggressive, financial manager named Harry Mann, who came from the Walter Kidde Company. Mann instituted needed controls, but from Anderson's point of view, he also was driving a wedge between the two cofounders in the hope of creating a position for himself near the top.

DEC's manufacturing reflected the greater chaos. Many more orders came in for modules than could be filled. Like the rest of the company, manufacturing was broken into dozens of small groups, some interconnected to others, some independent. The total manufacturing operation couldn't produce enough. Stan, with the help of inexperienced managers like Jack Smith, tried to stabilize the situation, but the order delays lengthened.

In early 1963, engineers at Atomic Energy of Canada's Chalk River plant were complaining about the complexity of the PDP-4, which they had purchased from DEC to control their nuclear reactor. They needed a smaller, simpler machine as a front end to the PDP-4.

Mazzarese and Bell flew up to Canada to discuss solutions with John Leng (who joined DEC later that year) and other Chalk River engineers. On the flight, Bell turned to Mazzarese and said, "You know, I think it would be possible to build a little computer that would do what they want but would also do what a lot of other people want." Bell took out paper and pencil and sketched the machine he already had drawn in his mind. "Maybe we can sell this idea to them," he said. The Canadians bought the design for the machine they had requested, not realizing that Bell had actually sketched a general-purpose, low-priced computer that would be the forerunner of the minicomputer industry. It was tabbed the PDP-5.

Bell, the prolific architect, was simultaneously designing the PDP-6, a 36-bit, large-scale computer conceived for time-sharing. It would sit at the high end of DEC's product line, a powerful machine priced at $300,000. But it was far too ambitious for a $10 million company. Olsen himself described the PDP-6 as "a bold product for a small company because it is equivalent to the very large computers used by scientific laboratories." DEC delivered the computer in the fall of 1964, trailed by a long list of complications and cost overruns.

Leng, who would later manage DEC's large systems, saw

the problems with the PDP-6. "It was a complex machine," he says. "It took a lot of resources. It was a time-sharing machine, so inherently you have a lot of users on-line. When the machine hiccups, it shows its unreliability very quickly because you affect a lot of users."

The fatal flaw may have been technical, a basic electrical design mistake: "They assumed the electronics would work," says Howard Hubbard, who was in line to be the product's promotion manager. "No one was given the task of making sure it did." A half-dozen PDP-6s were sold to places like MIT, Brookhaven National Laboratory, and Lawrence Radiation Laboratory before a customer discovered that the electrical signals were degrading not far from the CPU.

Anderson and Bell championed the PDP-6, and Olsen participated in its planning stages. Only when the technical problems began to arise did he disavow responsibility. He realized that the PDP-6 was not just a large project for a small company to take on, it was more than DEC could handle. He turned to the board, hoping the directors would ax the product. But they felt DEC should keep trying.

It was not Olsen's style to stand up and dictate openly to his company. He worked each issue—forming countless committees, setting up competing product development groups to seek a single answer, and constantly asking more and more questions. He counted on the truth working its way into everyone's view. But he also hand-lettered the road signs, so that the truth everyone eventually found was the one he was after.

Out of the tempest came an idea. Anderson believes it was a thought he himself had expressed in somewhat different form more than a year earlier. After lying awake one night struggling with the issue, Olsen hit upon his own version of the concept that would change DEC dramatically and fuel its stunning success. The idea was deceptively simple: a senior executive would take ownership of each product line. The manager would have to develop it, market it, nurture it, and turn a profit. Profit and loss accountability was his. He would, essentially, become an entrepreneur within Digital.

The product-line manager would stand before the Works Committee with his plans and budget. If they were accepted, he assumed the obligation for carrying them out. If later there turned out to be a problem or deviance from the plan, he would have to come back before the committee and explain. He would have responsibility.

Divisional structures, such as at Hewlett-Packard, built iron fences between divisions. Olsen's product-line arrangement purposely avoided barriers between groups. DEC built bridges among the product and functional managers. Line managers would share such resources as sales, manufacturing, and marketing, negotiating to buy these services from the central functions. This organizational structure, DEC's hallmark, came to be known as the *matrix*, a term that was unused in 1965.

Olsen declared to his managers, "Now we're a new company. Nobody tells anybody else what to do. Each of you has the responsibility for your part of the company. You, you, you, and you are now entrepreneurs, and everybody else is a service."

The matrix structure was not unique to DEC; the aerospace industry employed it to some degree with some success. But DEC came to symbolize matrix management because in Olsen's hands, it became the perfect mechanism for explosive growth. The matrix by design gave virtually everyone in the company at least two bosses. And it further encouraged corporate democracy. With influence over decisions spread around so widely, proposals could spring up from anywhere in the organization. The matrix encouraged creativity. Unlike strict hierarchical companies, DEC suddenly opened up, allowing ideas, action, influence, and responsibility to flow at all angles through the organization.

Olsen came to dislike the term *matrix*, rejecting a label for his management structure. Nonetheless, matrix-style management made Olsen famous. More important, it let DEC grow.

Not surprisingly, however, many in the company felt demoted. Managers accustomed to the hierarchical past suddenly saw their power dissipated. Control was far less clear.

Their subordinates now had a second and sometimes third boss to answer to. "It went over like a lead balloon," says Olsen.

Some, like Anderson, felt even worse than demoted. He believed that after Olsen created the product-line structure, he saw it as a means of dumping the PDP-6 on Anderson and eventually shoving him out of the company. "It was the first time," Anderson says, "he had ever identified and pushed a particular project onto me, as opposed to letting me be part of the general management. I felt like a scapegoat."

Whatever his motivation, Olsen was given full credit for devising a business structure built for high growth. The board accepted the suggestion with just a little lingering sentiment in favor of a centralist point of view. The board meetings had become tension-filled as Anderson and Forrester debated openly what was happening within DEC, much to Olsen's discomfort. He didn't like airing the family business, even to the directors.

Stan initially pressed for more divisionalization, because he felt the company should be developing general managers. But he got over his concerns within a week. Stan believes that if there were any doubters, it was because Ken didn't sell the structure well enough, despite the genius of the idea. "If you've been going in a different direction and someone says, 'This is where we are going now,' you need to get sold on it, and Ken doesn't quite sell enough."

Nonetheless, the plan was bought. Olsen put Mazzarese in charge of the PDP-5 and gave Stan the modules business and Win Hindle the new MIT-developed Linc computer, along with the memory test products. And to his cofounder, Olsen assigned the PDP-6. With this, Anderson was essentially being handed a one-way ticket out of the company.

The strain between Olsen and Anderson had grown to intolerable proportions. Though never close friends, they had been close business partners. They had shared long walks, deep in discussion, in the woods around the Mill and talked every night over the phone about their company. They were bonded by the experience of starting Digital together and watching it expand. Both were privately anguished now at the conflict. Some, like Norm Taylor, who had supervised both men at Lincoln Lab, were not surprised at the deterioration of the relationship. He saw a basic mismatch from the start—Olsen's dynamism versus Anderson's cool reserve. "There was no harmony there," Taylor says.

In his frustration, Anderson turned to Forrester, Doriot, and all the board members. He told them about Olsen's "bizarre behavior and harsh treatment of engineers." Mazzarese, for one, felt Anderson was obliquely testing whose allegiance he could count on. Olsen read Anderson's maneuvering as a threat to his power, possibly even an attempted coup. He agonized over a possible civil war, fearing that it would tear DEC apart. But he precipitated no direct confrontation with Anderson. Instead, Olsen handed Anderson, who was already standing in a swamp, a heavy rock and let him sink.

Anderson believed that larger computers were important for the company. But he was not married to the PDP-6 and felt that Ken should bear as much responsibility for its current plight as he. Olsen divorced himself from the PDP-6. And then he helped make it fail. Mazzarese, in charge of the PDP-5, suddenly found himself the beneficiary of Olsen's largesse. Resources were pulled from the 6 and given to the 5 team. The PDP-5 shipped in early 1964 at a remarkably low price of $27,000. As the least expensive core-memory computer available, the PDP-5 sold far beyond expectations for Bell's simple idea. DEC planned to sell ten machines—enough to write off engineering expenses. In fact, the company sold about 1,000.

In the dark mood that enveloped Olsen, the PDP-5 was a bright light. He personally pushed the system, revealing an affinity for small computers that continues to this day. The PDP-6, on the other hand, failed terribly. Only twenty-three machines were sold before the newly formed Operations Committee voted to kill it. It rests in DEC's history as the least-selling machine ever produced.

By early 1966, with the fledgling product-line structure

blossoming, Harlan Anderson quit. "I decided it was the best thing for my sanity," he says. "General Doriot and Dorothy Rowe begged me to stay." He is convinced that Olsen believed his departure was the right move for the company's sake. If Digital was to continue to grow and thrive, it needed only one leader. And that leader was Ken Olsen.

"Take responsibility."

—*Ken Olsen*

8
Start the Revolution

ENGINEERS AND SCIENTISTS calculate significant changes in structures by the measure called *order of magnitude*. In general terms, it is a generational change, a quantum leap forward. By 1966, Olsen had changed Digital by such an order of magnitude. The creation of the product lines was the basis for the transformation; the stagnation in revenues and earnings suddenly turned into dynamic growth. There was a sense of manifest destiny, that DEC was forging not just a market but a revolution.

Digital passed through its wrenching transformation free of the glare of TV lights and the sharp pens of a later decade's business writers. The departure of a cofounder (Anderson), followed closely by both a famous director (Forrester) and the lead engineer (Bell, who left for a long sabbatical), would today draw a pack of business reporters to the corporate front doors to find out what was going on. But in 1966, internal business fights were more likely to be a private matter. With the shades drawn, Olsen managed to turn what could have been a scandalous cover story into an opportunity to tighten control over his company.

Forrester had risen to challenge Olsen's basic philosophy on running the organization, and he lost. He could see no point in continuing on the board if his advice was unheeded. At the same time, MIT embroiled itself in legal suits with DEC and several other computer companies over patent infringements related to Forrester's magnetic core memory. Forrester left DEC's board, stating that it would be a conflict of interest for him to remain during the impending litigation.

Though Olsen had backed Forrester's entry to the board almost a decade before, he was now glad that he left. After Anderson and Forrester, no one from within DEC ever again held a seat on the board of directors—except Olsen. He could see that his management style and philosophy bred questions and confrontations, and he wanted just one point of view presented to the board from inside DEC: his own.

Bell avoided confronting Olsen directly by taking a sabbatical at Carnegie-Mellon University, then known as Carnegie Tech. At age thirty-two, he had masterminded every Digital computer except the PDP-1. He was burned out, his enthusiasm smothered by internal politics and Olsen's heavy hand. And besides, the last thing DEC needed in 1966 was another computer to develop. Bell wanted to teach and to learn about the far reaches of computing and so turned to a university. "I just didn't want the narrowness of the system anymore," Bell says. "And there were too damn many products for a $20 million company."

Bell was also unhappy about what had happened with the PDP-6. He considered the machine an intellectual achievement from an engineer's point of view, despite its commercial failure. He personally felt the sting of the black eye it received at DEC. When he left for Carnegie-Mellon in 1966, Bell retained a consultant's status at DEC, much to the relief of the engineering corps, which not only relied on his genius but was won over by his ebullient and unpredictable personality.

Olsen was shaken by the Anderson episode and remained insecure about the complex swirls of management that his new product-line structure was creating. He had anointed five key players with power. On the product side: his brother, Stan

Olsen, Nick Mazzarese, and Win Hindle. On the functional side: Ted Johnson, over sales, and a new manager, Peter Kaufmann, over manufacturing. Along with Olsen himself and Harry Mann, they formed the original Operations Committee in 1966. He told them to take responsibility and then banned hiring for a year. Resources were tight—manufacturing, research, and administrative expenses had jumped $4.4 million in fiscal 1965, and net income dropped for the second straight year. If the new entrepreneurs could thrive in this austere-budget environment, Olsen would know the product-line structure suited DEC.

Kaufmann, a manufacturing hotshot recruited from Beckman Instruments Company in California, was considered a "new age" sort of manager. He was a young MBA in a field generally populated by older, unschooled, process-oriented managers. He understood organizational dynamics and tried to meld the environment and the people who worked in it. Most of DEC's managers had started with the company, so Kaufmann brought a refreshing and much needed outsider's view to Maynard. He was also witty and irreverent, possessing the innate ability to relax a tense moment with the right word or look.

Kaufmann had been restless on the West Coast. He sought a new challenge, and when Mann called, he decided to look at DEC. On his first job interview there, Kaufmann spent an hour in the president's office. Olsen drew an organizational chart on the blackboard. "This is the screwiest thing I've ever seen," Kaufmann said to himself. "There's a million pieces. This guy's an idiot." Mann offered him the job, but Kaufmann turned him down.

Kaufmann returned to California, where his boss, a friend who knew he needed a change of jobs, observed, "No man who builds a $20 million corporation out of nothing is an idiot. Look again. Maybe you're the idiot." When Digital called four months later, still without a head of manufacturing, Kaufmann took another look.

Flying back to Boston, he met Olsen, but this time along with Doriot. The General was about to leave for Logan Airport and a plane to France, but he ended up spending four hours discussing the job and his manufacturing philosophy. This time, Kaufmann found Olsen more personable, more down-to-earth. But it was Doriot—smooth and glib, a manu-facturing-production man—who won Kaufmann over. This time Kaufmann accepted Digital and with it, Olsen.

In his first week, Kaufmann and Mann toured the com-pany's two floors and then went down to two more empty floors in the Mill. "I want to rent these," Mann said.

"But we won't need this much space in five years," Kauf-mann said. DEC, it turned out, filled the floors before the year was out.

Kaufmann walked into his first management meeting at the Mill—before Olsen formed the Operations Committee—and was stunned. Thirty-five people sat in the room, and all of them reported directly to Olsen. Later, Kaufmann was called into the president's office to discuss the specifics of his mana-gerial role. Olsen pulled out an old envelope and wrote down the people who would report to Kaufmann. He handed over the list, with thirteen names on it, and said, "Go find these people, and tell them you're their new boss."

Kaufmann suddenly became the overseer of nearly half the company's 700 employees. Several of his new reports were shocked at the method of introduction. One couldn't handle the breach of hierarchical etiquette and left. It was an odd beginning.

Within a couple of years, Kaufmann emerged as a rallying point for the vice presidents and managers—DEC executives looking for someone to handle the day-to-day running of the company. "I knew a lot about power and politics and how organizations worked and about people," Kaufmann says. "Ken isn't a real people man. He wasn't organizationally attuned. He had strong survival instincts. He collected around him individuals, some of whom were brilliant. But he wasn't much for organizing them or directing them."

Kaufmann got closer to Olsen than anyone else in the 1960s, as close as almost any Digital executive ever has. He became Olsen's confidante and legs of support inside the company.

Olsen needed management support, and he turned also to MIT's Edgar Schein for counseling and professional advice. Thus began a relationship with Olsen and DEC that continues to this day. It was a corporate culture unlike any Schein had seen: chaos built around a strong central figure, a founder who gained control by giving up control. Schein saw in Olsen an engineer who was keenly interested in the mechanics of leading a company. Olsen viewed management as a process, like engineering, which could be learned and taught and implemented. Early on he realized the need to motivate his people, despite a limited sense of how to do it. His introduction of the product-line structure served that function. Suddenly, motivation was there in the form of survival. Each manager controlled his own destiny to some extent within the matrix, but was, at the same time, dependent on countless others within the organization to get things done. While they didn't own unilateral power, the managers did carry great influence and responsibility. They were motivated to make things happen.

Schein's first function was to try to bring together DEC's feisty group of managers, who were flailing about in the new product-line structure, trying to figure out who did what for whom. He proposed afternoon get-togethers—Olsen hosting ten or fifteen engineers in his office for tea and conversation. Olsen accepted this social role for a month or so and then called a halt to the tea parties.

Schein was more successful instituting off-site meetings for the Operations Committee, which took place at Olsen's cabin in the New Hampshire woods near Lake Winnipesaukee. The gatherings came to be called "Woods meetings," a name that remains today at DEC for any meeting off-site.

Once a month, the Operations Committee drove two hours north to either Ken's or Stan's cabin on Governor's Island. Schein designed the meetings as a means of getting DEC managers away from the daily barrage of individual decisions and to contemplate, as a group, where they and DEC were heading. Olsen used these sessions to encourage his executives to reach for leadership. The cabins were big enough to sleep the seven or eight participants. The atmosphere was loose and informal. The Operations Committee members held no influence in the middle of nowhere. They made their own beds, cooked their own meals, cleaned up their own dishes.

In keeping with DEC's style, the Woods meetings were anything but quiet. Though the marching orders were to focus only on future strategy, the discussions swept all over DEC's past and present. The managers jockeyed for position, knowing that their performance here could either enhance or diminish their influence back in Maynard. A feeling of camaraderie cushioned the bursts of temper and tension that crackled around the room. The long stretches of discussions were broken up with hikes in the deep pine woods, skiing, skating, and sailing in this men-only environment. "We'd go for walks," Kaufmann says, "and then we'd get back and all of a sudden in ten minutes we'd make six major decisions about a new direction for the company."

The informality often led to an inability to sustain order. He who talked loudest or longest held sway. Sometimes order was imposed through an orange or a grapefruit—you couldn't speak unless you were holding it. When you had said your piece, you tossed the fruit to the next person. Olsen watched and monitored and occasionally led the discussions. Sometimes he spoke in parables to start the meetings—often vague, unexplained monologues that would leave everyone contemplating their meaning and intent for the two-day retreat.

As the organizational consultant, Schein attended many Woods meetings as a facilitator. He sought to work out better relationships among the vice presidents, and between the vice presidents and Olsen. Before heading to the meetings, he would poll DEC workers in various offices or on the shop floor, asking about the problems they faced in doing their jobs right. He carried these issues with him to the Operations Committee for resolution.

At one Woods meeting, Schein set up an experiment. He asked each Operations Committee member to take a turn sitting in the "hot seat." The others were to treat that person as if he weren't in the room and talk about him—point out his strengths, criticize his weaknesses. The person in the chair wasn't allowed to talk or respond in any way. The experiment worked well . . . until Olsen sat in the chair. He could not stay quiet when he was criticized. He immediately defended himself. "Interpersonal skills were not his strong point," says one vice president.

Perhaps because of his management insecurities at the time, Olsen did not recognize the full genius of his own product-line plan. He was simply aiming to pass out responsibility throughout the organization. Essentially, he had placed ownership of every part of the company in somebody else's hands. If there was an organizational question, the head of the product line was to figure it out.

The central functions, such as sales and service and marketing, became the checks and balances that kept the line managers from carrying power too far. If a product-line manager wanted a machine built or promoted beyond what his own group's limited resources could do, he had to appeal to central manufacturing or advertising to get it done. This system prevented overzealous line managers from running off and developing and selling products any way they saw fit. A strong functional manager could influence corporate direction as much as a strong product-line manager. The drawback of the scheme was that it put enormous power into the hands of the most influential and clever managers—not necessarily the ones making the best decisions. The culture became Darwinian: survival of those best able to adapt to the new structure.

In giving out ownership, Olsen got back a bonding of the manager to his project. The new product-line chiefs became parents to their machines, and their DEC careers lived or died with their success or failure. DEC's structure was a powerful tool for gaining full commitment.

The message from Olsen—"take responsibility"—swept down into the whole organization. Levels upon sublevels bought into the new structure. The company began running from the center, rather than from the top down. Midlevel managers directly affected how their product looked, how it functioned, how it was priced, how it was marketed. They were not shielded from the bottom line by layers of bureaucracy.

Olsen sat above it all, watching. He postured as if he had

nothing much to do with product decisions. He didn't "own" any of the projects, so how could he be responsible? He gave himself no product line to handle, so he was free to wander the company "overseeing the cooks and stirring the pots as he chose," as *Fortune* magazine put it in 1986. He could move in close, offer suggestions and criticism, even pull out a screwdriver and get his hands dirty. He gave up direct responsibility, but he retained indirect control through the Operations Committee, where his influence was supreme. Olsen discovered that he didn't need to issue direct orders to have his way. An extra question, a lingering sense of dissatisfaction, a prolonged period of silence sent the committee members and the managers off to find a way to satisfy Ken.

As vice president of sales and service worldwide, Ted Johnson oversaw two vital, functional parts of the company. He stood on a precarious perch, holding tight to the masts of two ships that zigged and zagged crazily through the sea.

"The product lines had the power; he who has the gold, rules," was a common view in the company, says Johnson. The line managers got their money by convincing the Operations Committee to back their products. "Ken let the middle run the company," Johnson says, "and the Operations Committee was the bank. The product lines came for investments, and we on the committee would fight it out among ourselves." Then Johnson, who ran a functional department as well as sat on the Operations Committee, had to go back to the product managers for his own funding. "We in sales went to them for our money. We had to contract with them and then put pressure back on them to deliver products."

A sensitive young manager, Johnson was on the battlefield between product lines. He not only had to handle the complexities of the new corporate structure, but he had to fight Olsen's inherent distrust of marketing. Olsen's father had taught him by example that one should never try to sell something that a customer didn't need. Build a good product, Olsen believed, and people will bang down the door to buy it. Johnson couldn't win: if a product didn't sell, he wasn't doing his job; if it did, the product was selling itself.

Midlevel managers took all the responsibility they could get, but often it was unclear what they should do with it. They needed direction. Olsen refused to give it. He saw the puritan ethic clearly at work: you pull yourself up by your bootstraps and find the way—in this case, the DEC way. He was not unmindful of the confusion. He saw that the product lines were selling similar products to the same audience, but he expected the central functions to clarify the confusion.

Stories of Olsen's puritanical values spread through the company, and people would not think of drinking alcohol or swearing in his presence. Employees were tremendously loyal to the man; he ignored formalities and insisted on being "Ken" to everyone. The campuslike atmosphere borrowed from MIT pervaded the farthest corners of the old Mill. Olsen walked the miles of hallways and stopped in to discuss product engineering as often with the technicians as with the product managers. New engineers were startled to come to work on a Saturday and find Olsen hunched over their drawing tables, studying their current project. He was not there spying, and he was not there to offer answers. Olsen the engineer just couldn't stay away from the hands-on designing.

Clashes began to take place in the Operations Committee as the managers, such as Mazzarese, Hindle, Kaufmann, and others, grappled for influence and resources. The tradition of decision through confrontation was born. Schein monitored the meetings and suggested exercises and skills to alleviate the tension. In his book *Organizational Culture and Leadership* Schein disguises his client Olsen as "Murphy" and DEC as "Action." He points out "Murphy's" stated commitment to broad consensus across a range of committees and managers. "That is the official, formal position," Schein says. "Yet many of his subordinates will say that he usually does know what he wants and is only manipulating the situation to have the answer come out of the group, so that he does not have to take sole responsibility." Schein concludes that Murphy both manipulates situations and, in some cases, genuinely discovers solutions through consensus.

The product-line strategy set a framework, but now the

company needed the products to make it work. In the fall of 1965, DEC had unveiled the PDP-8, a machine that Bell derived from his own PDP-5 design. The PDP-8 defined an industry and sent Digital sales into orbit. Riding this product, Digital grew between 25 percent and 40 percent per year in revenues as well as profits for the next seventeen years.

Perhaps because the PDP-6, a large machine, had fared so poorly in the marketplace, or perhaps because of his intense desire to do something—anything—different from IBM, Olsen hammered away at the concept of small. While the computing world was looking to the more complex and expensive, Olsen pushed DEC the other way. The PDP-8 was, like the PDP-5, a 12-bit machine, but far smaller and cheaper. Instead of one cabinet, the PDP-8 fit into half of a cabinet, which allowed users to put it on top of a lab bench. Its small footprint also attracted other vendors who wanted to integrate the PDP-8 into their own systems.

In 1960, Stan Olsen had hired Edson de Castro out of the University of Lowell as employee number 100. An ambitious, strong-willed, and often troublesome engineer, de Castro moved into the Special Systems Group, which handled missions apart from the standard product lines. Under Bell's tutelage, de Castro turned in a stellar performance carrying out the PDP-5 design and thus was given an opportunity to create the next generation of the machine, the PDP-8.

While the PDP-8 was getting set for production, Olsen suggested that de Castro use a new diode chip mounted on a ceramic substrate with a thin-film capacitor (called a Flip Chip), a method that drastically reduced the cost of the circuits. But the technique was untried, and despite Olsen's reassurance, de Castro doubted it would work. On his own initiative, he quietly enlisted a circuit designer named Dick Sogge to develop a conventional back-up circuit, just in case.

De Castro readied the PDP-8 for production, but despite Olsen's promise, the Flip Chip was not perfected. The PDP-8 would have been delayed going into manufacturing, causing DEC untold trouble in the marketplace, but de Castro pulled the conventional circuits from his back pocket to save the production schedule. De Castro is modest about his foresight. "That's what a good engineer is supposed to do, isn't it?" he says. Inside DEC, such cleverness usually brought forth high praise and recognition. In DEC parlance, he had slain a dragon. But such reward was not to be for de Castro.

The Operations Committee haggled over pricing the new PDP-8 at one of the first Woods meetings. The debate was whether to price aggressively, in order to dramatically improve volume, or to price conservatively, preserving higher margins. The proponents for radical pricing won out. DEC decided to sell the PDP-8 at a break-through level—$18,000. That figure was unheard of for a high-performance, general-purpose computer, far below any machines being sold by IBM or anyone else in the industry. DEC turned selling computers into a price war.

Even Olsen and his commanders were unprepared for the results. The PDP-8 quickly achieved a production run reserved for IBM computers. In all, DEC sold more than 50,000 of the machines over its fifteen-year lifespan. The PDP-8 opened up new markets for DEC and formed the basis for a new style of selling in the industry—the original equipment manufacturer (OEM). Such OEMs as scientific instrumentation makers or typesetting companies integrated their specific applications into the PDP-8, attaching their own hardware, writing their own software, and selling the resulting package as their own product. DEC assisted in the integration but let the OEMs provide the service and maintenance. The arrangement saved DEC the costly, labor-intensive job of writing its own software. Going bare bones helped DEC hold overhead in line, while revenues poured in. The engineers in Maynard began to earn a reputation as ironmakers—they'd turn out the hardware and let the software appear whenever it would, mostly from third-party vendors. Not long after, the OEM business accounted for 50 percent of all sales, lighting the fuse for DEC to skyrocket.

"To come out with a better machine and dramatically lower the price was a bold move," Stan Olsen says. "We provided a tremendous amount of computing power to the world to allow people to do their own thing with computers." Unmentioned but obvious to DEC was the absence of IBM from this segment of the computer market. Busy counting its billions from sales of large-scale computers, IBM took no notice of DEC and its emerging market. In fact, IBM had just completed a three-year, super-secret, $5 billion development effort—a bet-the-company gamble on its revolutionary System/360 mainframe computer.

According to Stan Olsen, DEC felt as if it was leading its own revolution in small, accessible computers. But many in business didn't understand the message of the PDP-8. In 1965, Stan and Ken visited the publishers of the *Wall Street Journal*, trying to sell them on the new machine's typesetting capabilities. The reaction from the *Journal*: no one is ever going to convince an editor to sit in front of a computer terminal all day. The Olsens pressed on undaunted.

John Leng, who started and ran DEC's Canadian operation until 1964, flew to London to establish DEC's presence in the United Kingdom. He sold PDP-5s and then PDP-8s with tremendous success. In the mid-sixties, miniskirt fever raged on London's Carnaby Street. Leng zigzagged through British traffic in an Austin Mini. He sent back sales reports: "Here is the latest minicomputer activity in the land of miniskirts as I drive around in my Mini Minor." The phrase caught on at DEC, and then the industry trade publications grabbed on to it. The age of the minicomputer was born.

The PDP-8 drove revenues through the roof at the Mill. DEC grew more than 50 percent a year, from $15 million in revenues in 1965 to nearly $23 million in 1966. Between fiscal 1965 and 1967, profits multiplied six times, to $4.5 million. By bringing affordable computing within reach of thousands, DEC presaged the personal computer era of a decade and a half later. Suddenly, DEC began to get noticed as a serious mainstream computer maker. According to Ted Withington, a former consultant with the noted research firm Arthur D. Little in Cambridge, Massachusettes, Digital began creeping into computer industry reports in 1965, the year it launched the minicomputer business.

As with every good idea, imitators quickly appeared. The possibility of selling lots of computers cheaply appealed to a range of electronics vendors, such as Hewlett-Packard, Varian Associates, Computer Controls Corporation, and Scientific Control Corporation. By 1970, about seventy companies were manufacturing minicomputers. But none seriously challenged Digital's domination of the market it had created. Most of the pretenders to the throne were immersed in other businesses both before and after they jumped into minicomputers for an expected quick killing. Olsen never gave in to temptation to stray from computer making. He has long credited this single-mindedness as key to DEC's success. "We don't go into random businesses like everyone else," Olsen says. "We decide what we want to do and what we want to be good at and concentrate on it."

Success also breeds merger and acquisition fever. Control Data's president, Bill Norris, sent Norm Taylor to Olsen with an offer to buy DEC. "CDC was really rolling," Taylor says. "The P/E ratio was sixty to one and Norris is an old poker player. He said, 'Let's use this Chinese money and buy something.' He wanted Digital." Taylor already knew Olsen's answer, but he asked anyway and dutifully reported back to Norris Olsen's refusal.

Hewlett-Packard came to Olsen in the mid-1960s with money in hand. "We'll compete with you if we can't buy you," HP told Olsen. Again, he refused. So HP jumped into the market on its own. Others came shopping over the years— Singer, Xerox, Harris. Olsen said no to them all. He never forgot the policy he adopted when he started DEC—do not look for a quick profit and then sell out.

And he didn't look to buy others, either, even though he was amassing the cash to do it. "Acquiring other companies takes up too much time and emotion," Olsen says. Though DEC has made numerous strategic agreements, it has never acquired another company in its thirty-one years. In an industry as merger-prone as the computer field, this isolation is remarkable. Olsen is determined to go it alone.

At that particular turning point of DEC's history in 1966,

there was no emotional energy to spare. Olsen had, in his view, steered the company back from a dangerous course. He had staved off what he perceived as Anderson's power play. He had implemented the product-line structure—a framework built to handle rapid growth—just in time to reap its benefit with the PDP-8. Olsen was in control, the foundation was solid, the company would survive. But Ken Olsen was anything but satisfied.

"Now I can buy a second canoe."

—Ken Olsen

9
Building the Matrix

CHANGE BRED MANY things at Digital but never calm. The company thrived on chaos. The product lines assigned responsibility but did little to settle the disorder. If anything, the new structure replaced one form of management turbulence with another. The matrix had transformed what was essentially one big brawl into an interwoven net of smaller squabbles.

From the start, Olsen was not simply an engineer's engineer. He had a collateral interest in the practice of management—how one motivates people to produce in their jobs. Designing the Memory Test Computer at MIT had given him a taste of leadership in the early 1950s. But that project required a single-minded focus on one goal, not directing different groups of people on different projects over the long haul. He had also taken over running the Park Street Church's Sunday school the year prior to starting DEC. That nonsecular task was a quick study for Olsen, and profit wasn't a complicating factor. He liked to believe that the means to accomplishment in the spiritual world translated into business achievement. But DEC was demanding much more out of him.

Olsen felt he needed to be everywhere, seeing everything, and sometimes he seemed to be. Jack Smith told the *Wall Street Journal* in 1986 how he had purchased a $7,000 soldering machine early in DEC's history—"a huge investment at the time"—and it proved unreliable. He worked nights and weekends to get the machine to function so that Olsen wouldn't notice. Finally, Smith bought a replacement machine, moved the lemon to a storeroom, and covered it with canvas. "Whew, I got away with that," he thought. Several years later, he came across the machine and lifted off the covering. He found a hand-lettered sign that read, "Smith's Folly, Ken Olsen."

Olsen could be a clever manipulator. He needed people to want to do it his way. And early on, through the very tangible power of his personality—the sheer presence of this large, intense man—DEC employees responded. Intuitively, Olsen set up situations in which he could win but not lose, which created an aura of invincibility around him. The matrix was the perfect form by which he could invisibly orchestrate his company.

The product-line structure perfectly suited a young company that needed flexibility and speed of response in an unstable marketplace. In the dynamics of a product group, "If you tell someone 'Your job is the following,' that guy will die to make it happen," says Julius Marcus, a former vice president who operated in that structure for fifteen years. "That's the way you get a cause championed. You find somebody and pin it on his chest." A strong functional organization, on the other hand, provided more stability when a mature business was seeking cost efficiency. Marrying the two together, as Olsen did, balanced form with function.

Rosabeth Moss Kanter, a noted behavioralist at the Harvard Business School and longtime consultant with Digital, described the characteristics of the product-line matrix in her 1983 book, *The Change Masters*. "In a matrix organization, employees or managers may combine two or more dimensions in their jobs—a functional specialty, such as sales, and a responsibility to a particular product line or market area. This combination," Kanter wrote, "is reflected in reporting to two or more bosses, one for the function and one or more for the product areas. Thus, whereas in the classic unitary chain of command, authority could be directly and relatively easily exercised, in the matrix, influence down the line must substitute for authority to gain compliance, since neither boss has complete control over the employee. Traditional authority virtually disappears; managers must instead persuade, influence or convince. The subordinate is expected to be the resolver of the conflict, integrating the demands in these two dimensions. Conflict is thus built into the matrix."

Conflict is built into DEC. Olsen fostered it from the beginning of the product-line structure. He dichotomized the environment as well, treating his executives one way and the rank and file another. Those close to him, the vice presidents and line managers, thrived or withered under the harsh scrutiny. Lower-level workers rarely witnessed Olsen's outbursts of anger. They were not burdened with the same responsibility for success or failure. Olsen became a legend to them.

Though Olsen was often particularly rough on the engineering managers, calling them prima donnas and blaming them for product problems, he clearly favored the engineering staff. He molded the company to fit an engineer's needs and temperament. An engineer, Olsen knew from firsthand experience, worked best when greatly challenged and allowed a wide berth. His message to the company was that the product drove the market, marketing did not drive the product.

The engineers responded with enthusiasm and passed that feeling on to the programmers and technicians who worked with them. "DEC was a fabulous company, everyone loved it," says Henry Burkhardt, who dropped out of Princeton to join at age nineteen. "I was a computer programmer by day and a computer-checkout technician at night. We were trying to ship computers, but some of the machines didn't work, so we all worked on a voluntary basis in manufacturing at night. We got ten or fifteen machines shipped that way."

This dedication pervaded all levels of the Mill, but it was imperative that it exist among DEC management. Olsen could see that it took a special kind of executive to succeed in DEC's barely controlled chaos. It was especially difficult to find experienced managers in traditional companies who could tolerate the Digital style. So recent college graduates, people in their first or second job, started to populate the Mill. "Grow your own" became a Digital axiom of how to get good managers.

In August 1966, after holding off for nine years to avoid the pressures of Wall Street, Olsen and his directors decided to take the company public. The initial offering on the Over the Counter exchange was priced at $22 per share—a level Olsen and the board insisted on. The underwriters, Lehman Brothers, believed that $17 per share was more reasonable. The stock opened at $22 and quickly dropped to $17. Analyst Martin Simpson remembers there was great confusion on the Street over this new public company: Was the stock overpriced? Would DEC be bought out? And who was Ken Olsen?

To the financial community, he was a mystery man—an engineer, rather than a trained corporate chief executive. And his company was selling computers, not renting them, even though hundreds of millions of rental dollars were flowing in yearly to IBM. What were his chances of surviving?

"Olsen was very worried about being acquired," Simpson says. "Even though the stock was selling at thirty times earnings, which is a very high price, they were terribly concerned about being taken over."

Digital offered 375,000 shares to the public on August 16; 235,000 "company shares" and 140,000 owned by a selling stockholder—Harlan Anderson. He heard the news while vacationing in California that going public had netted him $3 million. Olsen's 13 percent take—350,000 shares—earned him a fortune, on paper, of more than $7 million.

Though suddenly a multimillionaire, Olsen didn't change his lifestyle or his outlook on the company. He still drove a small Ford car. He still wore rumpled, baggy suits. He still felt more comfortable in work clothes and preferred a seat in his canoe to a table in an elegant restaurant. On the day of the public offering he told Kaufmann, "Now I can buy a second canoe."

But it was ARD, owning 1,750,000 shares, or 65 percent of

the company, at the time, that enriched its coffers on paper by $38.5 million that day. In nine years, ARD's original investment of $70,000 had multiplied by 500 times.

The product-line strategy was working better and faster than even Olsen hoped it might. But now there were stockholders to perform for. Short-term gains—what Wall Street always demanded—meant nothing to Olsen if the company's health over the long haul suffered. "Explaining to Wall Street why growth wasn't a goal was impossible," he says. "We gave up and just mouthed the words because they wouldn't understand."

Learning to live within the product-line matrix was not easy for managers. The newly designated internal entrepreneurs felt their way along. As Kanter points out, "The managers themselves sometimes wondered how much of the entrepreneurial activity was really beneficial to the company; frustration was occasionally expressed with duplication of effort and difficulty of transferring good ideas across organizational boundaries, slippage of schedules and changes of ground rules as new players entered the action."

Olsen worked the organizational issues hard, and he used the Operations Committee meetings as his forum. Though he felt awkward in one-on-one settings, he was comfortable sitting as the overseer of the corporate mission in the Operations Committee. He didn't necessarily hold a place at the head of the table. And often he said little, just listened and took in the messages.

The Operations Committee met every Monday morning. The original group—Ken, Stan, Hindle, Kaufmann, Johnson, Mann, and Mazzarese—first discussed basic corporate business. They argued over every kind of issue, from important product questions to turf battles over the shared resources, such as advertising or finances. Then they were joined by key department managers, both product-line and functional. The meetings were ostensibly open to any manager who wanted to attend. But no one came simply to observe. In the natural conflict of the matrix system, the Operations Committee meetings got brutal at times.

The petitioners either proposed a product direction or

solicited resources. Olsen listened. Sometimes he chatted quietly with the person next to him, seemingly oblivious to the impact such inattention had on the meeting. He regularly waited with his own hidden agenda, a thought or issue that was bothering him. And when the unfortunate executive whose area touched on that particular, bothersome subject got up to speak, Olsen lashed out.

He was relentless. The verbal attacks, such as the one Mazzarese witnessed directed at Stan, were loud and angry. He tore apart the issue piece by piece and, in the process, sometimes tore apart the person as well. The object of his wrath usually stood and took the frontal assault. At times, the attacks turned toward a manager's professional capabilities, striking at his weaknesses. Olsen's face got red and the veins in his neck bulged, as his frustration came to the surface. There was no answering or objecting. If someone argued, Olsen raised his large frame from his chair and yelled louder.

A rare few managers, like Mazzarese, yelled back. He went toe-to-toe with Olsen on several occasions, after his people in the small computer group had been attacked over a proposal. Even as he was shouting, Mazzarese saw the absurdity of the moment. This, he thought, is not how to reach a decision. Shaking and full of fury, Mazzarese fled the meetings, hopped in his car, and sped down the highway in a straight line away from DEC, trying to vent the anger. "His method was effective, though," Mazzarese says. "I worked harder for him than for anybody else, just to show him."

Others bore the attacks as physical assaults, shrinking in their seats. Not quite understanding what had gone wrong, they would be dazed and anguished as to how to get back into Olsen's favor. Johnson came under intense pressure, not only from Olsen, but from the product-line managers, who so desperately needed his group's services.

What drove Olsen ceaselessly in these meetings was the need to create responsibility. Line managers were given no direct orders from Olsen but had to respond as if they had. They could only try to sift his desires from his parables or his anger. In *Organizational Culture and Leadership*, Schein relates an incident from inside the Operations Committee that illustrates Olsen's message: "A newly hired treasurer was asked to make his report on the state of the business," Schein writes. "The treasurer had analyzed the three major product lines and brought his analysis to the meeting. He distributed the information and then pointed out that one product line in particular was in financial difficulty because of falling sales, excessive inventories and rapidly rising manufacturing costs. It became evident in the meeting that the vice president in charge of the product line had not seen the treasurer's figures and was somewhat embarrassed by what was being revealed.

"The treasurer finished and all eyes turned toward the VP. He said he wished he had had a chance to look at the figures, but since he had not seen them, he could not respond immediately. At this point, Murphy (Schein's pseudonym for Olsen) blew up at the vice president, to the surprise of the whole group."

The grand-standing treasurer did not offend Olsen. The unprepared vice president did. "Suddenly everyone realized that there was a powerful message in Murphy's behavior. He clearly expected and assumed that a product-line vice president would always be totally on top of his own business and would never put himself in a position of being embarrassed by financial data. The fact that he did not have his own numbers was a worse sin than being in trouble. The fact that he could not answer the troublesome figures was also a worse sin than being in trouble."

"If you are too successful," Olsen says, "You can delegate the learning to someone else, and suddenly you find you can't run the business. I asked a vice president, 'What happens if you raise the price 10 percent?' He answered, 'I don't know, I'll ask my financial analyst.' But a good vice president should be able to do the calculations himself—at least to within plus or minus 10 percent to 20 percent."

Olsen constantly threw new messages at his executives, messages that were sometimes straightforward and obvious but more often vague and open to several interpretations. As Bill Long, a former vice president, told *Fortune* magazine,

"Sometimes they're like little paper airplanes aimed at a particular person; sometimes they're like leaflets from the Goodyear blimp, aimed at anyone who picks them up."

Olsen was no less oblique in reviewing performances of his vice presidents on the Operations Committee. These annual sessions were brief, with little discussion about salary, since all Operations Committee members received about the same pay. Reviews might consist of just a quick sentence or two. One year Olsen said to Johnson, "Just don't intimidate people." Johnson walked away and spent the next several weeks trying to figure out the message.

Kaufmann, still relatively new to the fold, had a sixth sense in dealing with Olsen, an ability to read what he was really thinking. "Ken sometimes doesn't say what is really in his head," Kaufmann says. "And sometimes what he says sounds just awful. He'll get up and give a speech and say things that will just turn everybody in the room off. But somehow I could hear the philosophy of what he was saying and ignore the way he said it. I had a way of telling Ken he was full of shit and doing it in such a way that he could accept it."

After Kaufmann had been on board for just over a year, Olsen started to depend on him more and more. Every week-night for six or seven years, Kaufmann remembers, Olsen called him at home. "Between 9:30 and 9:40, the phone rang, and my wife let me answer it," Kaufmann says. "It was Ken. He'd talk about whatever was on his mind, some personnel problem or a product question. Sometimes we'd talk for fifteen minutes, sometimes an hour and a half."

Surprisingly perhaps, Kaufmann's favored status didn't bother his peers, even in the competitive environment DEC was becoming. Rather than being jealous of his position, the other top managers looked to him as an ally with the ear of the leader. "Pete is a very down-to-earth guy," says John Leng. "His language could be rough at times, but he injected a sense of humor into the situation. And he was a great help to Ken; he helped him through a certain stage in the company's develop-ment. It was amazing to see the effect he had. Ken didn't change his beliefs, but he matured. He saw that people were still good people even though they would drink or smoke or get a little wild at times. The person who helped him through that as much as anyone was Pete Kaufmann. He was really the first one to stand up to Ken, mostly because he was so good at what he did."

Kaufmann was savvy enough to know how far he could push. He tested Olsen's attitude with a pointed comment or two; if he wouldn't budge, Kaufmann didn't press the matter. Kaufmann also picked up on the subtle realities of the new management structure. Initiative, if it paid off, was rewarded, even if it went against agreed-upon boundaries set by the Operations Committee or a product-line manager. "I broke a lot of rules in that company," he admits, "and did a lot of things opposite to what Ken was saying."

"Kaufmann," Olsen would declare, "you do everything wrong but somehow the results always work."

Kaufmann realized that in the Digital structure, manufacturing was a relatively stable environment in which he could maneuver more freely than managers in the product lines or even in the other functional areas, such as Johnson in sales. Manufacturing was almost like a separate company, at least the way Kaufmann ran it, and he could do pretty much as he pleased.

Kaufmann helped create an atmosphere that allowed the front-line managers to survive in what seemed like an impossibly complex environment. Intimidated in the past by Olsen, the other vice presidents and top managers found comfort in Kaufmann's irreverence. His style caught on throughout the company. People felt more free to say what they thought. They could confront their peers with a resounding, "You're full of crap!" As long as Olsen felt secure in his patriarch's role, the members of the family could argue and battle with each other and still be welcome home.

Olsen's ambiguous style brought his subordinates closer together. The managers knew that their turn on the firing line could and would come. There was, at the least, a brotherhood of the embattled.

By letting go of his own direct power, Olsen gave people the freedom to grow in ways impossible in a traditional corporate environment. Managers new to DEC found themselves with inordinate responsibility in relation to their experience. If they could navigate the matrix, they could gain skills that would take years to garner in another company.

Olsen believed in certain principles: honesty and integrity foremost, and giving value to the customer next. "We had a very clear idea," Stan says, "that the customer must receive value. That's a much clearer statement than 'the customer is always right.' " The words didn't sound corny to the people at DEC. They were simple to understand and easy to embrace. Olsen could be hard on executives, but employees sensed that he wanted them to succeed for everyone's benefit, not just his own.

"His great genius was stepping aside and letting other people run the company, trusting us not to oversupervise," says Johnson, "and to give people responsibility and a chance to grow and learn. We spent a lot of money on communications, money no other company would spend, because it was critical to running a complex organization. Ken believed in that."

The product-line managers were given so much power that they could revive a dead machine, even one Olsen himself had buried. In late 1966, with the PDP-8 driving up revenues, the engineering group that had created the fallen PDP-6 quietly began to resurrect it. Despite Olsen's dislike of big computers, the group, led by Win Hindle, unearthed the concept of a large, expensive, 36-bit machine that would sit at the high end of DEC's product line. They convinced Olsen—or as one former engineer puts it, "pulled the wool over his eyes"—that the new version, the PDP-10, or DECsystem10 as it was marketed, was really geared to process control and would come with only limited memory. The problems the PDP-6 suffered would be avoided. And it would not be sold for time-sharing, a feature that amplified the potential for customer problems.

Before he left for his sabbatical, Gordon Bell felt that building a follow-on to the PDP-6 was a simple matter. His engineering group, partners in the three-year odyssey to failure with the 6, begged him to stay and help create the DEC10, but Bell saw no point to his involvement in it. "There was simply no technical or even managerial risk or challenge in building the 10," he says. So he took his leave at Carnegie-Mellon.

The 36-bit DEC10, a repackaged PDP-6 with new circuits, shipped in September 1967. This high-end machine drew a small but loyal group of users, who ensured its spot in Digital's product lineup for the next sixteen years. The computer came with several scientific languages built in, such as Fortran and Lisp. The DEC10's construction was modular so it could evolve easily, allowing users to build large systems from a relatively small initial investment. Despite what Olsen was told by its creators, the DEC10 was always intended for powerful, time-shared use in scientific and, later, commercial environments. Just as its backers had hoped, the field salesmen reported to Olsen that "customers only want time-sharing and big memories," says Burkhardt, one of the project engineers. "So we had no choice but to sell that to them."

The DEC10, however, would create a major problem for the company in the long run, making Olsen wonder whether its architecture should not have been left for dead in 1966.

"The wisest thing we ever did was not sue Data General."

—Ken Olsen

10
Birth of a Competitor

I N 1967, DIGITAL celebrated its tenth birthday as a $39 million company. Ken Olsen, at forty-one, was the embodiment of the American entrepreneurial dream. A dedicated husband, father of three children, and a millionaire, he had pushed and tugged his company, piloting it through uncertainty and doubt into a period of explosive growth. For fiscal 1967, DEC made $4.5 million in profit, more than double the previous year and six times greater than 1965.

It could have been a time to celebrate survival. Olsen had already outlived business wisdom, which said fast-growing companies fast outgrow their founder. He was firmly in control, not only the unquestioned leader at the top, but also the dominant influence throughout all levels of the company. And yet, Olsen would learn in the next twelve months, it is precisely when everything is apparently going right that the man in charge should worry most about things going wrong.

The timbre of success often obscures individual voices of discontent. At DEC, the engineers—most in their twenties—were itchy to push the envelope of technology. The PDP-8 was dominating the minicomputer market, fueling DEC's growth.

But the machine used 12-bit words, a technological border the computer world was already pushing past. Engineers could see that 16-bit and even 32-bit machines based on emerging integrated circuits were going to spawn much faster, more powerful machines. The excitement in engineering wasn't in refining old technology but in stretching into unexplored territory.

A trio of DEC engineers—Ed de Castro, Henry Burkhardt, and Dick Sogge—was among the restless. Led by de Castro, they had played key design roles in the PDP-8. But de Castro and Olsen were star-crossed. Their personalities could not coexist in the same company.

Quiet and moody, de Castro was a manager's enigma, and Mazzarese was his manager. To be sure, de Castro was bright and instinctive as an engineer, a valued asset. But he was also an engineer who wanted to do things his own way without interference from the rest of the company. In a short time, he earned a reputation for being uncommunicative. "He was a clam," says Mazzarese. "You just couldn't talk to him."

Only a novice manager himself, Mazzarese searched his management texts but found nothing to help him get through to de Castro. Olsen, himself awkward at interpersonal communication, managed to push hard at all the wrong places with de Castro. Olsen was DEC's packaging engineer. His image was reflected in how a product looked and how it was used—its ergonomic design. When the power supply of the PDP-5 was being designed by de Castro, Olsen went down to the model shop to see it. It was, in his view, a monstrosity—big, unwieldy, poorly designed. Olsen knew power supplies, and this one fell far below his standards. At the next product meeting, Olsen threw the power supply down on the table. Then he picked it apart. "This is ridiculous. This could be smaller. Look at all these wires. The thing is a kluge!"

The attack was aimed at de Castro, of course. He didn't fight back. He didn't defend his design. He took the public ridicule quietly, just as he took everything else. But inside, he brooded. He was a skilled computer designer, and he didn't need Olsen or anyone else dictating how he should do his job.

As de Castro was designing the PDP-8, Olsen decided to name a product-line manager to oversee the project. De Castro wanted the job. And he felt he deserved it because of his engineering on the PDP-5 and the work he was already doing on the 8. It is the engineer's credo that the one who designs a project should be the one to lead it. But de Castro had established a reputation for being a rebel within engineering. He disdained what he viewed as DEC's bureaucratic and arcane procedures and routinely expedited work by setting his own rules. In designing plug-in boards for the PDP-1, he refused to follow drafting standards. He assumed the freedom to operate as he saw fit to get his job done. This attitude rankled Olsen. De Castro insists there were other engineers who swam against the tide, that he was just the most visible. And anyway, wasn't he doing what Olsen espoused, taking responsibility?

Mazzarese questioned de Castro's capabilities as a leader. His style seemed the diametric opposite of all a manager needed to be. But Mazzarese believed de Castro deserved the chance to run the PDP-8 anyway, based on his contributions and desire. Besides, DEC wasn't blessed with battalions of great managers; many were young and untested like de Castro. "Let's give him a shot," Mazzarese argued. "We'll keep a close eye on him." But Olsen stayed steadfast. He didn't want de Castro to run the product line. It was not an argument you could win with Olsen.

Instead, Harvard Business School graduate John Allen Jones was handed the job. Jones brought with him a reputation in DEC for selling the PDP-4 to physics labs for pulse-height analysis. He had been a top student at Harvard a couple of years before and had taken Doriot's class on manufacturing. Jones liberally quoted the General around DEC, which earned him the label "Doriot's boy." Some saw Jones as the General's eye inside DEC. Though he was as inexperienced in managing as de Castro, Jones possessed all the communications skills that de Castro lacked. He became de Castro's boss.

Bell believes that making de Castro report to Jones was the surest way for Olsen to get rid of a person he no longer wanted at DEC. "De Castro simply had no respect for John Jones,"

Bell says. "And the best way to get rid of an engineer is to have him report to someone he doesn't respect. Understand that Ed had made the basic revenue for the company as the project engineer for the 8." Burkhardt is even more emphatic: "The PDP-8 made 120 percent of the profit and propelled the company onto the front pages of all the technical journals." Surprisingly, de Castro didn't walk out in disgust—at least not immediately. He just dismissed Jones from his mind. "I felt that I could get done what I needed to do either through him or around him, over him or under him," says de Castro.

As Jones settled into his new position, Mazzarese knew that trouble was brewing. He tried to figure out how to keep de Castro motivated. If he could have been content to remain a product designer rather than a product-line manager, de Castro might have found his place at DEC. But he wanted more than a comfortable slot; he was not only denied his opportunity but insulted to boot. Looking outside DEC, de Castro saw vast opportunity in the untapped minicomputer segment of the computer industry. He was already thinking about starting his own company.

Mazzarese tried to soothe the open wound by assigning de Castro to work on the next-generation DEC computer, the 16-bit machine. It was a prize engineering assignment because it would provide the hardware to take DEC into the 1970s. Burkhardt and Sogge joined de Castro in conceptualizing that machine, code-named the PDP-X. What drove their design was more than a desire to create another winner for the company. They wanted to stretch their engineering talents to new limits. DEC was starting to become a bit stodgy, already less fun for computer engineers than just a couple of years earlier. The company was earning millions of dollars, yet these engineers had no equity in the enterprise in the late 1960s. Their salaries were about $12,000 per year, average for the industry but not enough to put them on the fast road to financial independence. DEC was tight-fisted with stock options; only the vice presidents and top managers were eligible.

The desire to create something of his own began to surge within de Castro. "The idea of starting my own company was in my bones for a long time, even before I went to DEC," he says. "Having been in the small computer area and seeing it from multiple points of view—the marketplace, sales support, product design—I felt there was going to be a real growth opportunity in the business. That combined with the frustrations with some of what I tried to do at DEC led me to think more seriously about it."

By 1967, start-up fever was spreading in the computer industry. Venture capital, so dry a decade earlier, was flowing like a swollen river. Lunch-time discussions at engineering companies like DEC centered on where to find investors, how to write a business plan, and where to rent cheap space. Burkhardt and an advertising manager named Allen Kluchman talked about launching a computer typesetting business together. Many such ideas never got past the dream stage, including, for the moment, de Castro's.

Burkhardt and de Castro had their minds full defining the PDP-X. DEC was looking for a simple design, something like the PDP-8, to take the company into the 16-bit arena. There was a sense of urgency to the project: competitors that had recently jumped into the mini market were leapfrogging Digital technologically. Hewlett-Packard had already announced a 16-bit machine, and Computer Controls Corporation/Honeywell had joined the fray with its DDP 116. CCC, in fact, appeared to be a highflier until it was acquired by Honeywell and lost its technical edge in the mire of postacquisition bureaucracy.

IBM's System/360, introduced in 1964, had dramatically changed mainframe computing by making the 8-bit byte—and its multiples—the industry standard. This unifying maneuver by IBM made it clear in the marketplace that DEC was fighting a losing war with obsolete weapons in its 12- and 18-bit computers.

De Castro's group plunged into the PDP-X project with some radical notions about the future, ideas that seem ahead of their time in hindsight but were clearly misplaced at DEC in 1967. De Castro says, "I was pushing the idea that it was time for Digital to make a major departure from its product lines, move to the 8-bit standard and integrate the product lines into something that would fit smoothly together.''

Over several months, he presented to the Operations Committee his PDP-X plan in its various stages of development. The scheme elicited strong and swift opposition from around the company. De Castro was proposing that DEC redo its entire product line. He was not just treading lightly into other territory, he was stomping hard on turf that didn't belong to him. Already considered a troublemaker, de Castro did nothing to enhance his corporate standing with such a presumptuous plan. He lobbied hard, ''yelling and screaming and trying to get it done,'' he says. He was not easily derailed from his course.

In late 1967, de Castro unveiled the final PDP-X plan internally. It turned out to be anything but simple. The concept was, in fact, too forward-looking: a series of compatible products built using a new chip design and medium-scale integration that would function with the same software and the same peripherals. The basic 16-bit system would evolve up to 32-bits, allowing users to grow their machines, rather than replacing them each time they needed more power.

The PDP-X was an idea a full decade ahead of its time. It is ironic that DEC embraced the concept of it—a family of compatible machines with a broad range of power—in its VAX strategy of the mid-seventies. But in 1967, the idea was outrageous. De Castro's team essentially suggested that DEC replace its entire product line—products that controlled 85 percent of the minicomputer market—in favor of this new design. If the concept itself wasn't enough to do in the project, the way the young team tried to sell it sealed its fate. Burkhardt and de Castro visited Carnegie-Mellon where Bell, in his role as DEC consultant, approved the outline of the PDP-X. He was shocked later at how they pitched it internally. When they got back to DEC, they billed their plan as a mammoth project, even bigger than the PDP-6. That comparison was fatal; the PDP-6 had been at the center of the terrible storm just a year or so before. In Olsen's mind, that machine had almost brought the company to ruin.

Burkhardt, a gregarious and popular twenty-two-year-old engineer, told anyone who would listen that the PDP-X would make DEC's other computers obsolete.

By now, de Castro decided to hedge his bets. Whether or not the Operating Committee went for the plan—and it seemed clear that Olsen would not risk his money-making product lines on this ambitious and complicated strategy—de Castro had about had it with Digital. He and his friend and former boss in the Special Systems Group, Pat Greene, were talking about starting a new company together. Based on what they saw at trade shows and in the field, they believed that DEC was missing the market for a small, 8-bit machine. The two brought Sogge and then Burkhardt into the plan. They put together a prospectus for a machine and the company to make it.

By the time the proposal for the PDP-X came before the Operations Committee, all the company's product lines had mobilized against it. De Castro had argued and butted heads with countless opponents during the plan's conception and found few allies at the meeting. Stan Olsen, as head of the small computer area, ostensibly sponsored the PDP-X but without any real enthusiasm. The business plan was poorly written, the benefits obscured by complicated technical details. De Castro admits that he clearly didn't have the wisdom then to judge whether the PDP-X was really right for DEC. "From the technical point of view, I sure thought it was," he says. "But what it meant in terms of customer migration, revenue streams, and all that was far beyond my ken at the time." The proposal was so ambitious, and so risky, that Olsen gave copies of it to each Operations Committee member and several other confidantes for critiquing. The response was uniform: the PDP-X would never fly.

Olsen informed the group that the project was being killed. No one was surprised. Burkhardt believed that the PDP-X was doomed not just because of its bold scope but because the project came under Stan Olsen, who he says was not one of DEC's more influential managers. Mazzarese was only moderately supportive, realizing as the project developed that it went up against overwhelming opposition.

Despite knowing all along that the PDP-X was only a longshot, de Castro's team was disappointed and bitter. Burkhardt says the group would have stayed at DEC if the PDP-X had been accepted. "We were really anxious to build interesting machines," he insists. A better proposal, written around the technical merits of the plan, could have been presented and modifications made to give the PDP-X a better chance at approval, but no one stepped forward to do the work. It was as if the script were already written, and the actors could only follow their lines. For his part, Olsen painted the plan as a bad idea proposed by bad engineers who didn't have the company's best interests at heart.

De Castro felt the rejection as the final blow to his engineering ego. Suddenly, his alternate plans to start his own company took center stage. Simultaneously, Herb Richman, a flamboyant salesman from Fairchild Semiconductor in California who had sold de Castro chips, heard that the PDP-X was canceled. He spurred them to find venture capital to strike out on their own.

The group stayed on for several months, searching for capital. And while still working at DEC, they designed a prototype for an 8-bit computer to be the first product of a new company. According to de Castro, the machine they envisioned incorporated a mix of DEC and public-domain technology. "There is a very thin line," he says, "between what is corporate proprietary technology, what is one's general experience, and what is information that is in the public domain." The original design for an 8-bit machine, he insists, was not a direct copy of any DEC computer. And by the time the new company actually got on its feet a year later, that design was scuttled in favor of a newer and better one.

Greene was to be president, the others vice presidents. Even though there was as yet no company, the four put in equal sums of their own money toward getting back original investors' stock. The search for venture funding took longer than expected. One reason, according to Greene, was that they initially asked for too little money—$300,000—and the investors shied away. When they raised the ante to $800,000, venture capitalists took the plan for a new computer company seriously.

In the spring of 1968, Greene had a falling out with the group. He wanted to go to Olsen as soon as the PDP-X was killed and tell him about their plans. He believed that as a DEC employee, he owed the company honesty. De Castro says that Greene simply got cold feet about the idea and was holding up the group. And he wasn't demonstrating the leadership qualities expected from him. The three were now ready to quit their jobs and start a computer company, but Greene hesitated. Burkhardt went as emissary to tell him that they were ready to move on without him.

On returning from a business trip to Japan, Greene discovered that the others had in fact jumped from DEC. The trio left on April 15 without Greene. They informed their immediate boss, John Jones, of their intent in the morning, and by lunchtime they were escorted out of the building by DEC security guards.

Greene was enraged at being abandoned, as well as by the manner in which his colleagues had bolted—without telling Olsen. "That wasn't my way or the plans that I had," he says. "You are employed by a person, confront them directly; say, 'This is what I am going to do, and you may not like it, but I want to move on.'"

No one was more furious than Olsen. Disloyalty—leaving the company to start a competitor—was sin enough, in his mind. But the dishonesty he saw in the group—designing their own company on DEC's time and with what Olsen perceived to be DEC technology—struck at the core of his business ethics. Greene went to him immediately and turned over the prospectus and other plans that he and de Castro had created in the past several months. "I gave him all the paperwork," Greene says, "because I felt an obligation being paid by DEC that any work that I'd done belonged to them."

"We have a copy of their log for the two years before they

formed the company," Olsen says, "so we know exactly what went on in that period. We've never exposed it."

Though the 8-bit machine de Castro sketched out while at DEC was soon scrapped, Olsen was convinced that he was taking DEC technology with him to start a new company. Some speculate that Olsen even believed the PDP-X group had purposely designed an impossibly complex and radical 16-bit machine in order to set DEC back and give their own start-up a window of opportunity in the minicomputer field.

"What they did was so bad, we're still upset about it," Olsen told *Fortune* magazine in 1979, eleven years after the fact. Eighteen years later, Olsen's voice still pounded with emotion when recalling the incident: "We've never had vindictive or vicious feelings about them, never threatened them. All of that is made up by the press, or maybe by them."

"In this business, you have to be prepared for people to leave," Stan Olsen says. "When you are dealing with people with an entrepreneurial spirit, they're going to go on their own. And we specifically selected people with that capability. But we also like to have complete honesty and integrity in our people, and we didn't believe what they did was the most straightforward act. It became clear they were not working for the same company, that they were pulling in a different direction."

Burkhardt insists that the group never took any Digital technology with them nor used any to create a separate machine on Digital's time. On the day they left, de Castro and Burkhardt went directly from the Mill to Burkhardt's house and sat down at the dining room table to design a 16-bit computer for their new company, Data General Corporation.

De Castro denies the story that has grown up around the legendary departure—that his group took the PDP-X plans with them. They were far too ambitious for a start-up to tackle, he says. Burkhardt argues that the soul of their new machine could not have been conceived while at DEC simply because the components used in the Nova, Data General's first computer, didn't exist until just a few months before it shipped, near the end of 1968. Olsen refuses to accept that explanation. Nonetheless, DEC took no legal action, despite the veiled threats made to the investment community. Burkhardt says, "We never did any deeds or committed any acts that would have formed a basis for any possible claim that would prevail." If they had, Olsen would surely have sued, Burkhardt says. "He was angry enough." De Castro didn't worry about losing a lawsuit because he believed no case could be made. But he feared being sued because the start-up had too much to do to get involved in a protracted legal fight.

Olsen is thankful now that he held his anger in check twenty years ago. "I'm quite serious when I say the wisest thing we ever did was not sue Data General. Things were pretty bad," he says. "Anger tears your heart out. The emotions would have been so negative, it would have torn us apart. We made computers instead." The Operations Committee decided DEC would look foolish, like a bully, suing a tiny start-up. So Olsen tried to look the other way.

With Pat Greene out, the presidency of Data General was vacant. None of the three other principals wanted the job. Fred Adler, the major venture capitalist backing the new company, took on the role for six months until Burkhardt and Sogge convinced de Castro that the position should be his. He continues as president of Data General, now in his twentieth year, trailing his arch competitor Olsen by a decade in leading his own start-up.

Data General set up shop in a former beauty parlor in Hudson, Massachusetts, another small mill town bordering Maynard. Richman joined them in June to develop and head the sales force, and they pursued Allen Kluchman to come aboard as director of marketing. Kluchman was reluctant to leave, but clearly, he wasn't going to get rich at DEC. Equity was the only way to earn significant money. He saw a potentially lucrative opportunity at Data General and accepted the offer. In the summer of 1968, Kluchman went to his boss, Nick Mazzarese, and resigned. "Wait a minute," Mazzarese said. "I know what the problem is. I've been fighting the board about getting equity for key people. I'll be right back."

Mazzarese went down to Olsen's office and returned a few

minutes later with a proposal for stock options, options that would give Kluchman a substantial stake in DEC. His opportunities had clearly opened wide, and Kluchman pursued them. "I'm tired of running a functional organization," he said. "I want P and L responsibility. I want to run a product line." Mazzarese took him to Olsen, and Olsen agreed, "You should run a product line." Olsen was angry enough at the Data General crew to suddenly offer a big stake in DEC to keep a valued executive from going there.

With promises of stock and a product line now in his pocket, Kluchman went back to Data General and told de Castro he was staying at DEC. De Castro doubled his initial offer. With an inducement from Data General too good to refuse, Kluchman went to Olsen for the last time—to say goodbye. "I understand what you're doing and why you're doing it," Olsen said. "But I don't think you understand that those guys are going to fail. After they fail, we'd like you to come back."

Olsen let it be known throughout DEC that Data General was an unethical enterprise doomed to failure. The message went out through DEC's sales force to its customers, and it said, "Don't talk to DG."

"That," says Kluchman, "was like putting gasoline on the flames." Suddenly, DEC customers were calling up Data General to find out what it was they weren't supposed to know. Rumors of a lawsuit also increased the small company's visibility. Olsen finally realized that focusing so much attention on the start-up was only helping it gain credibility.

By 1969, Data General had effectively launched itself into the swirling minicomputer industry with the fast-selling Nova. It was the hottest new company in 1969 and a thorn in DEC's side from the start.

Inside Data General, the frenetic pace masked the new company's own problems. De Castro reluctantly took the president's mantle but did little to create a team spirit. His quiet, standoffish manner hardly inspired his new company. Kluchman believes that the immediate success of the product is what held the new enterprise together; had there been a greater struggle to sell the Nova, the whole thing might have come apart. "What you had was a tiger by the tail, and everyone was just holding on," he says. "What helped us was that we were the only new company in the business to come from Digital, and we understood the fine details associated with what was successful in the minicomputer business." As Tracy Kidder writes in *The Soul of a New Machine*, his inside look at DG, "Data General was the son, emphatically the son, of DEC."

The stunning success—Data General shipped 200 Novas in its first year and was in the black by its second—quickly catapulted the company into the third spot among mini makers. It continued to grow at 45 percent annually from 1973 to 1979. The two geographical neighbors competed as bitter rivals for more than a decade, until DEC pulled far ahead in the early 1980s.

The bitterness would not go away for Olsen. He referred to Data General often at Operations Committee meetings, each time embellishing the story just a little. "The Nova is simply a blinding star that burst in the sky and will disappear like all Novas do," he said.

De Castro can understand Olsen's initial anger—after all, with the Data General group gone, DEC was left without an engineering team in place to develop the crucial 16-bit computer. But de Castro can't understand the lasting enmity. "I always wondered," he says, "how Ken could have jumped out of Lincoln Lab and moved ahead with his business plan and yet found it so difficult to accept the fact that we did the same thing eleven years later. Every minute I spent at Digital, I felt I gave them my absolute best, and I think I did a lot of good things for them and for the business. I gave them a fair day's work for my pay, and I frankly don't understand the animosity."

In DEC history, de Castro is now just a footnote, despite being the implementer of the PDP-5 and designer of the PDP-8. As Kidder says in *The Soul of a New Machine*, "They expunged de Castro." Relegation to obscurity in Digital's official view of its past doesn't surprise him. "I was kind of an embarrassment to Ken and the corporation," de Castro says.

Today, Olsen claims that it is better to forget past hurts. "If we made one mistake with Data General, it's that we've ignored them," he says. "We never thought they'd succeed."

But there were more pressing issues to attend to in Maynard than the start-up of a competitor. By 1969, Olsen faced yet another crisis, this time with a certain innocence gone forever.

"Just because you can design a car in your basement doesn't mean you can go out and compete with Detroit."

—Ken Olsen

11

Hired Guns

THE DEPARTURE OF Edson de Castro and his engineering team caused barely a blip, at least initially, in Digital's financial performance. Profits for fiscal 1968 grew by 51 percent over the previous year, to nearly $7 million. In fiscal 1970, revenues and profits more than doubled over 1968 levels. After his fury over Data General subsided a little, Olsen took an elder statesman's view of the industry he had created. "The woods are full of people wanting to get into the small computer business," he told *Business Week*. "But just because you can design a car in your basement doesn't mean you can go out and compete with Detroit."

Olsen's words belied a serious problem brewing. Without de Castro—or more important, without the PDP-X they had been counting on—Olsen and DEC were stuck in a 16-bit hole.

Mazzarese had been ready to leave DEC even before the DG crew fled. He was tired and frustrated with the internal battling he found himself caught up in. He felt in over his head as manager of small computers and wanted something new. He was good at getting things done himself, but once DEC had grown into a $20 million company in 1966, he had to work through layers of people. He was fed up with the struggle and the verbal abuse. Still, he let Olsen persuade him to stay at least until the 16-bit follow-on to the PDP-8 could be built.

DEC's computers had developed organically up to now, natural outgrowths of previous technologies. The new machine was going to be much more complicated. Mazzarese knew the project required dynamic organizational skills not readily available inside DEC, and so he decided to go against the tradition of promoting from within. The Operations Committee backed him. He needed aggressive hired guns, people skilled in the ways of big companies, who could push a system through quickly. He brought in Andrew Knowles from RCA, Julius Marcus from General Electric, and Roger Cady from Honeywell. And he enlisted Gordon Bell at Carnegie-Mellon to be the technical guru.

The PDP-11, as the machine was named, turned DEC in a new direction of computing. Competitors were already chomping into DEC's minicomputer dynasty with 16-bit offerings. The PDP-11 had to be completed quickly, and it had to be better than any machine on the market. But change doesn't come easily at a company increasing profit by about 50 percent each year. The powerful product-line managers were pushing their own 12- and 18-bit machines into the marketplace. What, they asked, is the hurry if our products are selling so well?

"The management of the PDP-11 was a horror story in itself, given the fact that the only decent designers had left to go to Data General," says Bell. "No one really cared about the 16-bit machines because the product lines were fighting wars to sell the 12- and 18-bitters."

In Knowles, Mazzarese found a tough, seasoned warrior eager to make his mark in DEC's chaotic environment. Knowles got an early taste of the DEC way before he was even hired. A headhunter told him about the opportunity in Maynard in the summer of 1969. Though not unhappy at RCA, he saw great potential in this fast-growing computer maker and agreed to talk. But it wasn't until months later that he was granted an interview with Mazzarese in Building 5. "Most of

the Mill was in a state of disrepair and not air-conditioned,"
Knowles says. "The trip through the Mill was interesting to a
nine-year veteran of RCA who had his own parking space."
Knowles and Mazzarese hit it off immediately; they shared
views on where the minicomputer business was heading. But it
would be a month and a half, three visits, and eighteen interviews before Knowles was finally offered a job. He joined
DEC in December 1969 as product-line manager for the PDP-
11. His task was to get a product designed, introduced, and
into production within nine months to a year. Starting from
scratch, this was no minor challenge.

Knowles carried tremendous power. He was given line
responsibility for engineering and marketing the machine as
well as P and L responsibility. Control was exercised through
the funding, which Knowles had to negotiate, like other
managers, through Olsen and the Operations Committee.
Knowles came soon to the opinion that the Operations Committee members rendered very little operational help to the
product-line managers and almost no strategic direction.
"They played mostly a role of critic after the fact," he says.

Knowles was used to action. He found DEC's consensus
management slow and contradictory. On the one hand, the
task was urgent, with speed of the essence. But on the other,
Olsen needed to work over ideas endlessly, seeking more and
more input from various sources within the company.

Mazzarese gave Knowles a quick lesson on internal strategy.
During the initial budget sessions, he said to Knowles, "Andy,
the Operations Committee wants to go over the PDP-11
budget next Monday. Here's how we should handle it. I'll get
you on the agenda for 11:15 A.M. You come in, propose the
budget, mention Data General, sit back, and say nothing
further. They'll get into a big argument over why de Castro
will or will not succeed, get hungry, and throw you out. We'll
then assume the budget has been approved." And that was
about how the meeting went.

The design process on the PDP-11 was long and frustrating.
From April 1968, when de Castro departed, until late 1969,
DEC's engineers tried out idea after idea. Finally, Mazzarese

felt the limits of time had been reached. DEC was two years behind the industry in introducing a 16-bit machine. "We've got to have something now," he said. "We'll go see Gordon." Knowles, the driver of the project; Marcus, the marketing chief; and Cady, the engineering manager, traveled with Mazzarese and a handful of other DEC engineers to Carnegie-Mellon in Pittsburgh. They asked Bell and professor William Wulf their opinion of the PDP-11's early design. Bell and Wulf agreed: "We hate it." So they went to work to fix the machine.

Under Bell's direction, the PDP-11 was redesigned following ideas set forth by one of his graduate students, Harold MacFarland. The group settled in at Carnegie for a long weekend. They worked all night into Saturday and then on Sunday as well. On Sunday night, Bell called Mazzarese and told him the design was ready. The changes would cause a few months' more delay, but now, Bell knew, the PDP-11 "was just good enough to beat Data General's Nova."

What Bell orchestrated was a family of minicomputers with larger memories and more processing power than any small machine DEC built. Unlike the other systems, the PDP-11 was designed to span a range of computing performance. Most of all, the PDP-11 offered such ease of use that novice users could embrace a computer as never before. It was a breakthrough machine built on a technology that would far outlive and outperform any expectations. The PDP-11's simplicity and elegance quickly made it an industry standard, a model for a generation of computer designers. These engineers felt that DEC taught the world how to build small computers.

It was not an easy birth. The PDP-11 was speeding toward introduction when a flaw was spotted: an incorrectly designed input/output structure. The machine needed to accommodate higher data rates or no one would buy it.

Mazzarese was aghast—not another delay. That meant facing the Operations Committee again without an answer to the question, "Is the PDP-11 ready yet?" Surprisingly, Olsen tolerated the postponement. He badly wanted a 16-bit machine, but he never said, "Just build a machine fast. I don't care if it's good." He followed one of DEC's mottos—"Do the right thing"—just as he expected every employee to do.

The PDP-11 was finally announced on January 5, 1970, at a price of $10,800. But it was just a paper design. DEC engineers hated going out on a limb by announcing products far in advance of test machines and shipping dates. But if the company was to avoid losing customers, a machine had to be promised. Data General had announced and shipped the Nova just months after its founding and was a year ahead of DEC in the 16-bit race.

Knowles marshaled the resources and went at completing the PDP-11 with a zeal that only a fresh newcomer could summon. Mazzarese ran interference with Olsen, keeping his probing eye away from the engineers so they could get the job done. The team ran scared through the first quarter of 1970, working eighty-hour weeks. The company desperately needed to take a new income-producing machine to market. The recession of 1970 was flattening sales and earnings. Revenues rose just $11 million in 1971, to $147 million; profits actually dipped to $10.6 million after hitting $14.4 million in 1970.

Analysts blamed the stunted growth on the recession, but DEC insiders knew that the cause was their lateness getting into the 16-bit world. Varian, Hewlett-Packard, and Data General were cutting into DEC's customer base. Any further delay could be disastrous. With Bell's guiding hand, Cady's design prowess, and input from talented software designers like Larry Portner, the PDP-11 scored big.

The PDP-11 was selected by Industrial Research as one of the most significant technical products introduced in 1970. By mid-1971, DEC was shipping 100 machines per month. Two more powerful models were swiftly brought out, and by 1972, DEC was back in control of the minicomputer market from top to bottom.

"The Christian and the scientist should always seek the truth."

—*Ken Olsen*

12
The Modern Puritan
and the Palace Revolt

IN KEN OLSEN'S view, the best a businessman can do for the social good is provide jobs for people who can then make their own way. He believes the cliché people must pull themselves up by their own bootstraps. The less fortunate, the struggling, the poor do not reach salvation on the backs of others. In 1968, he told *Business Week*, "There are all kinds of pressures on senior people in organizations to do things peripheral to their business. Right now, for example, there is tremendous pressure to solve the Negro problem. After awhile, these demands can take up 300 percent of your time. It's somewhat unfair of society to expect people running a business, responsible for thousands of jobs, to also solve these other problems. The thing that destroys business management is working on these other things."

Olsen did not ignore the plight of his fellow man. Over the years he has donated 2 percent of DEC stock to the Stratford Foundation, which he established to aid Christian philanthropies, and has supported a small Christian school, Gordon College, in Wenham, Massachusetts. One family member points out that Ken is "terribly generous and interested in the common man," and it is simply his intense desire for privacy that keeps the public from knowing the depths of his philanthropy. But when it came to his business, Olsen did not bring his religion inside DEC's doors, aside from quoting from a hymn or two to make some management point. He was an isolationist, not an activist, in social affairs. He wanted DEC to change the world through the computers it made, not by becoming a social agency.

Olsen discouraged his managers from involving themselves in community affairs. Though DEC was the largest employer in Maynard by the late 1960s, neither Olsen nor any of his senior staff belonged to the chamber of commerce. The corporate population at the Mill and satellite plants surpassed 4,500 by the end of the decade, but DEC was a sociological unit, a world unto itself. The insular feeling of this unusual, but productive, environment came from a work force uncommonly dedicated to the same goals as its leader.

DEC cultivated honesty—rewarding the person who spoke the truth. It fostered fairness—every idea or grievance was given a hearing. And it encouraged doing the right thing—letting employees diverge from the corporate path as long as that road turned out to be the right one. Disobedience was not the sin—being both disobedient and wrong was. This environment reflected Olsen himself, the moral man—a Christian and a scientist, as he says, who should always seek the truth.

Olsen lives a modern-day puritan's life. His abstinence from drinking, smoking, and cursing is well known. His material needs are modest. He and Aulikki moved from Bedford to Lincoln, Massachusetts, soon after DEC was founded and still live in the same unpretentious home. He is known to mow his own lawn, shovel his own walk, do his own grocery shopping, and grow vegetables in a backyard garden. He does not act like a $300 million man.

In the puritans, Olsen saw two characteristics that he embodied in his own life. First, they believed that mankind was fallen. This observation did not make them cynical; they simply were never disappointed in how men acted. "If you believe this," Olsen said, "it has a very important meaning to your relationship with others in business and how you approach business." Second, the puritans believed that every night they should systematically review what they had learned that day about their fellow man, their relationship with God, and themselves.

Peter Kaufmann, the powerful manufacturing vice president by 1968, pushed against the limits of Ken's moral corporate world. "I loved working for Ken Olsen," he says. "I learned a lot in a philosophical sense; he is basically a good man."

Kaufmann set out to incorporate Olsen's moral views into a business plan. He directed DEC into opening manufacturing plants in such economically deprived areas as San German, Puerto Rico, and Galway, Ireland. These investments not only boosted these cities financially but earned the company major tax benefits as well.

Kaufmann also pushed DEC into dealing with the growing unrest among blacks in America. Riots were tearing cities apart in 1967; black America was tearing at white America. Kaufmann understood that blacks weren't demanding handouts, they wanted a fair chance to contribute.

Businesses venturing into the ghettos often created "do-good" plants that weren't expected to return anything to the bottom line. They were social projects or image builders, not business opportunities. In 1970, Kaufmann picked out an inner-city neighborhood in Springfield, Massachusetts, and said, "Let's build here." DEC refurbished the old Springfield Armory and soon occupied 450,000 square feet of space. This manufacturing plant would be like any other DEC facility turning out power supplies and cables and then building up to tape drives and disk drives—integral pieces of the company's product lines. The workers would be hired from within the city and trained not only to work in but to run the plant.

The board of directors split on the idea, so Kaufmann backed off for a year. Olsen feared turning DEC into a company with social, rather than business, ends on its mind. In late 1971, Kaufmann pressed ahead with implementing his plan on his own. He recruited Leroy Saylor to manage the

Springfield plant, opened in January 1972. Olsen said simply, "You'd better make it successful."

The plant eventually pulled hundreds off welfare and into meaningful jobs. "We had blacks providing a major contribution to DEC products, not just secondary work," Kaufmann says. As a profession, engineering traditionally didn't attract many women or minorities, but Kaufmann's efforts helped bring blacks into all levels and disciplines of the company. Kaufmann realized that the time was coming when DEC's growing work force would need men—and women—of all races. Eight years later, DEC opened a second inner-city plant, this one in the Roxbury section of Boston.

While Kaufmann's efforts at sensitizing DEC management to social issues were lauded by the communities in which DEC operated, they did little to solve the growing internal turbulence caused by the matrix. Even Kaufmann's tension-deflating manner could not stem the increasing frustration at the top levels of the company.

Dennis Burke, a management consultant and former priest, was brought in by Win Hindle in 1969 to help managers cope with the chaos that was engulfing the Operations Committee and the product-line managers. Burke found inside DEC a form of corporate pantheism. Olsen was basically "the great Buddha—a fundamentalist Buddha." The Olsen Burke encountered in the late 1960s was extraordinarily permissive, tolerant, and supportive of different people doing their own thing. "He is a kind of genius at that," Burke says. "He understands that certain things are key to making the company successful, and that's where he puts his energy. He is a father figure to most people there, so what he supports, likes, or values gets supported, liked, or valued by everyone else."

But Olsen also was a master of management by conflict, though, as Burke says, he would never admit it. "Ken Olsen likes to take two engineers, strike them together, and see if he can get sparks," goes an old saying at DEC. He would do the same with product and functional groups as well, pitting them against each other and watching the ideas shake themselves out. The product-line strategy augmented this thinking perfectly. Olsen waved the carrots—prestige, power, success—and the managers chased after them. But the checks and balances of the funding process prevented them from knocking each other out. They had to learn to negotiate and compromise to enlist support—budgetary as well as verbal—from their peers.

The process is called *buy-in* at DEC. An internal company handbook on the corporate culture describes buy-in as "the process of talking with interested parties to gather support for a project. When a party expresses interest in the job, buy-in can be achieved. Buy-in can be more powerful if the interested party provides 'real' support by being a part of a committee, providing resources or working difficult political situations. Sometimes buy-in requires horse-trading."

For the executives on the Operations Committee, buy-in was a tortuous process. The members found themselves going at each other constantly, vying for money for their product lines or power for their functional groups. Without clear direction from Olsen, the path to getting something done was an obstacle course of competing interests. The sentiment was widespread that the vice presidents couldn't wait for the Operations Committee meetings to end so they could return to the sanctuary of their own provinces. The company was growing rapidly in the early 1970s—sometimes up to 50 percent a year—and so was the lack of organization and control.

Olsen, Burke says today, is the quintessential entrepreneur consumed by developing a product and taking it to market. When such people find themselves at the head of a company, "They become very conscious of needing to be powerful to stay on top," Burke says. "And they become more conscious of their power as they use it."

Kaufmann used his influence to try to balance Olsen's power. He walked the line between being the trusted right-hand man free to speak his mind and being just another executive pushing beyond what Olsen would tolerate. Kaufmann also understood that Olsen tended to spread around his grace; fair-haired boys routinely appeared and disappeared at DEC.

Ed Schein's role as a part-time consultant to DEC was more to suggest than solve. He was essentially Ken's man and operated only at the highest executive level. In *Organizational Culture and Leadership*, Schein writes, "I was never asked for a recommendation; if I gave one, it was usually overridden immediately by various ideas from the client, which were then debated among the members. The company is comfortable with ambiguity and has its own system of pragmatically moving toward action alternatives."

Burke, on the other hand, was brought in specifically for conflict resolution, to help build bridges between competing executives. Hindle had actually started looking for help in 1967 and found one or two clinical psychologists, who proved to be of little value. Burke was working in management development at Raychem in California. He also ran T-groups and taught at the University of San Francisco.

Burke sat as a full member of the Operations Committee from 1969 to 1973, and from that vantage point he witnessed the conflict that he had been hired to resolve. Olsen put one manager after another on the firing line and fired away at them. "You always knew who was in the barrel," Burke says. Olsen sometimes seemed near to physically exploding with anger. One day in Hindle's office, Burke asked Schein how he would characterize Olsen's management style. "Weirdly participative management," Schein answered.

"What's that mean?" Burke pressed him.

"He beats the hell out of people to participate," Schein said.

Burke sees the effective side of Olsen's style. "Ken would yell at people, but he was out front about it," Burke says. "Problems were incredibly visible to everyone in that company. It was only bad when he was on your case. But then, a few weeks later, he'd come around smiling, asking how things were going."

Burke had a certain easy way with people, and he understood business issues. He gained the confidence of the vice presidents and facilitated many of the earliest Woods meetings. People trusted him, because he never gave names, ranks, or serial numbers when he reported complaints or problems. He took the issues to Olsen and the Operations Committee, while protecting the managers.

Among the biggest issues was the constant conflict between Ted Johnson's sales force and the product lines. In the matrix structure, sales was independent, not attached to the product lines. The roles were ill-defined. There was no mechanism for agreeing on projected manufacturing and sales numbers. For example, a product line might request 1,000 machines be built; manufacturing, knowing that the line managers always overestimated need by 30 percent, would assemble only 700. Sales might find it could sell 1,200. Each side always remembered the numbers differently and used their own financial analysts to rationalize their position.

The Operations Committee finally invoked the "magic charts." Ken said, "Let's put the figures on paper and tack them to the wall." This simple device, such an obvious solution to the accounting anarchy, suddenly made clear to all the numbers that the product lines wanted made, that manufacturing agreed to produce, and that the sales force agreed to sell.

In early 1970, the vice presidents were finding Olsen unmanageable. He frequently went out visiting customers and, in his customary style, refused to make hard decisions needed to run the Mill. His treatment for most problems was to form another committee and work the issue.

Nearby in Westboro, Massachusetts, Data General's Nova was blazing, not burning out, as Olsen had predicted. De Castro's company was succeeding, and it shouldn't be, according to Olsen's view of justice in the world. His temper exploded in Operations Committee and Woods meetings. Why were so many products late? How was Digital going to survive the recession the way things were going?

The Operations Committee worried that Olsen was losing control of the company. Schein talked to all the executives, and several, including Burke, Stan, Mazzarese, and Hindle, agreed that DEC needed an executive vice president, someone who could take some of the day-to-day management pressure off Olsen and help steer the drifting ship.

Schein and members of the committee, with the exception of Ted Johnson, met at Kaufmann's home and told Kaufmann that he was viewed as the best manager in the company, the natural choice to be Olsen's executive vice president. "He seemed to be the obvious successor to Ken if there was one," Burke says. "He ran half the company and ran it better than anyone else. He always met his goals and did it under cost. And he was a charismatic leader whom everyone respected." Kaufmann was stunned, caught unprepared for the strong vote of confidence. He knew Olsen would never believe the plan wasn't his idea. But if these key executives had faith in him, he would go along. He was scared at the thought of doing that job—as well as exhilarated. "I was innocent enough to think I was capable of being executive vice president," Kaufmann says.

Hindle and Schein took the suggestion to Olsen. He was shaken. Despite his anger, Olsen wouldn't confront Kaufmann in person. Instead he called him on the phone. "I understand you want to be president of this company," Olsen said.

"No, no," Kaufmann protested. He knew what Olsen was thinking. It wasn't his idea, Kaufmann said. He didn't want this proposal to undermine all he had built at DEC.

It was too late. Olsen believed Kaufmann was leading a palace revolt, and this apparent insurgence touched sensitive nerves within him. No one was going to take his company from him. He spent the next two months wandering through Digital, deep in thought. And then he returned to visibility. The bitter memories of Harlan Anderson's perceived power play and the thought that he could lose control of his company spurred Olsen. He took control in a way that he never had before. He was decisive and vehement. Digital was his company, and if there was to be a successor, he would name him. And that wasn't going to happen for a long time. The "palace revolt" was squelched.

For Kaufmann, the episode signaled a dissolution of his power. The evening phone calls stopped, and suddenly, it was Kaufmann under Olsen's thumb at Operations Committee and

Woods meetings. He thought he was going to be fired. "I was lucky that I made it through somehow," Kaufmann says. "We got back to a certain level of trust, but not to where it was." It is ironic that Kaufmann had intended to leave when DEC reached $100 million in sales, feeling that such a size corporation was the largest he ever wanted to work for. But now, with DEC already at $135 million in annual sales, he decided to stay, to ride out Olsen's anger. In order to avoid further controversy, Kaufmann consciously divorced himself from the major corporate role he had played over the years. He no longer took part in marketing or strategic decisions, preferring to keep a more humble appearance and to stick to his manufacturing duties.

When Kaufmann was about to leave DEC in 1977, he met with a newly hired consultant. In their first conversation, the "palace revolt" came up. It was obvious to Kaufmann that Olsen had mentioned it, that Olsen hadn't forgotten. "Seven years later and he was still paranoid about it," Kaufmann thought. "The scars must be very deep."

For six months after the executive-vice-president idea was buried, Olsen was a bear, and Kaufmann was the main meal. The developing language of DEC culture included aggressive and violent images. People were constantly getting "beaten up" or "killed." Kaufmann was getting beaten up at virtually every meeting. Olsen came down hard on manufacturing, demanding accountability.

Olsen's frustration went beyond Kaufmann. During that period, from 1970 to 1972, Olsen was reaching for something he couldn't explain even to himself. He seemed intuitively bothered by the misfirings at the very core of the company. The top managers weren't working together, and the meetings were constant battlegrounds. Olsen couldn't make clear what was upsetting him, and the vice presidents were at a loss to figure it out. Schein, who has studied Olsen's impact on DEC for more than twenty-five years, concluded that Olsen typically sends inconsistent signals concerning simplicity and complexity to his vice presidents. "He always advocated simple structures in which accountability was clearly visible; yet his decision-making style forced high degrees of complexity as various managers worked their proposed solutions through various committees," Schein wrote.

Over time, Olsen's longevity served to imbed DEC's culture with a "solution" to his ambiguous messages. Since he was so powerful, he had the right to be inconsistent. The internal structure would have to accommodate him somehow; the staff could not change the leader, so the rules would be set up around him and his idiosyncrasies. In extreme cases, a leader/founder whose style becomes an apparent detriment to corporate health is driven out by his board of directors. Not at DEC. Despite his inconsistencies and his angry outbursts, Olsen displayed a willingness to listen to critical messages about products and strategies.

Olsen looked to Doriot for counsel. He didn't want business answers, but rather, spiritual guidance and support. Doriot saw his role at times like these as one to "watch, push, worry, and spread hope." The General knew instinctively what to say. "Spring is a period of creation," Doriot would point out. "If things go well and you grow, you acquire good habits. Spring is hard because nature isn't on your side completely. In the summer, things are easier; it's warmer. If it's your company, your product may have been accepted. I'm not saying you get lazy, but you don't feel so much pressure. Toward the end of summer, you find the leaves are falling, the orders aren't coming in as easily, the clients aren't satisfied with the product. Now they don't pay so willingly. Unless you've regenerated the spring atmosphere and constructive attitude, then summer comes and goes, and fall comes. But if things go all right, the company goes on and reaches a state of stability I call 'inner strength.' The company can mature and draw on its own strength for success."

To Olsen, a fall chill seemed to be always in the air. He searched for inner strength and then set about to make things right.

"It's absolutely immoral to overpay someone."
                                    —Ken Olsen

13
No Commission

THE BARELY CONTROLLED chaos at the top of DEC was rarely seen by lower-level employees. Olsen's penchant for unadorned simplicity created an egalitarian state. Olsen has dressed DEC in his own image. Andy Knowles says, "He maintained a company that was for the people and by the people. You'll never find anything in Digital that smacks of anything illegal, immoral, or irrational. That comes from the man."

The architecture and office layout of the Mill reflect Olsen's assumptions about human relationships. He insisted on open office environments, with few private offices, no executive dining room, no formal dress codes, no executive parking spaces. At DEC, the saying goes, the only way to get a good parking space is to be the first one to work. Peter Smith, the current marketing vice president, tried once to circumvent the rules by arranging with a guard to let him park near a loading dock. On the second day, he left work and found the side of his car crushed. He had parked in the path of the huge delivery trucks backing up to the dock. "We still don't have reserved parking, and if you want it, you risk getting your car crushed," Smith says wryly.

There are no floor-to-ceiling walls, except in the corners of DEC buildings, so everyone can see window light from their cubicles. Windows convey status in many large corporations. DEC's policy is more democratic and pragmatic. When Smith joined the company as a young engineer in April 1970, he was assigned an office with huge windows overlooking the beautiful pond next to the Mill. He reveled in his good fortune for several months until winter came to Maynard, and he felt the cold drafts from the old and cracked windows. As he sat and shivered, Smith understood why no one wanted a window office.

Olsen disdained ostentation. While driving down Route 2 in Concord one afternoon, Dennis Burke was surprised to spot Olsen behind the wheel of a gold Mercedes. At the next Monday meeting in Maynard, Burke mentioned the strange thing he had seen—Olsen driving a Mercedes. Embarrassed, Olsen assured the group that the car belonged to his wife. At DEC, sales managers get the same cars to drive, regardless of rank in the organization.

Dick Berube, the former corporate communications director, joined DEC in the early 1970s from CBS Broadcasting. Like other new employees from traditional corporate backgrounds, he found the change dramatic. "It was 180 degrees from that of CBS," he says. "CBS was largely form, very little substance. I came from a forty-fourth floor downtown office with fancy furniture and desk lamps to the Mill, where I had a little cubicle, dirty windows, and cobwebs. It's a culture not distracted by trappings." "We are dull on purpose," Olsen says. "Our job isn't to prove how successful or bright we are. It's to manage the company."

Returning from lunch at a Main Street restaurant one day, Olsen and one of his managers strode across the huge corporate parking lot. Bothered by the old papers scattered on DEC property, Olsen started zigzagging his path, picking up the litter by the handfuls. The surprised manager did as the boss—picked up trash on his way back from lunch.

New employees immediately sensed they had joined something special, a club rather than a corporation. More than anything, Olsen seemed, and very often was, accessible. "When I joined the company in the late seventies, I'm willing to bet that 80 percent of the employees felt that they could walk right into Ken's office and tell him what was on their mind," says a former employee. This feeling of connecting to every part of the organization overshadowed traditional employee complaints. DEC paid its people adequately, but not spectacularly. "If you overpay someone, you ruin his life," Olsen says. "He has to keep bluffing, struggling to keep that pay, or take a cut in pay, which some people can never tolerate. It's absolutely immoral to overpay someone. Sometimes we'll overpay someone because they force us into it. I'll even tell them, 'Sure, we'll overpay you, you've got us over a barrel.' If I warn them, I don't feel morally obligated."

Olsen and Johnson agreed early in Digital's history that salesmen would work for straight salary—no commission—a virtually unheard-of method of compensation in big business. "I worked without commission, and I liked working that way," says Johnson. "As we started growing, there was pressure to have commissions, but Ken wasn't for it. He didn't like to overpay people, get them used to making too much money so that if anything happened, they wouldn't be able to support their families. We felt the company was generous to us. It wasn't this hot venture capital kind of deal. The money wasn't that important to us. We were career DEC people. You went to work at DEC for life." As Olsen told *Fortune*, "Since people want to work, all you have to do is treat them well."

After the engineering exodus to Data General, DEC liberalized stock options. Olsen had been particularly tight-fisted about giving out shares in the company prior to going public. John Leng, for example, tried to get a piece of DEC when he joined from Atomic Energy of Canada in 1963 but was refused. Not until two years later, as European manager, was he awarded one of the company's first stock options—thirty shares for $12,000. Leng benefited handsomely as his stock split fifty shares to one when DEC went public, in 1966. Below his level, few engineers shared the good fortune until start-ups like Data General forced Olsen to loosen his grip.

Stock options came to be a good indicator of a manager's worth. In a case study of DEC culture done at MIT's Sloan School in 1982, graduate student W. Gibb Dyer, Jr., spoke with dozens of DEC employees. Getting a first option, one manager told Dyer, signals acceptance by upper management. "The first time I got a stock option, it was the greatest thing that ever happened to me," the manager said. "It means, man, I'm in the club, I'm recognized. They must really value me. It's a recognition that you're doing something that's a little extraordinary, because not everybody gets options."

The people most likely to get significant stock options were, and still are, engineers. Other DEC employees displaying outstanding initiative and performance also receive small options periodically, but rarely in the amounts aimed at engineers. Engineers, in Olsen's mind, are the company's lifeblood.

DEC was regarded as the ultimate employer by engineers. The company was founded by an engineer and created in the image of the perfect engineering work environment. Managers of support functions learned quickly that the road to the top of DEC was through the ranks of engineering. One former manager chose to start in a low-level engineering position rather than pursue a marketing slot higher up because he knew that to go anywhere in DEC, one had to pay his dues in engineering. Even today, midlevel engineers have essentially the same status as functional managers.

Engineering graduates from the country's top schools were drawn to the Mill. DEC was hiring frenetically—10,000 people per year by 1975—but it was still difficult to get a job there. Each candidate faced seven or eight interviews before being hired. A consensus was called for. Will this person be right for the job? Will he fit into the group as well as into DEC's complicated and unsettling atmosphere? Each person on an engineering team was asked for his input, and many had the chance to question the candidate.

Once a person joined, however, they were welcomed to the family. There was the sense of a Japanese-style company, employment for life. Getting hired into DEC, one employee told Dyer, is like getting married: you meet your wife's mother and father and her aunts, uncles, and cousins. It is a bonding process to an extended group of peers, as well as executives higher up and workers lower down. DEC sought out people who wanted to become career employees and avoided the job-hoppers. Turnover has traditionally been the lowest in the computer industry. "I've never even been slightly tempted to leave Digital," says Hindle. "I couldn't imagine competing with Digital. It would just feel terrible."

Though a no-layoff policy never existed formally, employees believed in it as part of the "DEC way." For most of the company's history, there was simply no need to consider letting workers go. But at the beginning of 1970, the economic recession challenged this DEC tradition. Computer-industry companies were laying off people by the hundreds. DEC stretched to keep everybody busy. One oldtimer spoke to Dyer about that period: "I can remember seeing a line of men, all DEC employees, sweeping the parking lot by hand. And we were doing that to make sure that everybody was working, that they kept their jobs." Junior recruiters hired to work in personnel were asked to sell products instead. Most were happy enough to take any job available to stay with the company. Digital never wrote down the no-layoff policy—limiting future options did not make business sense. But managers took great pride in adhering to the tradition.

Ten years later when suffering through another difficult economic period, Olsen explained his position to Wall Street analysts. "We never promised never to have layoffs," he said, "but it seems common sense to avoid it. When a company has to have a layoff, it's most often the management's fault. So at least for a while, we should take the licking, not the employees. In a recession, people want to test me to see if I'm brave enough to have a layoff. I'm willing to take that ridicule because it has paid off to hold on to our people. I don't have layoffs to prove how brave I am. At some time, if it's the wise thing to do, we may do it."

The no-layoff tradition not only helps keep the company union-free, but it creates an aura around DEC as a place that takes care of its own. Olsen said about his employees, "Their faith in the company is important. It's good business for our people to have confidence that we will not lay them off just to help our short-term profit."

It was expected that new employees would flounder for several months, trying to make their way through the maze of the DEC matrix. If an employee fails at his first job, DEC's philosophy is to find another position for him, with responsibility better matched to his skills. Firing at DEC is seen as more a failure of the supervisor than the employee. Consequently, few get fired, except for such transgressions as lying or stealing.

One manager told Dyer the story of a young woman trying to be a secretary. "She was lousy," he said. "But we stuck with her and finally found her a slot in data processing as a technical operator. I think today she is one of the most respected operators around. That was exactly the right spot for her. And she came within probably a week of getting her severance pay. When you see that happen, you realize the importance of giving people an opportunity to try and find a slot."

Executives weren't always treated as sensitively. If a top-level manager failed, Olsen sent him to the "penalty box," "dog house," "Siberia," or whatever word in the DEC vernacular was popular at the time. That person was what Bell terms "the walking dead." One current DEC engineer, a veteran of several decades, remembers Olsen's "death row"—empty offices next to the president where he moved unwanted executives. The message was clear: find a new job. To some, letting people twist in the wind, stripped of responsibilities, seemed heartless. But Olsen saw it differently. "It's not cruel," he explained. "They've got a secretary. They can take as long as they want to find a new job."

For a time, the manager in the penalty box is without a portfolio—no responsibility of any consequence. He has fouled up his project, and everyone knows it. He needs to find a way back into Olsen's graces. One way is to hang on until his particular skills are needed on a new project. But that opportunity might never come. A better angle is to find a dragon to slay, a crisis that only he can solve to bring himself back to the living.

For some, the fate can be similar to that of Anderson. A manager is given enough rope to either climb up or hang himself. Though outright firing is unlikely, the manager who isn't performing as Olsen wishes faces no pleasant alternatives in staying with the company.

Leaving DEC is often a traumatic separation for executives, whether the person leaves voluntarily or with subtle prodding. Olsen brooks little sentimentality about emigrants or defectors from his company. Few find a way to leave on friendly terms. Those who are obliquely shown the door can certainly return for quick hellos and a handshake. But for long-term executives who devoted their lives to DEC, that kind of polite posturing is tormenting.

For those who leave of their own free will, there is no return. "If you're stupid enough to cut yourself off from the mother church," says one executive who recently did just that, "Digital's attitude is, 'Don't bother to come back.' " Once a high-level person leaves, his memory is shredded. Often he is labeled a failure who will fail again on the outside. Olsen, Kaufmann says, sees his family in vivid shades of black and white. "You're for me or against me" is Olsen's perception.

As sales of the PDP-11 began to take off in 1972, few top managers found any reason to leave DEC. This decade promised to be explosive in the computer industry, and DEC was the place to be for anyone with a distaste for the pinstriped suit of IBM.

"Do the right thing."

—*Ken Olsen*

14
Controlled Chaos

While scouring the business books at Lexington Library in 1957 looking for corporate successes to emulate, Ken Olsen found no specific model to his liking. Thus, he and Anderson created a company with no precedent as to style or form in American business.

As the 1970s began, the product-line strategy was in full flower, driving high-pitched, aggressive competition. Within this environment, the culture was solidifying. Passed along at Digital from level to level and generation to generation was a simple rule that later appeared on a list titled "DEC Corporate Philosophies." Of the fifteen tenets, this one, labeled "First Rule," actually came last. It read, "When dealing with a customer, a vendor or an employee, do what is right to do in each situation."

"Do the right thing" took on various meanings over the years, depending on the person choosing to invoke this rule. Basically it meant: don't blindly follow instructions from a superior if you believe he is wrong; take the initiative and find out what is right to do. Most companies would grind to a halt if employees consistently questioned directives and went off searching for what they perceived to be "the right way."

Rules and structure are what keep order and avoid chaos and anarchy. At DEC, the rules almost cultivated anarchy—what one employee calls "wonderfully controlled chaos." There was no "no" at Digital. People with proposals were encouraged or redirected, almost never flat-out refused. That attitude created both an encouraging and confusing environment. Someone making a proposal clearly wrong for DEC ends up "rock fetching." As former DEC vice president Jeff Kalb describes it, "You realize what you are doing is fetching rocks, looking for one with the right shape and color. But given all the selection of rocks in the world, you are probably not going to find the right one. You eventually drop the project on your own."

For Olsen, the new decade brought an opportunity to finally take stock of what he had created. With the PDP-11 hitting the market on all cylinders, DEC was in firm control of the industry it had spawned. He felt his ideas were paying off. A well-engineered organization should run itself, Olsen believed, and DEC was doing just that. A good manager should never have to make any decisions at all. One of Olsen's convictions is that management should not own decisions. Management should guide and advise. The minute an executive makes a decision or forces some action, he owns the problem. Olsen believed in this management style for several reasons, according to Kalb. First, the person working on an issue probably knows it far better than the executive and will likely do a better job in the long run. And second, if the executive stays clear of routine decision-making, he can provide more objective input. More important, he won't get saddled with blame if something goes wrong. This refusal of management to own decisions or problems is frustrating to those outside DEC, such as vendors negotiating contracts. They must struggle to find someone who will finally decide.

The decisions are left to committees—engineering committees, marketing committees, design committees, and review committees of every conceivable nature. Early on, Olsen sat on almost every one. He used committees to wear away the complexities of an issue—working it, discussing it, analyzing it until the correct path inevitably made itself clear. As the company outgrew his ability to sit on every committee, Olsen picked the ones dealing with issues closest to his heart— packaging, small computers, and power supplies. Managers vied to get him to sit on their committees because his presence brought importance to their projects. According to Modesto Maidique writing in the *Sloan Management Review*, "One DEC manager had been championing a project whose approval had become mired in red tape. Olsen sat in on a meeting in which this man's difficulties emerged. Olsen asked about the project and wondered out loud why such a promising idea was finding so little support. 'Suddenly, the barriers to the project came down,' the manager reports. 'What normally might have taken a year or more to complete became a six-month project.' "

Olsen created informal networks within the technical organizations to keep him informed. He often worked with engineers levels below product-line management. "You had to be really attuned to that," says a former vice president, "or you could easily get blindsided."

"A lot of consensus is required on ideas before they get to be accepted into the corporate strategy," says Win Hindle. "If you keep talking, generally the right idea will emerge. I don't think that's well understood about Digital. Ken's name and Digital are so linked together that people assume that a strong manager—and Ken is a very strong person—must be making all the decisions himself. That's not the way Digital operates."

"Sometimes people have a vision of Ken Olsen with a harmonica and cymbals strapped to his knees clapping together as a one-man band," adds Jack Shields. "But you don't orchestrate a company this size with this much growth and success as a one-man band."

Though he didn't order his company in this direction or that, Olsen still maintained a strong sense of responsibility for its course. Simply stated, DEC is Olsen and Olsen is DEC. His ability to let go of major portions of power was tempered by an equal ability to maintain wide control. He was personally and emotionally tied into the company in ways that few could see or understand. Some DEC veterans saw the committees as a complex front for Olsen's intense need for control. "Ken makes a lot of noise about delegating responsibilities. All of that is public relations hype," says a former vice president. "Ken keeps very tight control on that company . . . always has and always will."

Whatever the degree of Olsen's control, he never portrayed himself as knowing all the answers. He allowed diverging opinions to be expressed in public confrontations. Ideas came from individuals but then had to run the gauntlet of the group, being worked and tested. Olsen believes that unless the parties who are critical to an idea's implementation are completely sold, they will either misunderstand or unwittingly sabotage a decision. Until he achieves consensus and commitment from everyone, Olsen will not allow a proposal to become a product or strategy. Burned in the past, when all responsibility fell in his lap, Olsen didn't want to be out there leading if he could not count on the troops behind him.

Olsen quickly embraced a philosophy—"Don't lose sight of your product"—that became gospel at DEC. Though the company always spent heavily on research and engineering (about one-fifth of revenues from 1965 to 1970), Olsen never advocated really long-range development. "Ken generally doesn't have a lot of patience with long-term things," says a former vice president. "He can't get interested in projects until they are nine months away. He has a tendency to put multiple teams in place to work on a single concept, and he doesn't like to get committed to any one thing until he's pretty much sure which one is going to win out. He won't go out on a limb for something unless its success seems imminent and apparent."

Olsen's experience at Lincoln Lab driving a single assignment to completion never really left him. He favors action, trying out possibilities, rather than debating them theoretically. At DEC, he earned a reputation as a cut-and-fit carpenter, someone who goes into a project, fiddles around a bit, puts it in the corner and cuts, molds, and shapes it until it fits.

Other traits began to emerge in the president's character.

Olsen had a sixth sense about trouble spots in the organization. Even during the boom times of the seventies, in fact especially during those times, he began to probe to find out what was happening in the outer reaches of the company. "I kept Ken informed," says Kaufmann about his manufacturing operation. "I made sure there were no surprises for Ken, that he knew what was going on. And so he felt a certain safeness that he didn't have to investigate. If you hid things from Ken, he would get nosy. I was real open about what the problems were, and he was real helpful in solving them."

One of Olsen's best resources for problem solving—General Doriot—joined the board of directors in 1972. ARD was bought out that year by Textron, and Doriot retired from the venture capital business. By joining DEC's board, Doriot was able to take a more active hand in the company that had provided him his greatest wealth. Textron paid $400 million for ARD, most of it for the value of DEC stock that ARD owned.

By the time Doriot became a director, DEC was a well-established name in the scientific and engineering side of Fortune 500 businesses. Through its OEMs, DEC computers were being incorporated into a variety of innovative applications, from calculating scientific problems to running the electronic scoreboard at Boston's baseball stadium, Fenway Park. To its direct customers, DEC was earning a reputation as a company that built excellent products and had the technical-minded support staff to make buying and running computers relatively trouble free. Olsen understood the people DEC was selling to; most were in environments he was familiar with—the research labs and engineering departments populated by his brethren. DEC even called its salesmen sales engineers. As Shields says, "The way you sold was to solve a problem for a customer. You might design an interface. You might connect up some sort of X-ray defractometer. You might run an experiment with a customer. You had technical people talking to technical people. That was the selling approach, contrasted to companies who were selling computers for traditional data-processing applications."

Computing was at a point of transition. DEC had brought computers out of the hands of the data processing high priests and now there were legions waiting to get at them in corporate settings. It was unexplored territory, especially for the inquisitive scientists and engineers who formed the core of DEC's customer base. DEC listened to its customers to an extreme; the user group DECUS was more like an extension of DEC engineering than an organization of customers. Digital engineers often returned from DECUS symposiums with long lists of product changes and enhancements to implement.

DEC engineers formed close relationships with their big customers, such as AT&T, DuPont, and General Motors. Together, buyer and seller created novel applications for DEC computers, incorporating them into environments that had heretofore lacked computing power. Suddenly, computers could be used for process control, design work, and product simulation.

But like most computer makers of the time, DEC paid little attention to software. The company supplied the hardware and suggested uses it could be put to. Application software was left to the customers themselves or third-party developers to devise. As DEC machines hit critical mass in the early seventies, software developers saw the potential rewards of writing programs for them. DEC itself retained its reputation as a supplier of iron.

As the PDP-11 began to fly in 1972, the influence and reach of DEC was felt in all corners of industry. Olsen's dream of bringing computers to individuals had worked. The rewards came home in the form of explosive sales and massive growth. The PDP-8 was followed by enhanced models—one selling for below $10,000—which propelled the small-computer business to greater heights. The PDP-11, the machine that was two years late to market, sat atop the 16-bit world and was on its way to becoming the most popular minicomputer of all time. More than 250,000 PDP-11s were eventually sold. Eighteen years after its introduction, DEC still releases add-on features and options. Even the DEC10 was finding a growing market in time-sharing. Selling for between $300,000 and $400,000, it was beating IBM mainframes in many accounts, including academic environments.

As the company reached $200 million in revenues, DEC's world began to expand well beyond the borders of Maynard. The company established a permanent European headquarters in Geneva, Switzerland, in 1969. Kaufmann opened manufacturing plants in Reading, England, and Mountain View, California, DEC's first West Coast assembly operation. DEC turned next to the Far East, launching core memory manufacturing operations in Taiwan and Hong Kong.

By June 1972, DEC had 7,800 employees around the world. As plants began to open both domestically and abroad, a strange phenomenon occurred: rather than reflecting the local culture, DEC offices and plants displayed the company's culture first and foremost. An employee visiting a facility anywhere in the United States or abroad immediately felt the familiar twinge of the world of DEC—the open office environment; familiar posters and marketing memos tacked on the walls and in people's cubicles; and the location itself, typically in a country setting. "No matter which facility you walk into, there is a feeling that you belong to this family, this club," says one long-time employee. Everyone on the DEC payroll understood the tenets, regardless of the language spoken there. "Do the right thing; always seek the truth; stay humble during the good times" were understood as well in Geneva or San German as in Maynard. "Ken's presence was felt, even though he wasn't there," says a former DEC Europe vice president.

With the PDP-11 under Knowles's control, Mazzarese finally left DEC in 1972. It had been a frenetic, fulfilling, and frustrating decade for him. Mazzarese came into DEC having managed no one and left, at thirty-eight, a vice president in charge of more than 1,000 people and the entire small-computer product line. He believed that the company had changed, that people willing to sublimate their own egos for the sake of Digital were losing influence to a growing corps of aggressive, new managers. And he was not alone. At Mazzarese's going away party, Kaufmann came over to him and said, "Nick, you're leaving. I'm next."

Mazzarese and Kaufmann were responding to a subtle change in Digital—the passing from adolescence into corporate adulthood and the ranks of big companies. In the 1960s, Kaufmann says, DEC was open in a way that was unusual in business. Even the struggling periods of indecision were marked by a team spirit. "There was a lot of infighting, but it was all done in a very open way," Kaufmann says. "We sort of went through our divorces and changes out in the open. It might have seemed ugly, but it was open." By the time Mazzarese left, however, the environment was hardening. People began to build walls around their territories. The openness, to a degree, ended. "There was much more manipulating behind the scenes," Kaufmann says of the early to mid-1970s. There was nothing inherently wrong with DEC's transformation. But it was not an environment either man wanted to be part of any longer. Wealthy at thirty-eight from his DEC stock, Mazzarese left more than a few envious friends behind as he bought a sailboat and sailed around the Caribbean for the next year.

Saying that he was never formally notified, Knowles was made vice president of small computers. He joined Hindle and Stan Olsen as heads of product lines. By now, each product line was creating new product lines, a generation process that by the late 1970s filled the company with thirty-three independent product domains. Friction began to develop between product managers as to who would sell to which markets. To make the territories more clear, the company redirected its product lines into a market-oriented scheme in 1972. Rather than simply selling products, DEC identified markets to target and pushed the product lines in a more focused approach to selling. One of the key reasons for the reorganization was that the product lines were starting to build and market competing products. Customers were barraged by various DEC salesmen representing different product lines targeting the same account. By redefining according to vertical markets, Digital smoothed away the overlap, at least for the time being.

Despite the redirection, the new setup didn't alleviate the scrapping for resources within the matrix. The frustrations of trying to win the hearts and minds of various internal functions—from sales to finance—continued for the line managers. Olsen firmly believed in the value of internal competition. "History keeps proving," he says, "that when we allow healthy competition, no secrets, no disruptions, we get a better product." A new tenet took form: "Survival equals responsiveness to a changing environment." This statement recognized the matrix as the basis of management and reorganizations as a fact of life at DEC. The manager would be judged by the results he obtained negotiating his way through the matrix. Success required solving cross-functional, time-to-market, and product problems.

Knowles personified the next-generation DEC manager. His ability to get the PDP-11 designed and out the door within a year of joining the company earned him his vice presidency in 1972. Knowles was known as a top-flight manager, a doer who could rally the troops and muster resources. But he was also blamed for politicizing DEC in a new way, adding a sharp edge to the internal competition. Unlike the previous generation of managers, Knowles coveted power and aggressively sought to build his own empire within the company.

In the spring of 1972, Knowles's PDP-11 group presented a new concept at the Spring Joint Computer Conference in Atlantic City. Dubbed the DEC Datacenter, the machine packaged a PDP-11/20 with a VT05 terminal and a printer into a desk. The prototype, along with a marketing brochure, was shown to curious attendees. The promotional pitch proclaimed: "The DEC Datacenter brings the computer to the people. All the people. Secretaries, programmers, bookkeepers, engineers, clerks, students, businessmen, scientists and more."

This "low-cost tool for on-the-spot computation" featured all the characteristics of the personal computer, a machine still half a decade away from existence. But only three DEC Datacenters were built. The Operations Committee killed the idea. "There's no such thing," Olsen said, "as personal computing."

The DEC Datacenter was the first of many attempts by Digital executives to personalize computing. None succeeded.

The company founded on the principle of bringing computing to the individual passed up the opportunity in 1972 to go the next logical step in the evolution that it had begun.

Olsen didn't view the world in terms of missed opportunities. "We always want to have more products than we can use and sell, because the only alternative is to have too few," Olsen says. "Sometimes it looks like we have more products than we've exploited, but it is just so much safer to have more."

In 1972, Olsen prevailed upon Gordon Bell to return to DEC as vice president of engineering. Bell was averse to large organizations, and with nearly $200 million in revenues and 8,000 employees, DEC now fit the label. But he could see trends emerging in the computer business, such as the large-scale integration of microprocessor chips. He saw a revolution coming, and he wanted to be at the forefront of building the computers that would come from the downsizing of circuits onto a chip. To build machines that would make a difference, he needed a company with deep pockets. Academia, even with its research grants, certainly didn't have them. So Bell came back to the Mill with a new mandate from Olsen and a head full of concepts.

Initially, he avoided staff or line responsibilities as much as he could. He just wanted to consult on technical advancements. But by the end of his second year back, he couldn't keep his distance. He was a hands-on computer architect, not a hands-off consultant.

Olsen demonstrated his view of Bell's worth by locating Bell's office directly across the hall from his own in Building 12. And in no time, the two were shuttling back and forth between offices to confer on ideas and product directions. A new sight turned the heads of DEC employees—the hulking Olsen with the smaller, frenetic Bell jabbering away in his ear, walking together through the Mill.

With Gordon back in the fold, DEC's engineering future suddenly seemed bright.

*"Who looks over the whole system to say that it
is a product we'd be proud of?"*

—*Ken Olsen*

15
On the Frontier

BURKE AND KAUFMANN were swimming
against the current of disinterest, dragging DEC forward in its
personnel policies. The pair's actions were aided by the federal
government's new hard line on affirmative action. DEC, like
other companies, came under the scrutiny of the Department
of Defense despite not going after government contracts.
However, unlike many conservative companies, which took
years to follow, DEC assumed a pioneering role in human
resource activities. The inner-city plants, the no-layoff tradition, the lack of a rigid hierarchy, and the ability of employees
to directly influence decision-making were the characteristics
that made DEC different.

Fundamental values that spilled down from Olsen were
formally written as policy in 1974.

On honesty: "We want to be not only technically honest, but
also make sure that the implication of what we say and the
impressions we leave are correct."

On profit: "Success is measured by profit. With success
comes the opportunity to grow, the ability to hire good people
and the satisfaction that comes from meeting your goals."

On responsibility: "Plans are proposed by managers or teams. These plans may be rejected until they fit corporate goals or until the Operations Committee feels confidence in the plans. But when they are accepted, they are the responsibility of those who proposed them."

On customers: "We must be honest and straight-forward with our customers and be sure that they are not only told the facts, but that they understand the facts."

On simplicity and clarity: "We want all aspects of DEC to be clear and simple, and we want simple products, proposals, organization, literature that is easy to read and understand, and advertisements that have a simple obvious message. Our decisions must always consider the impact on the people who will be affected by them."

First rule: "When dealing with a customer, vendor or an employee, do what is 'right' to do in each situation."

Unlike the old smokestack industries, the emerging computer industry was attracting highly motivated, intellectual young professionals, some with an offbeat sense of business. Michael Weinstein, a former reporter for a new industry trade publication, *Computerworld,* came to DEC at the start of the 1970s to do marketing and advertising. He found a company unlike any in the industry. "DEC was a wild place, the Wild West," he says. "You could see it in the terminology—there were wizards and gurus, a whole underground of technofreaks. The feeling got picked up later by Apple. There we were in this cruddy old mill, with nineteen buildings and secret passageways. Some places you had to go downstairs in the middle because otherwise you couldn't connect to the bridge to another building. Ken used to say that the primary difference between the balance sheet of DEC and Honeywell was the cost of facilities. It was a company that captured an image and a spirit, a counterculture," Weinstein says. "We lived out in Maynard on the frontier, and we knew that we built the best computers. We knew we were going to win."

This spirit lived in DEC's engineers, programmers, and technicians. Here was a company that not only understood the quirks and eccentricities of creative technical minds but fostered them. Inside the Mill, they were not the social misfits of high school and college. At DEC, they were the heroes, respected and appreciated for what they could build. It was an atmosphere of pragmatic deviation: lights burned in Mill windows throughout the night. Few engineers watched the clock. "I wore a ponytail all the way down my back and wore jeans, a T-shirt, and a beard," says Dan Bricklin, a former DEC programmer. "Some of the conservative managers tried to make sure my desk was not visible from theirs. But it was always done in good fun, and I was treated very well by those same people."

Olsen was the role model for work habits. Someone driving past his home in Lincoln at 2 A.M. would quite likely see a light burning in an upstairs window as he puzzled over his drawing table. He had no compunction about picking up a phone and calling a DEC manager or engineer regardless of the hour. His sloppy dress, some believe, was an affectation. By appearing as an unsophisticated engineer, he could constantly surprise colleagues and competitors with his ability to solve tough business or management questions.

Beyond engineering, however, Olsen's views of the world were old-fashioned in many respects, particularly when it came to women. But at DEC the need to get the job done outweighed his biases. Programmers, for example, were scooped up as fast as they could be found, and the company cared not a bit about skin color or gender. If you could do the job, that was all the qualification needed. It wasn't due to discrimination on DEC's part that the majority of technical and engineering employees were white males. Few women or blacks were attracted to careers in computer science or engineering in the 1960s, and so the budding profession quickly took on a men's club feeling.

Following Kaufmann's lead, Burke did much to integrate the company. When he started, there were no black or female professionals out of 60 in the personnel area. By 1976, when Burke left, blacks and females made up 50 percent of the department. In that time, he pushed DEC to recruit from eighteen black colleges. Kaufmann hired John Sims as affirmative action manager in 1974 for his worldwide manufacturing operation. Sims was prepared to move to Stamford, Connecticut, with AT&T but decided to take a quick look at this computer maker in Maynard. Though he found few blacks in this Assabet Valley community, he liked what he saw and heard from the people at DEC. "There was an air of openness, honest competitiveness, and anxiousness to do what was right that I hadn't seen elsewhere," says Sims. He joined the company and quickly rose through the ranks, eventually becoming DEC's highest ranking black executive, vice president of personnel.

But although the company could be commended for aggressively hiring blacks to fill a variety of roles early on, the same cannot be said for how it dealt with women. Growing up in a male-only profession, engineers like Olsen and his executives brought certain assumptions about women's roles to DEC. Starting from the day the doors opened at the Mill, women were employed in nonprofessional clerical, secretarial, and assembly-line jobs. Women who hoped to advance in the corporation rose into managerial positions through the personnel or finance departments.

Olsen didn't help matters much. When he wanted to demonstrate the ease of use of a DEC product, he often reverted to calling a secretary from the audience and having her try her hand at a particular machine. "It's so easy, even a girl can do it," Olsen would declare, smiling.

One young woman hired in 1971, as an administrative assistant in personnel, decided that the best place to start up the ladder would be as a corporate recruiter. She approached one of the senior people in her department and told him her objective. "Well, that's very nice," he replied. "But you can't do that. Women can't be recruiters because they would have to travel."

"So what?" she responded.

"First of all, their husbands wouldn't like it, and we don't want their husbands upset. And secondly, the way we do these trips is to send two or three people, so we'd have to send men and women together. The wives certainly wouldn't like that."

The woman was shocked but undaunted. She tried to overcome the stigma of her sex by grabbing the next opportunity that came along—and then the next. She switched jobs seven times in two-and-a-half years, searching for a route upward.

Another woman undeterred by the male-dominated environment was Mary Jane Forbes. As Gordon Bell's new secretary when he returned from Carnegie-Mellon, she soon realized her influence as the key assistant to the chief of engineering. She tried out DEC's first word processing system, a crude text editor on the DEC10. She mastered the complicated system but found the massive machine too hard to move around the office. She asked the engineers if they could put wheels on the computer. They complied and began calling the innovation the Mary Jane wheels.

Her legend grew. By 1975, when Stan Olsen's group devised the company's DECmate word-processing computer, Forbes was given an early prototype to test. She was thrilled with the new machine and told everybody about its potential. She wrote a five-page review—including suggestions for changes—and handed it to engineering. Many of her ideas were implemented, and thus was born the Mary Jane test. From then on, Bell insisted that any general business product be reviewed by Forbes. He would often ask his engineers, "Have you done what Mary Jane suggested?" Bell, in his own inimitable style, believes that people should be measured logarithmically. "Mary Jane," he says, "is an order of magnitude better than any secretary I ever met."

Forbes went beyond being a product barometer. On her own initiative, she organized full-day seminars to teach word processing to the secretarial staff. The first one attracted 900 secretaries. "DEC just about shut down," she says. Realizing the potential of these seminars as a sales tool, she organized several free seminars open to the public. In two sessions, 2,000 secretaries showed up for demonstrations of the new products. Forbes eventually wrote a book on word processing, published by Digital.

But aside from exceptions like Forbes, women were not likely to possess much power at DEC through the 1970s. No woman had ever sat on the Operations Committee nor run a major product or functional area. Not until 1984 did DEC name its first woman vice president, Rose Ann Giordano.

The feeling pervaded DEC that managers had to be able to take the beating that came with the job. They had to be aggressive enough to propose and criticize ideas and, in turn, receive harsh criticism from their peers. DEC's male leaders, with Olsen as the standard bearer, didn't feel comfortable putting women in such a position. Staff managers in ancillary disciplines such as personnel were off the firing line, and so these jobs, therefore, were deemed more suitable to women. One of these exceptions was Gloria Porrazzo, who moved up from assembler to group manager in manufacturing. "Ken was never too comfortable," she says, "with a woman in my position. He wasn't used to women in business."

Several managers commented to Dyer during his study of DEC culture about the risks of putting women in line positions. "It's a pure leadership function, and the guys are reluctant to play on a team with a girl captain," said one manager. "Women are sisters or mothers or wives for most of these guys," said another. "Most of them have not had women friends or colleagues. You don't 'clobber' your wife, your sister, your mother—it's just inappropriate. That's not the way a good boy behaves." At meetings where the few women with power were present, they were often treated with deference. "With them it wasn't, 'You're full of shit.' It's 'What do you mean? What are you getting at?' Very gentlemanly kind of treatment."

Women who achieved success at DEC often copied the behavior exhibited by their male peers, several managers told Dyer. "The women I see surviving usually try to become like their male counterparts. They swear more than any of the men, and they're more vulgar," said one manager.

In the heat of tremendous growth toward the mid-1970s, women's issues were not a paramount concern at DEC. From 1971 to 1975, the company surged from $146 million in sales to $533 million. Profits more than quadrupled. In March 1974, DEC shipped its 30,000th computer system and entered the Fortune 500 list for the first time—the 475th largest company in America.

Like a teenager who grows eight inches taller in a single summer, DEC was bursting at its seams. Expansion fever struck. In June, the company that began on one 8,500 square-foot floor of Building 12 purchased all nineteen buildings and 1,069,359 square feet of the Mill. But it wasn't enough. DEC began renting space, buying buildings, and constructing new ones all over Massachusetts in order to accommodate its work force. DEC spread out on purpose, says Kaufmann, the ideal being no more than 2,500 people working in any single plant. In small plants DEC could maintain the feeling of being a small company.

In Maynard, the multibuilding Parker Street facility was erected. DEC hunted for any square footage it could find, buying up shopping centers and retail stores that had closed. Knowles, the former RCA man, heard that his old company was ready to sell a huge, nearly completed facility in nearby Marlboro. As fast as DEC was rising in the industry, RCA fell. In 1971, RCA had suddenly hit bottom and sold its way out of the computer business.

Knowles toured the never-occupied facility. It was a magnificent 700,000 square-foot building located on Route 495, the outer ring of Boston's highway network. The facility was valued at nearly $40 million, but DEC managed to purchase it unfinished in 1973 for $12.8 million.

The company was on its way to becoming the largest employer in Massachusetts. DEC started purchasing aircraft to transport people quickly between the new facilities. The fleet started with a couple of helicopters and in the 1980s became the state's largest corporate airline. Olsen made sure that manufacturing plants were located close enough so that the people building DEC's machines could easily get in touch with the people who designed the systems. They were never more than a thirty-minute helicopter ride away.

In early 1974, Knowles, Stan Olsen, and Bell began coaxing DEC into new businesses. This was no simple task because Olsen was generally immovable when it came to expanding beyond basic computing. But the suggested new territories were logical extensions to DEC's existing business, not radical departures. Knowles saw vast potential in both the terminals end of computing and in large-scale integration of circuits. He decided to propose the formation of a Components Group that would make products in both areas. For months Knowles lobbied for his concept. As usual at DEC, he would get no quick decision.

As the newest member of the Operations Committee, replacing Mazzarese, Knowles formed a coalition with Hindle, Johnson, and Al Bertocchi, DEC's financial vice president—the golfers. On the important question of where to hold the February Woods meeting—either at Ken's cabin in New Hampshire or at the famed Pink Beach Club in Bermuda—the four golfers always voted for Bermuda and won, 4-3.

In February 1974, Knowles arrived at the Pink Beach, armed with golf clubs and a thick proposal for creating the Components Group. The golfing members of the Operations Committee had gone down on a Friday night to get in as much of the game as possible before the Sunday afternoon meeting. But this year, it rained constantly. No golf. The Operations Committee was grouchy.

The meetings began on Sunday, and Knowles was scheduled to speak last. He had his flip charts and overheads ready. But as it came time for him to speak after a break, the sun came out. And Digital's executives grabbed their golf clubs and motor bikes and headed outside.

Standing on the veranda of the Pink Beach Club, Knowles said to himself, "I'm proposing spending hundreds of millions of dollars and everyone's gone." He took the 5 P.M. flight out of Bermuda. Back at the Mill, he told the secretary of the Operations Committee, "I assume my plan has been approved." Then he moved his group to the Marlboro plant.

Knowles pushed aggressively into large-scale integration. He advocated the downsizing of the PDP-11 circuits onto several chips at first, then onto a single chip. The first microcomputer-based product from DEC, the LSI-11, came out in 1974.

Also that year, Bell centralized DEC's engineering group. Under the previous structure, each product line engineered its own machines; the small central group was only asked for advice. Bell felt that the pulse of DEC came from engineering. And a $500 million company shouldn't divide up its talent.

By consolidating engineering, Bell hoped to address the technical and organizational issues that he found plaguing DEC when he returned from Carnegie-Mellon. In a memo proposing the change, Bell said, "A strong central group with dotted-line reporting to product lines seems to be the way to go." He also pushed, along with Kaufmann, to tighten the relationship between engineering and manufacturing.

Bell brought to DEC an eccentric view of the world. Like a hyperactive child, he could not sit still in a chair when an idea was percolating in his mind. And ideas were always percolating. He might suddenly leap onto a conference table during meetings, surges of energy, like electricity, pumping through him as he made a point. His analytical power to abstract a problem—to see it as a shadow of reality—was without peer at DEC. His mind ran four or five thoughts ahead of his fellow engineers, racing toward architectures and machines and concepts that he would sketch down on whatever bit of paper was at hand.

Bell's engineering meetings were rituals within DEC. They started out quietly, with fifteen-minute overviews of the agenda, but inevitably dissolved into shouting matches of apparent chaos and animosity. Somehow, they always ended on a high note, engineers streaming out of the conference room smiling.

Bell's enthusiasm was infectious. His quirks and idiosyncrasies endeared him even to those who didn't understand a word he said.

He and Olsen coexisted uneasily. Bell believed strongly that an engineering company such as DEC must be run by an engineer, someone who understands machines and what it takes to build them. In assessing chief executives in his mathematical model, Bell believes Olsen to be a good standard of measurement, with the average CEO "about a one-tenth Olsen." He respected Olsen as a packaging engineer—but not as a computer architect. "Ken was the most demanding person I ever worked for," Bell says. "But I felt he had several blind spots. He's a very physical-thinking person. I could not communicate with him at an abstract level. I'm used to massive abstractions. Sure, he deals with abstractions—he had circuit theory—but I was enormously frustrated trying to get him to see things abstractly rather than physically."

For years, the pair pushed hard at each other. For the most part, Olsen trusted Bell's engineering instincts and stayed out of strategic architectural discussions. Olsen's hands-on computer engineering essentially ceased in the early days of the PDP-1, except for one area—packaging. Three decades after beginning Digital, Olsen still attends to the look and feel of many products. He once ordered a new DEC printer delivered to his home. The day it arrived, he drafted an angry memo to Bell, Shields, and Smith: "I've never seen such poor mechanical design and such poor system thinking. I'd like to know who looks over the whole system to say that it is a product we'd be proud of? This is absolutely atrocious, and I want to know who did it and who approved it. It took two people to carry it in, they couldn't get it through the door, there were loose screws, one of which fell into the machine and I worry about it when I turn it on." To a packager like Olsen, the trim and fit of a product is the signature of the man.

Sometimes Olsen and Bell worked together. "Occasionally it was fun to build things with him," Bell says. "But mostly it was a pain because he would ultimately resort to bossing and ridicule instead of logic to win his way . . . which was often wrong."

"If you let people set their own goals, they are going to work harder and do more."

—Ken Olsen

16
Brothers

A COMPANY THAT considers itself a pioneer must accept that there are no trails to follow. By the mid-1970s, Digital was experiencing both the profit and the pain of creating an industry. Competition from some seventy mini-computer competitors was forcing DEC to constantly reevaluate its products and positioning. The General reminded Olsen: "Always remember that someone, somewhere is making a product obsolete." This warning applied to the fast-changing computer industry above all others.

But at companies growing at 30 or 40 percent a year, the employees don't feel vulnerable. They don't look over their shoulders. Bounding growth is all the younger workers know; they breathe it like an intoxicant. Some of the old-timers are more sober, moving at 78 rpms in a 45 rpm world. In a talk to employees in 1975, Olsen allowed himself a fanciful thought: if Digital grew as fast in the next eighteen years as it had in the first eighteen, he said, the company would equal France in output and population.

Dennis Burke, often referred to as the do-gooder by Olsen, could sense change and the tension it was creating. To his quarterly report to the president, he appended a one-page essay on how DEC was shifting from a trust culture to a power culture. Some of that change, he wrote, was inevitable because of the increased entanglements of managers within the matrix. But the stress was excessive—the overenthusiastic response of managers who could not abstain from the elixir of power. They were "beating up" too many people. Digital, Burke said, needed to understand and face up to the kind of company it was becoming.

At the next Operations Committee meeting, Olsen confronted his personnel manager. "What's this memo you wrote about power and trust?" he asked. "I don't understand it."

"I thought it was pretty clear," Burke replied.

The Operations Committee debated Burke's thesis hotly, but reached no conclusion. Finally Burke said, "Ken, you pay me to be perceptive and that's my perception." It was not a view of the company Olsen wanted to face. For Burke, the public confrontation was the beginning of the end of his reign as a resolver of conflicts and arbiter of confrontations. He left the company in 1976.

But Burke was right. DEC was becoming a power organization, and people like Knowles and Shields were thriving in it. Others, like Kaufmann, Johnson, and Leng, were getting frustrated. They missed the old days.

Olsen rode the change like a skilled surfer on a big wave, shifting his weight from side to side to keep from getting wiped out. Less steady was Stan Olsen. Like other long-time veterans, he was constantly racing to stay a step ahead of the organizational changes. There had never been an easy period for him at DEC. As Ken's brother, Stan was subjected to stricter standards. Ken worked to avoid the impression that his brother received preferential treatment. Nonetheless, many in the organization believed Stan worked at DEC simply because he was the president's brother.

One former manager in Stan's group says that the two Olsens tried to create the illusion that they were not brothers. They treated each other as boss and employee. Everyone else saw this posturing as a facade. There was some sense, as the years went by, that Ken wondered whether having a brother in such a visible role in the company was a mistake. He did not allow the situation to be repeated: no other family members, be it his youngest brother, David, his sons, Glenn and James, or his daughter, Ava, were invited to join the business. He was adamant that as a public company, DEC owed its allegiance to the stockholders and not members of the Olsen clan. Unlike corporate neighbor An Wang, who groomed his son Fred to take over Wang Laboratories in Lowell, Massachusetts, Ken has no interest in passing along his legacy to an Olsen.

Ken trusted Stan over the years to take on projects he wouldn't give to anyone else. He knew his younger brother looked up to him with unquestioned loyalty. Some engineers, like de Castro and Burkhardt earlier on, didn't respect Stan's engineering capabilities. They felt he was riding his brother's coattails. Yet Stan was doing a creditable job running the modules business as its first product-line manager. Later, he helped DEC recognize the potential of the commercial side of computing. The perceptions of Stan tended to fall from how close a person got to him. Those who saw him from a distance were apt to question his lofty position within DEC. Those who worked closely with Stan found him warm, considerate, and insightful—without any hunger for power in his motives.

One former DEC employee says that when she joined the company in the early 1970s, the reputation was, "Oh, Stan . . . Ken's younger brother. The image I got was that this was the Smothers Brothers—one smart guy, one dumb guy." On meeting Stan, her view changed considerably. She discovered Stan's attributes: he brought an inventive, probing mind to DEC. She found that the differences between brothers had little to do with mental capabilities. Though there is a vague family resemblance, Stan is shorter and less imposing than his brother. He wears glasses and sports a moustache. "I thought, here's a guy wearing a red-and-white striped shirt; that's so different from Ken, who always wore these clunky ancient suits. Maybe they're not that much alike," she says.

Though general wisdom said Ken and Stan talked routinely each evening by phone about Stan's projects and ideas, in reality, the conversations didn't take place. Stan carried his proposals to the Operations Committee, just like everyone else.

Stan developed an ability to roll with his brother's punches. He looked for the sense in Ken's reasoning even when he totally disagreed with it. Early in DEC's history, for example, Stan took charge of the sales operations. He was in Rochester, New York, setting up a sales office, when Ken called and told him, "Forget about it. Come on home."

"Wait a minute," Stan said. "I've been working too hard on this. I'm going to set this up. I'm dedicated to it, and I believe in it." Ken insisted, and Stan came back to Maynard. "Ken was concerned about the economy at that time and thought that maybe we weren't ready for any more offices, not just Rochester," Stan says. "But he didn't explain it well, and I got upset. About a week later, I figured out what he was talking about and agreed with it."

With or without Stan present, Ken would go on occasional tirades about his younger brother, leaving those in the room embarrassed by such an attack on a family member. Stan's friends wondered why he tolerated Ken's periodic outbursts. Stan explained to one vice president, "You've got to understand that our family background, our religious background, is such that we have a head of the family, and that is Ken. He sets the direction for the family, and we go along with it, take his guidance." He was patriarch of the Olsen clan as he was of DEC.

Stan did not further a positive reputation by his attitude toward organizing and managing. He hated meetings and would push quickly through the agenda to get out of them. Left on his own, he rarely called his staff together, so they set up their own meetings. Stan sat in but didn't seem to listen to what was going on. He would open his mail or look at memos. In one meeting, a heated debate raged about a software product that was late to market. Stan sat cutting up a newspaper with his Swiss Army knife, making a book cover out of it. He didn't say a word. "I think that's where his reputation for not being very capable came from," says one former staffer.

"When he wasn't interested in something, he just didn't pay any attention to it. And he wasn't interested in managing."

As DEC headed into the 1970s, Stan's main interest was getting the company into the emerging word-processing business. He and Jack Gilmore, a former Lincoln Lab-Whirlwind engineer, saw the potential of building off an earlier machine aimed at the education market. Stan's organization at the time was stocked with engineering and marketing talent—people like Julius Marcus, Tom Stockebrand, and Irwin Jacobs. And there were outstanding programmers and marketers working on the project, such as Dan Bricklin and Steve Watson. Bricklin later created the first electronic spreadsheet, Visicalc; Watson opened Boston's first Computerland store.

"Stan had a lot of ideas, not all of them good," Marcus says. "The trick is to surround the idea guy with some people who are implementers. I felt my job was to sit with Stan and catch some of the good ideas and go off and implement them."

Using the now-aged PDP-8 technology, Stan and Gilmore created DEC's entry into the word-processing market, the DECmate. The product had great potential to work from—proven, even if slightly dated, technology and a virgin market in which it could grab a commanding share. But compared to what competitors such as IBM and Xerox were offering, the DECmate was a big-ticket item, priced at $22,000. According to *Business Week*, the new business was "murderously competitive." Stan insisted that DEC's course would avoid confrontation with IBM. "Our approach is the same in word processing as it is in the rest of our products," he explained. "Our system is not an automatic typewriter like IBM's, designed to speed up the secretary's job. It is interactive—we take the person who is composing and put him in the center of the composition, working with the CRT screen."

DEC sensed that it had only to beat Wang Labs. That competitor, driven by its inventive Chinese founder, An Wang, was moving from a lucrative business in electronic calculators into word processing. The DEC group believed that it could build a superior product to Wang's; but in this case, Olsen's belief in the build-a-better-mousetrap theory of customer acceptance didn't work out. The DECmate simply cut against the corporate grain. DEC's own product-line structure hobbled the company in the lucrative word processing market. More than twenty Digital product lines had sprung up by the mid-1970s. The product managers who exceeded their financial goals earned the biggest budget increases the following year. In this competitive environment, Stan couldn't muster needed support for the DECmate.

Ken was unsympathetic, believing that this survival-of-the-strongest theory produced superior products. "If you let people set their own goals, they're going to work harder and do more," Olsen told the *Wall Street Journal*. But in reaching for their goals, the product lines were duplicating each other's research and marketing.

Knowles was pushing hard to win enough resources for the new Components Group to fund projects like the LSI-11 and his entry into the terminals business. He and Stan butted heads, fighting for internal support. Knowles had the sexy new technologies that were steps to the future. Stan was backing a machine, the DECmate, that was based on a ten-year-old technology.

Though the DECmate did well initially, it lost any chance for momentum by being undermarketed. According to Mary Jane Forbes, Bell's secretary and an active proponent of the machine, the company didn't aggressively sell it. "They would tell us, 'We can't go out and sell this, people have to come to us because we can't make enough money on such a low-end product,' " Forbes says. "I said, 'You don't understand. This is the best product we've got.' " Wang outmarketed DEC and became the major force in word processing. DEC missed the opportunity to command the office market.

Meanwhile, the Operations Committee decided that DEC had grown too large for its home state. Ken felt it was unsafe to continue building the company under just one political structure. Massachusetts, run by its new governor, Michael Dukakis, was an uncertain environment for business growth in 1975. Taxes were so high that residents came to call their state "Taxachusetts."

Also in the mid-1970s, DEC developed a policy that it should not employ more than 5 percent of a community's work force. DEC wanted to be a good public citizen—but no more important than anyone else. Standing out is not Olsen's or Digital's way. The company asks for reasonable roads, reasonable taxes, and the approval to build when it needs to build. In return, DEC provides high-quality, stable employment. "We didn't want to dominate the scene," Marcus says. "So we looked for other places to colonize."

Stan saw a move to New Hampshire as a way for him to get out from under the pressure of the battle to push DEC into the commercial arena. If he was out of the corporate line of sight, he could get more done. In 1975, he took 650 DEC employees to a new facility in Merrimack, New Hampshire. Over time, DEC expanded to more than 7,000 employees and became the largest employer in the state.

Stan began investing his own money in New Hampshire real estate. He bought high ground—hills, lakes, and open space. His purchases sometimes didn't seem to make financial sense. He bought at times simply because he liked the land. The more he invested, the more Stan's interest in real-estate development grew. In time, he owned a measurable percentage of New Hampshire.

But the investing was not enough of a distraction. In June 1977, DEC broke the $1 billion barrier in revenues. It controlled 41 percent of the worldwide minicomputer business. It now employed 38,000 employees. For Stan and others, the frustration of working for a corporate giant was growing. Pete Kaufmann didn't like the way the environment was causing him to use his own power. He found himself forcing his opinions and ideas on people where once he could explain and persuade.

Ted Johnson was also under the gun. DEC's sales and service organizations were doubling in size in step with revenue growth. And the customer base was changing. Commercial customers required a more sophisticated sales pitch than DEC's technical salesmen could often provide. Johnson, many inside DEC began to feel, was not up to the task. He did not delegate easily; he needed to have his hand in every decision. And the market was moving too fast for second thoughts.

Jack Shields, who had built a smooth service organization under Johnson, was flexing his muscles. He understood the subtleties of DEC. He was a master at the power brokering necessary to maneuver or get things done in the matrix. More important, he understood Olsen better than anyone. He knew that his president loved to hear good news, and that is what Shields provided him in his service reports. Year after year, Shields' records showed that customer satisfaction with service—Shields's service organization—improved.

Paradoxically, there existed at DEC a simultaneous concern for customers and an arrogance toward them. The original engineers and marketers believed they knew better than the customers themselves what the customers wanted and needed—the same thinking that pervaded IBM. The success of the minicomputers reinforced the attitude at DEC. Engineers often didn't listen to what sales and marketing had to say. Olsen, with a touch of engineer's arrogance, generally agreed with engineering's independence from marketing.

Shields could see the world changing. In his sixteen years at Digital, he had become the connoisseur of power, the man who knew how to work DEC to his own benefit. Computer users now had ideas that DEC needed to listen to, so he carefully started steering the company toward a new customer-oriented thinking.

Two DECs were emerging: the one seen from the outside as a paragon of corporate stability and intelligence, a humane and invigorating company that seemed a nearly ideal employer; and the DEC seen from inside at the executive level, where the corporate power game was taking its toll.

Ken Olsen held tight the tiller of this undulating ship, while Gordon Bell was quietly masterminding the course of DEC's future.

17
Soul of a DEC Machine

On APRIL 1, 1975, Gordon Bell led five of
Digital's best engineers to a small conference room on the
third floor of Building 12 in the Mill. The room was stark and
unpainted, with lanolin-soaked floors and dirty walls. The
group—Dave Cutler, Tom Hastings, Richie Lary, Steve Roth-
man, and Bill Strecker—spent weeks there, seeking an answer.
The men represented a cross-section of the DEC engineering
corps, from the studious Strecker to the boyish, curly-topped
Lary. They knew their mission was vital to the prosperity of
the company. Bell called the group VAX-A. A larger team,
called VAX-B, was formed simultaneously as a sounding board
for VAX-A's ideas.

The subject was the future. DEC was selling PDP-8s, 10s,
and 11s as fast as they could be produced. By September 1975,
the company had shipped its 50,000th computer system. Each
of the PDP lines had been enhanced with new models and new
price configurations, giving the appearance of a company
pushing at the leading edge. But the fact was that the PDP-11,
the most recently designed model in the overall product
lineup, was five years old. In computing lifecycles, the 11 was
entering its geriatric stage.

150

Bell realized even as he returned from Carnegie-Mellon in 1972 that DEC would quickly face the question, "What next?" His goal, and VAX-A's goal, was to move DEC to the next generation. Not an incremental step, not even a mere jump into the next generation—Bell was looking for an architecture that could vault Digital into the computing future. He could see by a complex formula of price and memory growth rates that the basic 16-bit PDP-11 was "born to have a short, happy, prolific, and profitable life . . . a life of six to nine years," counting from its creation in 1970. Bell was not an engineer who held onto old designs and old products. "One of the hardest things to know," he wrote later, "is when we should stop evolving (a product) and take a new approach. I think history provides good lessons in determining when a product is over-the-hill in terms of extendibility and hence lacks competitiveness. I strongly believe in product euthanasia."

But with the product-line managers owning their respective technologies, it was no simple task for central engineering to change a machine, let alone kill one off. The other option—adding a whole new architecture to DEC's computer lineup—required corporate resources that were already being stretched to support dozens of major products. Bell sponsored engineering teams to explore follow-ons to the 10 and 11. Could those architectures be effectively grown to carry DEC into the future?

There were persuasive arguments to create a smaller version of the DEC10 to cover the gap in the product lineup. The 10, DEC's large-scale machine, already had a huge library of third-party software written for its larger memory configuration. DEC engineers understood the 10 and had already solved many of the problems a new machine would only recreate. And the 10 was efficient at running Fortran, a key computer language in the scientific-engineering world. Most important, the 10 was already in the marketplace and supported by a cult following.

Unfortunately, the 10 was based on 36-bit, rather than 32-bit, architecture. DEC would be bucking the 8-bit standard if it held to 36-bit technology. The DEC10 was also a sophisticated machine, requiring knowledgeable users to handle it. Its complex operating systems demanded programmers devoted enough to spend months understanding it. For the future, Bell wanted to attract a broader, less sophisticated customer base to DEC computers. He wanted to free users from the centralized data processing authority that operated IBM's mainframes.

DEC's small-computer heritage argued most strongly against tying the company's future to the DEC10 architecture. The sales, service, engineering, marketing, and manufacturing forces were focused on the small computers, the PDP-8 and -11, which accounted for 90 percent of total sales. Going with a DEC10 solution would mean retraining and reeducating thousands within DEC to a new operating environment. The 10 solution was ruled out.

The PDP-11 also was found unsuitable as an architecture to build on. The extremely small address space meant that users ran out of memory too soon. If the hardware is the car and the software is the gas, then the memory is the gas tank. A tiny gas tank means you can only go so far with that system. By Bell's estimates, the 11's gas tank was too small to sustain a long journey.

But Bell knew that the company could not simply abandon the PDP-11 and start over. DEC's customers had invested too much money in the hardware itself and the software running on it. He had already begun efforts to extend the 11's address space, but his engineers kept hitting technological walls. In order to keep the 11 architecture intact, changes to components of the technology would have to be made, and those would affect compatibility. Users might not be able to run existing software applications on the new version of the machine without rewriting extensive code. In addition, the compromises necessary to force the needed performance from the underlying architecture would have caused a "kluge"—a system made up of poorly matched components, rather than a clean and efficient design. The conclusion: something radical needed to be done.

Bill Demmer, another among DEC's elite engineering corps, wrote Bell a detailed memo in February 1975, advocating a new 32-bit family of machines. Using this argument as a base, Bell's VAX-A group proposed the VAX-11. The machine would be 32 bits instead of 16; but more important, it included a fundamental—and untried—method of providing virtually unlimited address space or memory built into a minicomputer's architecture. If the VAX—Virtual Address Extension—could be pulled off, it would give DEC machines an overwhelming technical advantage.

Initially, the group's overriding concern for the new machine was to retain compatibility with the PDP-11. The VAX-A team finally decided to simply include a full-mode PDP-11 in the VAX design. Though he strongly believed that the PDP-11 architecture was doomed, Bell knew that the thousands of 11 users would raise Cain if they were suddenly abandoned. He made his opinions clear: "My position on the 11 is to get out of it so we don't have to support it, because we aren't making it there. We know the 11 isn't going anywhere in the long run. It's another code museum." But that was Bell's engineering voice speaking. He knew in his business heart that any change would have to be gradual.

Strecker, Bell's first Ph.D. student at Carnegie-Mellon and the architect of the VAX, wrote in 1978: "In principle, there is no great challenge in designing a large virtual address minicomputer system. For example, many of the large mainframe computers could serve as architectural models for such a system. The real challenge lies in two areas: compatibility—very tangible and important; and simplicity—intangible but nonetheless important."

With the PDP-11 "thrown in" to the design, the VAX-A group proceeded with its new architecture. Any feature that compromised ease of use was summarily rejected. The new project was called the VAX-11 so that customers would recognize the company's commitment to compatibility with the PDP-11.

Bell had a computing vision taking shape in his head, a vision bigger than the compatibility or ease-of-use issue. He wanted to build a machine that would represent an order-of-magnitude advance, taking DEC into the mid-1980s and beyond, based on a computer of unparalleled range of price-performance possibilities.

Bell's original VAX announcement memo, dated June 4, 1975, hinted at his thinking: VAX "will merge systems development to a single system to cover a large range." It would be several years before he formulated his entire strategy. But the foundation piece, the VAX, was under way. He put the project in the hands of Strecker as architect, Demmer as project leader, Dave Rodgers as head of hardware design, and Cutler as developer of the VMS operating system. The VAX-11 took less than three years to complete, a remarkably short time for so complex a machine. Bell, as head of engineering, served as what he calls "city planner" of the operation.

As VAX-A developed its plans, another group of engineers and marketing managers met every Tuesday night at the new Parker Street facility in Maynard to devise DEC's overall computer strategy. Over pizza and submarine sandwiches, the group, led by Andy Knowles, discussed how best to implement the plan set forth by Bell's team and how to focus the existing product lines to complement VAX. Knowles and Marcus insisted that the different VAX models—code-named Galaxy, Star, and Nebula—would have only one operating system, rather than the four created for the PDP-11.

Concurrently, a small software group, led by Stu Wecker, was conceiving of DECnet, a proprietary network to hook DEC machines together. Until the mid-1970s, computers seemed destined to operate in isolation. Then the federal government implemented ARPANET to link together Department of Defense offices. IBM introduced SNA (Systems Network Architecture) to connect its mainframes in American corporations. Inside DEC, the notion of tying great numbers of computers into a network was also being born. The task was so technologically difficult that many in DEC management argued not to proceed. But by a close vote, DECnet survived. Bell realized quickly that DECnet was not only a "major architectural triumph" but was as crucial to the company as the new VAX. He became its main supporter within the company.

By the time VAX was being proposed in the spring of 1975,

Knowles's Components Group was operating in Marlboro. He moved in with just a single secretary as the group's work force. It was only a half-hour drive to the Mill, yet Maynard seemed a world away. Senior management left Knowles to his own devices, and he operated the Components Group like an autonomous division. He almost never saw Olsen, except at Operations Committee meetings. Knowles was both amazed and content with Olsen's lack of interference in not only his group but with the emerging VAX-11 strategy. Olsen attended neither Knowles's Tuesday night meetings at Parker Street nor Bell's VAX-A group meetings.

The engineers, especially Bell, were also relieved that Olsen kept his hands off the VAX. They acknowledged his skill as a packaging designer but not as a computer designer. His involvement—or his interference—in the VAX implementation would have slowed down, and possibly destroyed, the grand scheme. To his credit, Olsen saw that his best designers were on the project and was content to drive the company's business side while they worked on the products. He wasn't interested in high-end machines anyway. His passion was smaller computers, where the packaging made a difference to the user. The larger minicomputers were like refrigerators, housed in racks and platforms—hardly a packaging person's challenge.

Nevertheless, Olsen's interest in technology hardly waned during this time. He still came to the Mill on Saturday mornings and wandered around the design areas—particularly in packaging and power supplies—to see what technologies were on the drawing boards. "For a chief executive, he had an enormous interest in the technical detail," says Henk Schalke, a former power-supply engineer. And Olsen had little trouble finding people to talk to on the weekends. The work week at DEC, at least for engineers, lasted six days, and for many, seven. Olsen loved to stop and talk with his dedicated team, rolling up his sleeves and grabbing a screwdriver to help put a box together. The engineers and technicians, according to Schalke, were flattered that he showed such interest, but were also uncomfortable that the head of the company wanted to be that close to their work.

Olsen's wanderings into the product development areas

were short escapes from the worries of the executive office. The company was growing so rapidly that he feared a loss of control as had happened in the early sixties.

Olsen saw his product-line strategy fraying at the edges. In fiscal 1975, recession cut DEC's revenue growth almost in half, to 27 percent. Time, money, and customer goodwill were being lost as DEC marketed overlapping products. But Olsen had no alternative in mind. Rapid growth seemed to mandate such a decentralized approach. He told *Business Week* in 1976, "We think the computer markets are so complex that you can't centralize—you must break the company into pieces. I can't see any other way to manage a computer company."

Suddenly, the minicomputer market, now one of the hottest businesses in the United States, was gaining increasing press coverage. Olsen, as de facto leader of the industry, found his insight and folksy quotes in demand by dozens of newspapers and magazines. *Business Week* put him on the cover in April 1976. Business writers couldn't resist comparing DEC to Data General, which was soaring like a hawk over DEC's territory.

Olsen was awkward and more than a bit innocent when it came to the media. His public-relations manager, Dick Berube, tried to coach him on what to say to the press, but Olsen followed his own instincts. His surprising candor offset his lack of communication skills. And his technobumpkin appearance was disarmingly refreshing to reporters used to the Brooks Brothers executive reciting corporate platitudes. With Olsen, what you see is what he is. "He doesn't have a little vacuum," Berube says, "where he can sit as an hermetically sealed CEO and play back the corporate philosophy."

Olsen would often utter inopportune statements about an issue or a competitor to startled reporters and then say, "That sounds bad; you fix it up for me later." He said what was on his mind while Berube winced alongside, knowing he would have to follow up later to explain to reporters. While DEC enjoyed record growth, Olsen formed a comfortable, if awkward, relationship with the business writers. Good numbers equaled good reviews and a tranquil coexistence.

In 1976, Olsen turned fifty. DEC, at age nineteen, was a

$736 million company. DEC was now listed among the major computer vendors in Wall Street reports. In October, the stock split three for one, and Wall Street stamped its "buy" label on the hot-growth company in Maynard. In Armonk, New York, a tiger stirred and then awakened. In the spring, IBM introduced its Series 1, a minicomputer ready to attack DEC's lucrative market.

"We are not competing against IBM."
— *Ken Olsen*

18
Going After Big Blue

Dᴇᴄ's sᴜᴄᴄᴇss, ᴛʜᴇ argument goes, has been inversely proportional to IBM's failure. IBM failed to recognize the potential of minicomputers, thus DEC lived and thrived.

In their 1986 book *Marketing Warfare*, Al Ries and Jack Trout observe that in the computer-market wars, DEC outflanked IBM by building small computers while everyone else—Burroughs, Univac, NCR, Control Data, Honeywell—tried to grab for portions of IBM's own territory, large computers. "Leaders tend to be easier to flank at the low end," they wrote. "IBM's ego got in the way of its judgment. Who'd buy a low-cost bare-bones, small computer without IBM software and IBM technological support?" The answer to this last rhetorical question—which expresses IBM's own view of the market—turned out to be a long list of DEC customers, including AT&T, Standard Oil, Banker's Trust, Bechtel, General Motors, Rockwell International, and thousands of others.

Could DEC have staked out this territory if IBM had been competing in the midrange in 1957? Could DEC have prospered if IBM had moved into the business even in 1970, when the PDP-11 was dangerously late, instead of waiting until 1976? "Strong competitive moves should always be blocked," wrote Ries and Trout.

To Olsen, the difference between his company and the one the Watsons built has always been more than just timing. It is a fundamental difference in philosophy: Olsen believed in bringing computing to the individual with small, interactive machines. IBM saw the world through colossal number crunchers, out of the reach of the single user. IBM told its customers, "Don't worry about your computing problems and needs, we'll take care of all of it for you." IBM often treated its commercial customers as computer illiterates—which in many cases they were—and showed little interest in educating them. This attitude contrasted with Olsen's vision of how computers should be sold and used. He didn't worry that Big Blue would sweep the minicomputer market because his rival so clearly didn't understand computing at that level. IBM had seemed unwilling or incapable of producing a computer that sold for less than $1 million.

But Olsen didn't want to rouse IBM's attention. He saw no need to anger the Watsons or their successor chief executives. "We are not competing against IBM" was the avowed DEC policy, even when DEC clearly was. Olsen followed Norm Taylor's advice: never publicly criticize IBM. In 1971, when IBM first offered a smaller computer (though still not in the minicomputer range), Olsen told *Forbes* magazine, "We love IBM. It focuses attention on the market."

Despite his humble public pronouncements, Olsen wanted to best IBM, to show the world what he saw in Poughkeepsie in 1953—that he could "beat these guys at their own game." But the time wasn't right in the mid-1970s. IBM had built itself into the monolithic force of the computer industry. Its revenues nearly doubled the combined annual sales of its top ten hardware rivals. There was nothing to gain for DEC by comparing itself to the model of American business.

Like many others in the industry, Olsen chafed at what he viewed as IBM's growing monopolistic ways. Years later, in an infrequent public slip about IBM, he angrily told the *Wall*

Street Journal, "I know what IBM thinks—they're the messenger right from God."

Particularly in the early days, Olsen refrained from using IBM as a motivational tool or rallying point for the sales force. "That was not our model at all," says Ted Johnson. "Our first model in the business was Tektronix. But from then on, we hardly ever talked about competitors, in the sense of trying to learn from them. We did our own thing. That was the attitude inside the company. It was always dangerous in the computer business to think about IBM because then you'd start doing what they did. We had our own sense of what was right to do in computing, and our skill was finding customers that were more adventurous, that we could satisfy. If they were brainwashed by IBM, we didn't waste our time. We sold where we could win."

In truth, DEC was quietly competing against IBM as early as 1971 with the DEC10 line. This large time-sharing system was going head to head with IBM mainframes and winning accounts in universities and research labs. But DEC salespeople were told not to talk about their very large competitor.

One of the reasons for paying the sales force salaries rather than commissions was to instill yet another difference in the customer's mind between DEC and IBM. Olsen believed that commissions created a high-pressure sales environment in which the salesman would push unneeded products on a customer. He wanted his salespeople to be free to work with the customer, not sell at the customer.

"I never did like commission houses," says Johnson. "I personally felt that it was more professional to work under direct salary. The commission idea was propagated by IBM. People were imitating IBM all over the place. Almost everything we did, when you examine it, was different from IBM."

DEC's open and democratic, campuslike atmosphere contrasted with IBM's secretive and controlled hierarchical order. As DEC grew in the 1970s, employees took a certain pride in being different. A cult thrived deep in the Mill that looked upon DEC as the brave, resourceful David saving the computing masses from the hulking Goliath.

An underground comic book called *CPU Wars* circulated through the Mill in 1980 in which IPM (Impossible to Program Machines) Corporation invades the Mill in Barnyard, Massachusetts, in an attempted takeover of HEC (Human Equipment Corporation). Armed with tanks and guns, IPM takes control. The reason: "Because HEC makes computers that are easy to use and more accessible to people, IPM felt a moral obligation to eliminate HEC before too many people had access to too much information."

IPM installs its corporate controls—"Those of you with interactive terminals will turn them in"—and forces HEC employees to wear gray suits. Soon an insurgent underground movement is born, and HEC's brave loyalists force IPM out of the Mill. Among the terms of surrender: "Batch cards are to be used only for telephone bills and toll tickets," and "No computer will be made mysterious and complicated on purpose."

The comic sold briskly around the Mill until its creator took the free enterprise concept too far to suit DEC executives (he set up a booth in the cafeteria selling comics and T-shirts).

In *The Change Masters*, Kanter illustrates one difference between DEC (called *Chipco* in the book) and IBM: "I remember being at a seminar with some Chipco people at a large elegant hotel that had an IBM meeting next door. At the coffee break, the beards, blazers, corduroy pants and polo shirts of the Chipco men could not have stood out more from the dark suits, white shirts and conservative ties that poured out of the IBM room."

Until the mid-1970s, DEC did not worry about being compared to IBM. In 1975, IBM shook the minicomputer world with the introduction of its System/32, a small business computer selling for $33,000, its lowest-priced machine to date. IBM aimed the System/32 more at the small machines offered by NCR and Burroughs than at DEC's products. But the pricing at the minicomputer level showed clearly that IBM had its eyes on DEC's territory.

DEC countered with the introduction of a PDP-8 model aimed at the engineering as well as general business markets, sold at $12,000. It went to market billed as "the world's lowest-priced, fully programmable computer system." DEC also unveiled its classic educational system, a PDP-8A priced at $7,900. But the DEC and IBM machines were still apples and oranges, products with vastly different capabilities aimed at completely different users. DEC sold its basic computers to OEMs and value-added resellers, manufacturers who customized the machines to resell or lease into niche markets. IBM took the opposite tack, loading the System/32 with its own software and extensive service options and generally selling or leasing directly to customers. It was a stretch to call the two companies significant competitors yet.

By 1976, however, Olsen's ability to avoid confrontation with IBM was slipping. DEC's minicomputer legions spurred the change to a new concept of computing—distributed data processing. For five years, engineers had been working on Digital's communication protocol called DECnet. Low-cost minicomputers tied together by DECnet could now handle the central data processing in some small and midsize corporations, as well as divisions of large companies. Distributed data processing promised even more—to distribute computing power to remote parts of the organization that had traditionally suffered delays in accessing computing services.

Few in the industry had recognized the enormous implications of DECnet and DEC's early commitment to an easy-to-use communications component. But DEC's message was starting to sink in. A 1976 report from the International Data Corporation in Framingham, Massachusetts, noted that users were getting more sophisticated and "drifting from hardline IBM doctrine." Many computer sites were starting to evaluate minis as an alternative to the traditional mainframe solution. IBM, which at $7 billion in annual sales was ten times bigger than DEC in 1976 and ten times bigger than its nearest mainframe competitor, Honeywell, was hardly quivering. In computers, IBM was the sun and the competition merely small planets revolving around it. IBM was also the master marketing organization. Inside DEC, marketing philosophy reflected Olsen: it was simple and direct. Build the best piece of hardware and it will sell itself. Olsen's attitude was reflected a few years later when an advertising agency suggested promoting a product on television. Olsen asked for the cost involved, quickly calculated the number of technical manuals that could be purchased for the same price, and just as quickly refused to retain the agency.

DEC marketers realized that the company's strength was its reputation for quality. They were content to let that image quietly spread even if the general public had never heard of them. The company was taking its anonymity to the bank. "People always think of marketing as how much you spend on advertising," says Johnson. "We worked quietly, finding niches, finding people we could satisfy, and built a broad base. That was great marketing."

Clair Goldsmith, a longtime customer and ex-president of the user group, DECUS, says, "One of the things we used to complain to Digital about was name recognition. There wasn't any." Corporate executives thought all computers were IBM.

Stan Olsen once brought in an advertising agency that suggested the company formally use DEC rather than Digital in marketing to avoid confusion with digital watches and other general industry uses of the term. Despite strong internal support and the common use of "DEC" by press, analysts, and customers, Olsen refused.

IBM realized that minicomputers already represented a $5 billion industry, and it wanted a piece. The Series 1 introduction in 1976 marked IBM's entry into that market, and suddenly, the business and trade press began to take the minimakers seriously. Data General, known for its pugnacious advertising, produced an ad that no publication would accept. It read: "They say IBM's entry into minicomputers will legitimize the market. The bastards say, welcome."

Olsen's response was less combative. "We don't mind competing with IBM—it doesn't worry us," he told *Business Week*. He saw the computer market as big enough for lots of players. DEC's bread and butter markets—scientific-engineering environments—were essentially safe from IBM. But Big Blue's vast customer base in business seemed ready to consider DEC-style computing.

"What terrifies people about IBM is the resources they can

pour into a problem," Olsen said. "But we're just about at that point ourselves. We're cheaper, but they offer a lot more service. IBM will say, 'We'll make your system work no matter how dumb you are.' We walk away from some customers." DEC had no plans to specifically increase its sales and service force to try to compete with IBM. The close relationships it had formed with third-party developers and OEMs helped obviate the need for a huge field organization of its own.

In truth, DEC had more immediate concerns in 1976 than IBM. While Bell's group settled into devising the VAX, other new products were testing the waters in new markets. Stan's group in New Hampshire leaped into the word processing market with its $22,000 DECmate. This product entrenched DEC in the business side of computing and brought the company into the early office-automation fray.

Knowles was experiencing difficulties getting the LSI-11 product into the black, but the terminals business was showing signs of solid returns. (Knowles knew his line of terminals had reached its pinnacle of visibility when it was used as a prop in Perry White's newspaper office in the movie *Superman*.) DEC's early terminal products suffered various flaws, which Knowles's group addressed one by one. What emerged in 1976 was the VT100, an "intelligent" full-featured computer terminal that would become an industry standard.

Knowles was a tough competitor and a demanding boss. He was obsessed with succeeding, showing Olsen and the Operations Committee that his little band in Marlboro could make it. He had fought Operations Committee members even to accept the Marlboro site. They feared that the glass and deep-pile carpet left over from the building's RCA days would be at odds with DEC's earthy Mill image.

The competitive times and spurting growth set the perfect environment for the unrelenting, hard-edge mentality that Knowles brought to his work. The squeeze was on DEC— from IBM at the top, from Data General and the other mini-computer vendors at all sides. Data General was reveling in its own phenomenal success. Whereas it had taken DEC thirteen years to reach $100 million in sales, it took Data General just seven. Data General was just one-fifth DEC's size. But that one-fifth represented $100 million worth of business that probably would have gone to DEC.

In the corporate images west of Boston, DEC was, ironically, now the stodgy old veteran, the IBM of the mini business; Data General was the glamorous employer to work for. *Forbes* published an article in January 1976 headlined, "The Long Hairs vs. The Stuffed Shirts," comparing DG to DEC. The article asserted that DEC had "become a stuffy company top heavy with management."

Still, DEC remained the employer of choice along Route 128. Berube estimates that DEC was receiving hundreds of thousands of resumes per year by the end of the 1970s for openings in a work force of under 50,000. DEC, for its part, hardly acknowledged Data General's existence anymore, despite Olsen's continued anger. Bell, upon returning from Carnegie-Mellon, had advised Olsen against worrying about Data General, insisting that the company was not a long-term threat. Still, the Nova had not burned out quickly, as Olsen had hoped. Data General was now a major player, an opponent to watch.

While the fires burned in the high-tech wars, two young inventors sat in a garage in Palo Alto, California, formulating another kind of computer. Steven Jobs, twenty-one, and Steven Wozniak, twenty-four, were putting the finishing touches on the first Apple personal computer, a crude version of the machine that would spark a new industry. Their opportunity was vast in part because DEC and Olsen, in a classic business oversight, failed to take interactive computing to its next logical step—personal computing—and thus left the field open to them.

"You've got nothing to offer society if you only follow."

—*Ken Olsen*

19
A Spider's Web

ONE MORNING IN early 1977, Pete Kaufmann told Olsen he would be leaving the company shortly. He hadn't planned to deliver his message that day, but Olsen was pressing him to take on more responsibility, including the personnel department after Dennis Burke's departure. Kaufmann, who had survived Olsen's wrath from the "palace revolt" in 1970, had reached his limit.

As it celebrated its twentieth birthday in 1977, DEC hit the $1 billion mark in sales. From the year Computing-Tabulating-Recording Company changed its name to IBM in 1924, the company took thirty-three years to attain the billion-dollar plateau. Kaufmann had targeted leaving DEC when it became a $100 million corporation, so he figured he had long overstayed his own timetable. He wasn't interested in huge corporate environments and the tangled webs of relationships that they spun. DEC had changed. That didn't surprise Kaufmann; it was inevitable as a company grew. Olsen was starting to lean on new shoulders, like those of Jack Shields. Kaufmann felt that the new club was not one he wanted to belong to.

Olsen asked him to stay. Once. And when Kaufmann

couldn't be dissuaded, the issue was settled. Though he would remain nine more months before officially resigning, Kaufmann was once again a nonperson. Olsen never called him at home or at work about any DEC matter.

Kaufmann's leaving reverberated throughout DEC. His strong personality had left an indelible mark on the company. To those in manufacturing, he seemed irreplaceable. Employees couldn't comprehend how he could just quit without being lured away by a much better offer. Kaufmann told them he was heading to the wilds of northern Maine to rethink his life, to decide which course to follow. Not only was he a spiritual leader and an inimitable nonconformist who represented the best of DEC's freewheeling individuality, but he was a ranking vice president. A vice presidency was an honored spot beyond even the power it carried; giving it up at DEC was like resigning being an uncle—you just couldn't do it.

Mazzarese had walked away five years earlier, but his departure didn't produce the repercussions of Kaufmann's resignation. DEC was in a period of financial growth and leadership in 1977. "How could Pete leave now?" was the question around the Mill. Kaufmann's exit signaled to the old-timers that an era was ending. People like Stan, Ted Johnson, and John Leng felt that Ken was somehow different now, less accessible, relying on new people they didn't always trust.

A new era dawned at DEC. There were 36,000 employees worldwide, and the lines of the matrix were crisscrossing like a spider's web. Gloria Porrazzo, one of the first dozen employees, had seen a dramatic change since she started twenty years before as an assembler. The feeling in the early days had been one of trust and openness—it didn't matter if somebody did someone else's job, as long as it got done. "When we started bringing in a lot of professional types, cataloging every job, it really lost that family feeling. It didn't seem like Digital anymore," Porrazzo says.

What seemed like a loss of the good old days to one group marked the beginning of a golden period to another. And the changes hardly regimented the company. When Tom Peters and Robert Waterman were looking for excellence five years later in their landmark business book *In Search of Excellence*, they found DEC's product-line organization. As Johnson told them, "Essentially, we act like a group of smaller companies." The "chaos management" at DEC was, in many ways, a catalyst for excellence.

Acting like a group of smaller companies, Peters and Waterman wrote, "means constant reorganization, product-line proliferation and overlap, salesmen out creating 'one customer niche after another.' People at Digital, and at many other excellent companies, regularly lament short production runs, inventory confusion and sometimes dual coverage of customers. They lament, we'd add, all the way to the bank."

Despite this appraisal from the outside, DEC's structure was wobbling on the line between success and failure. It is ironic that as *In Search of Excellence* sat atop the bestseller list in the early 1980s, DEC was phasing out the very product-line arrangement the book praised so highly.

Norman Taylor, Olsen's former boss at Lincoln Lab, saw firsthand DEC's difficulty selling into the commercial marketplace. As a consultant to Equitable Life in 1978, he evaluated DEC and Wang for a $50 million office system purchase. "I sensed there were problems within DEC," Taylor says. "The salesman promised one thing, and when we went to the engineer, he promised something different. There were two different groups within Digital trying to sell different products to us, and they'd actually get in front of us and compete with each other. They let the client see the contest. It was very confusing to the people from Equitable to have an engineer telling them that what the salesman promised was not going to happen. So they lost the sale to Wang." And Taylor wrote to Olsen: "Ken, you've got to straighten out this mess. It just cost you a $50 million order." Olsen didn't reply.

The two men ran into each other not long after, and Taylor told Olsen how lucrative the insurance industry could be for an aggressive computer maker with a coordinated sales effort. "I imagine that's true," Olsen replied, but he was not eager to get into the commercial arena. "Don't imagine, it is true," Taylor said. "How long are you going to wait?"

DEC branched slowly into commercial markets, such as banking and chemicals, at the prodding of Marcus, Shields, and Stan Olsen. They found that customer expectations there had already been set by IBM, Honeywell, Burroughs, and other mainframe vendors. These companies provided 100 percent hand-holding to their customers. DEC's sales and service organizations weren't prepared for that kind of relationship. DEC had established rapport with its users, but these scientists and engineers didn't need pampering. Suddenly, DEC faced providing more than iron; the new customers needed guidance and supervision, not just a machine, no matter how good it was.

Through his service organization, Shields hammered away at creating a reputation for providing quality service. He used innovative methods, such as sending out a detailed questionnaire to users years before the technique became popular. In 1977, he introduced the industry's first computerized remote diagnosis capability, the ability of a centrally located computer to monitor a customer's systems and prevent problems without sending a field engineer to the site.

Shields was DEC's service pioneer going back to 1961. With Olsen's blessing, he had made service a profit-making venture from the start, an unusual setup in industry. If a customer valued good service, he would be willing to pay for it, Shields reasoned. DEC has made a profit on service ever since.

In 1974, Shields was rewarded with a vice presidency of his service and support areas; in 1978, he spun his group out from under Johnson's sales organization. But Shields's vision of the new DEC customer was not yet accepted at DEC. Internally, the product lines remained oblivious or, perhaps, too entangled with each other and the functional groups to face the changes.

As Kanter pointed out in *The Change Masters*, "The legitimacy of crosscutting access promoted the circulation of all three power commodities: resources, information and support. Managers could go across formal lines and levels in the organization to find what they needed—vertically, horizontally or diagonally—without feeling that they were violating protocol. They could skip a level or two without penalty. Indeed, managers were frequently counseled that direct access was better than going through channels."

Olsen himself set the standard for direct access from the early days. He frequently checked in with engineers two levels down in the organization to work out issues, sometimes leaving the project manager he had skipped over feeling undermined. Conversely, DEC employees believed that they could go directly to Ken if they needed to, whether to propose a new idea or settle a problem.

To the customer outside looking in, DEC's organization often appeared to formalize duplication. A classic example is Clair Goldsmith, the ex-president of DECUS. "The product-line structure was a real problem," he says. "I work for an educational institution that is health-care related. DEC would have these wars sometimes internally because a certain product line would need revenue. That was a war that as a customer I shouldn't know exists. I would get a call from the education salesman to 'watch out, the Labs people are after you. And they can't do for you what I can because I better understand the business you are in.' They would compete against each other. Some days you could really play it to your advantage. Other days, you couldn't get any help because they'd say, 'No, you're the other guy's customer.' "

Despite the confusion externally and internally, the product-line structure held together from the mid-1960s to the early 1980s. DEC's middle managers earned their stripes by showing they could thrive in the matrix management setup. Upper management would not take ownership of projects; therefore, middle managers had to exert influence and initiative. The means of achieving decisions were so complex that managers brought in from traditional hierarchical companies took six months to a year to figure out what was going on. One high-level manager likened DEC to a Japanese-style company: He could find no one who would say no. At the secretarial level, this lack of decisiveness was just as clear. "The joke," says Mary Jane Forbes, "was, 'Don't let the proposal go to the Operations Committee, cause you'll never get a decision out of Ken.' "

Two-thirds of DEC's very low turnover occurs within the

first two years. The kind of manager DEC wants in the long run is the person who will take charge of his own path right from the first day. Advanced degrees did little to ensure the success of a candidate. In fact, MBAs traditionally didn't rise to the top of DEC as at many other companies. The engineering ranks were unimpressed by a business degree that could contribute so little to the technical, specialized environment that was DEC.

There are no seminars designed to tell new employees how to survive in DEC's matrix. Managers hand out assignments and expect the new employee to come back frustrated at not being able to do the job. From that first failure in the ways of the matrix, managers would build a model DEC employee. One manager who has been navigating through the matrix for twelve years says, "You don't go in to Digital, sit down at your desk, and get your job done. I don't care how good the electronic mail system is or the network is, you have to get out from behind your desk. You have to get face to face with individuals and groups to really make something happen."

The foremost trait of DEC's management culture that a new executive needed to understand was the need for consensus. In the absence of a central voice of authority, decisions could be influenced from virtually any part or level of the company. The trick was knowing whom to get to sign off on an idea to move it along. The right person might be two or three levels down in an organization; without his input and approval, a project would get stuck. "At times," one senior manager told Barbara Marchilonis for her Harvard Graduate School of Education thesis, "I think some people ask for, even pray for, some top-down direction. The majority of their day-to-day activities is spent trying to influence the direction of events so they can maintain control over their groups and produce on schedule."

With the power so well distributed, DEC managers became corporate Henry Kissingers, negotiating deals, building coalitions, gaining consensus or "buy-in." The diplomacy included a period of lobbying or preselling so that when an idea came up before a committee meeting, the votes were already secured. This tactic was called "loading" the meeting. Lukewarm or majority acceptance wasn't sufficient to move a proposal along. Unanimity was required for a project to make its way to the Operations Committee. As one manager put it, "A five-to-four decision is not a decision in this company."

Veto power still resides in many hands. There is the ever-present possibility of having the rug pulled out from under you just as your project seems to be on sound footing. A veto is often preceded by the comment, "Ken won't like it." But the veto has to be used sparingly, because a reputation for non-cooperation is antithetical to the consensus-building atmosphere. Sometimes buy-in is not completely clear. "It's hard to tell when you have buy-in, but it's easy to tell when you don't," says one manager.

Thus, DEC is a highly political environment in one sense; but because everyone operates under the same basic rules, the politics are at least democratic, not monarchical. Says Julius Marcus, "Despite all of the conflicts that occurred between product groups and the functions scrapping with each other inside, it was not the same thing as political whispering campaigns that occurred in the hallways of other companies. You could stand up and tell somebody that he was full of crap and get away with it. It wasn't taken personally. When it was a $1 billion and $2 billion company, Digital was the least political company of its size in the world. We used to laugh at Honeywell. Honeywell had all this seething, political, internal backstabbing, butt-covering behavior that you could smell from the outside. They were killing each other inside. They didn't know where the enemy was."

At DEC, the corporate enemy is always clear enough, and that enemy is poor quality. Hindle says that whenever he had to make a difficult decision, he would think about the outcome in terms of quality, profit, and growth—in that order. Olsen pushed harder at this point than any other and earned DEC a reputation for top-notch products. "We will never compete on price," he told *Computerworld*. "We believe that quality, features and ergonomics are what people want in a product. So our approach to selling is to do a job for people, provide good equipment." Olsen was also adamant that innovation must accompany quality. "You've got nothing to offer society if you only follow," he said. For the struggle of winning consensus, the payoff was carrying an idea into production as a machine and out to market. Money was not the primary reward for DEC engineers, who were generally paid at or just below industry averages. They saw little connection between their salaries and their effort expended in reaching product goals.

The need for buy-in in the matrix encouraged face-to-face meetings, whether by helicopter rides to New Hampshire or trans-Atlantic flights to Geneva. But influencing others also fostered an easier way to communicate. In the late 1970s, DEC created a sophisticated electronic mail network, which eventually grew to more than 50,000 users worldwide, in order to facilitate the messages that streamed through the work force. This system, the largest such private E-mail network in existence, continues to grow along with the company.

Olsen again set the model here, turning out electronic memos by the score. "I am in the market for a backhoe," read a widely known Olsen parable. "The other day I stopped at a Ford place to get literature on tractors. They had colored brochures with beautiful pictures and glowing descriptions, and plain black-on-yellow data sheets filled with numbers. The four models which I think may cover my needs seem to be made by four different product organizations that compete with each other in who can make the most expensive and beautiful brochure. But no way would the brochures explain why one Ford tractor might have advantages over another. The data sheets vary from two to eight pages, and there is no consistency in the way the data is presented. There is no way to compare the four tractors.

"If I don't get tired of the whole idea of a backhoe, I'll try seeing the salesman next time. But I am not sure he would understand the difference between the models, and I would feel intimidated by my lack of knowledge. I am always embarrassed when salesmen act surprised that I don't know how deep a ditch I want to dig, how heavy a load I want to lift or how high I want to lift it. Sometime I'd like to have you explain whether there is a parallel at Digital in this or not." While many managers puzzled over Olsen's message, the prevailing question was, "Why did he want a backhoe?"

"It was my job to say, 'We're one company, this is the strategy. If you don't like it, get out.' "
—Ken Olsen

20
The VAX Strategy

IN LATE AUGUST 1978, Gordon Bell stood out on the deck of a sloop sailing downwind through the Tahitian islands to Bora Bora. It was the end of a three-week tour of Japan and Australia, where he had lectured on and tried to sell the concept of the VAX. The sailing voyage was designed as a getaway, time off with his wife, Gwen, and their children, Brigham and Laura. In between his daily scuba dives, he read James Clavell's *Shogun* and then edited proofs of *Computer Engineering*, his history of Digital's computers.

As the warm Pacific winds angled the boat through the islands, Bell's thoughts ranged over the state of the computing world: the possibilities of networking, the hierarchy of computers, and the potential dominance of Japan. Bell reflected also on DEC's computing past; it was all in his upcoming book and fresh in his mind. He contemplated DEC's future as well, as he often did on trips. Bell came up with his best ideas far away from Maynard.

Most of all, Bell was thinking about the VAX. It represented an extraordinary, novel design that would change the face of computing. The VAX-11/780 "superminicomputer," as it had been named, was introduced in October 1977, less than three years after Bell and his VAX-A group conceived it in the Mill. Strecker, Demmer, Rodgers, and Cutler—DEC's engineering elite—led the implementation. "The message was, 'Go out and get it done,' says engineer Bernie Lacroute, who joined as the effort got going. "The VAX team was privileged, no question. We were highly motivated and determined to make this thing happen."

The machine needed to be expedited, and to Bell that meant steering Olsen away from it. Bell believed if Olsen got involved and demanded little changes or objected to certain design decisions, he might cool the fever that DEC's engineers were bringing to the assignment. "Ken had absolutely no role, as president or engineer, in VAX, beginning with its inception," Bell says. "He clearly must be given credit as president, though, for letting it come into being."

Olsen had been in poor health during the early VAX development. A gall bladder operation in 1977 and his recuperation sidelined him for several months, keeping him away from any hands-on engineering projects. But Olsen did not announce that a medical problem caused his absence from the Mill. Internal rumors circulated that perhaps Olsen had lost interest in running DEC and was ready to call it quits. When he did return, he came back stronger than ever. Olsen reportedly checked himself out of the hospital in Concord, Massachusetts, and walked several miles home to Lincoln through a blizzard. He was ready to take command again, and he made that clear to all, just as he had done in 1970 following the perceived "palace revolt."

The 11/780 was a welcome-back present. In a ceremonial gesture for DEC employees, Olsen powered up the first VAX prototype off the assembly line on October 25, 1977, and discovered the first operational bug. When he turned the power on, the metal handles to the module heated up and burned his hand. Olsen made the initial entry in the debug log: "Module handle shorted to +5 volts."

VAX represented more than just one dynamic machine. It evolved into a range of computers within an architecture that would span the 1980s and beyond. DEC always demonstrated the foresight to create long-lasting architectures—the PDP-8, DEC10, and PDP-11 were still selling briskly after thirteen years. VAX was different, however. It would leapfrog the technical obstacles that its brethren had eventually run into and would take DEC into a broader realm of computing power. At VAX's unveiling, Olsen called the machine "the most significant interactive computer of the last decade."

To the outside world, the VAX 11/780 was reestablishing DEC's supremacy in the minicomputer market. Rivals who were making strides against DEC's fleet of aging machines suddenly faced a younger heavyweight contender, and it had the look of a champion.

At Data General, the VAX announcement particularly disturbed Tom West. As one of Data General's chief engineers, he was immersed in developing his own 32-bit offering—a story that became legend in Tracy Kidder's Pulitzer Prize-winning book, *The Soul of a New Machine*. Kidder writes: "It had been painful for Tom West and for a number of engineers working with him at Westboro to watch DEC's VAX-11/780 go to market, to hear it described as a 'breakthrough' and not have a brand new machine of their own to show off. VAX was beginning to look like one of those bestsellers that come along once in a while."

Getting the VAX built was only the first step. Now Bell had to summon all of his standing at DEC to convince Olsen and the Operations Committee of the strategy he was formulating in his mind. He spoke many times on VAX in Japan and Australia. Finally, it came to him on the sailboat in Tahiti—a magic moment when random thoughts coalesced into an idea. DEC, he decided, should build only VAXes. All other product development should stop. DEC's resources should be directed into one framework—the VAX architecture. Computing was heading in a new direction, Bell believed, the opposite direction from IBM. DEC could lead the way in networking, as it had in the minicomputer business. Or it could follow, with its multiple products built on multiple architectures, scrambling like the rest of the minicomputer makers for small pieces of the overall computer industry.

When Bell returned to Maynard from the South Pacific in the fall of 1978, he set to work on what he naturally called the VAX Strategy. He sent a detailed memo laying out his plan to the Operations Committee. The idea was this: computing, traditionally oriented around a mainframe, was going to move to a three-tiered model. Mainframes would continue to function as huge corporate data processors, but minicomputers would serve the computing needs of departments within companies; intelligent terminals or personal computers would serve individuals within departments. Sophisticated new communications technology would create networks—lines of information flowing between the mainframe, the mini, and the desktop. The individual users at the ends of the network could thus tap immense computing power.

In Bell's internal memo, he wrote: "The essence of the strategy is simplicity through adopting a single architecture. Although superficially it appears to be possible to have numerous architectures that are segmented by size and by market, the user requirements to cross both size and application boundaries are significant. In fact, given that IBM is segmenting its products both by size and application, the main strength of the strategy is to have a single architecture with which a user can be comfortable rather than bounded by a manufacturer segmentation. The most compelling reason for basing the strategy on the single VAX architecture, besides the technical excellence of the product, is the belief that we cannot build the truly distributed computing system of the '80s with heterogeneous architectures."

Bell went a step further, explicitly bringing up the subject that usually went unstated at DEC. On page three of his strategy, he asked, "How Can We Win Against IBM?" Looking toward the 1980s, Bell believed that based on his new model of computing, the industry war would pit DEC squarely against IBM. He pointed out that IBM's philosophy was to introduce new products based on proprietary architectures to highly targeted, specific new markets. Big Blue seemed unconcerned about compatibility of its machines, as long as it achieved revenue and profit growth.

To Bell, this strategy was self-defeating in the long run.

Among its myriad products in the late 1970s, IBM sold its 360/370 family of mainframes, a new 8100 distributed processing system and a new System/38 small business computer. At the minicomputer level, IBM introduced the Series 1 in 1976. Each system came with its own architecture, making each one unable to talk easily or share applications with the others.

In his VAX Strategy memo, Bell wrote: "While on the surface, the 8100 stands to be IBM's most significant product, it seems to be a serious mistake as it introduces another incompatible computer system with which customers will have to deal. This means that the making of a compatible, fully distributed processing system will be essentially impossible."

IBM was painting itself into a corner, albeit a multi-billion-dollar corner. Bell could scarcely hide his disdain for his competitor's shortsightedness. "I wanted to beat the shit out of IBM—that was simple," he says. "It was going to be really easy if they didn't straighten out. They just totally played into our hands. I saw them getting worse and worse and deeper and deeper into it."

Bell argued for a diminished investment in PDP-11 software and suggested putting virtually all resources into developing VAX's VMS operating system, a sleek, expandable software design that would span the product range. He believed that the simultaneous evolution of DEC's several product lines caused vast duplication and cost far too much. "Since we provide many choices, we find our sales force and customers have difficulty deciding what to sell and buy," he wrote. "This makes us difficult to understand and to do business with."

Not surprisingly, Bell's magnum opus met with strong internal resistance. It was a radical plan, similar in unifying intent to the one made by Ed de Castro's PDP-X group in 1967. If accepted, it would spell the end of several of DEC's product lines. "It was the ultimate nail in the coffin of any business group in DEC oriented around a non-VAX computer," Bell says. The other lines would continue to be sold; there were too many customers out there to shut down production lines. In fact, Digital had shipped its 100,000th computer system in February of 1978. But the implications were clear: a machine would have to be a VAX to be accepted.

Bell drove the plan night and day from September to December of 1978. He continually fought engineers, such as Leng, and marketing people who had vested interests in perpetuating the old product lines. Knowles became a strong ally, even though he was leading the Components Group.

Jack Smith, who had been running manufacturing since Kaufmann's departure, sensed the confusion brought on by the new concept: "People said, 'Are you crazy? What are you doing? We've been growing at 30 percent per year. We're making a lot of money. Why do we have to leave the PDP-11?' "

Olsen neither favored nor rejected the proposal in the initial meetings. In his typical fashion, he pushed hard to expose the core of the issue. He sparred with Bell about whether the plan represented a true corporate strategy or just a simple product change. "Ken's harangues were always very painful," Bell says, "but also useful to me, because then I could go off and address the issues on his mind." After Bell convinced him that he was proposing an all-inclusive strategy for DEC, Olsen let the decision making proceed. The issues got aired and a consensus developed.

But Olsen worried. The company would be betting billions in development costs and potential lost revenue on this scheme. DEC would also be heading into areas where it had little experience, such as manufacturing its own microprocessors, building large disk storage units, and writing software to run on networks. Could Digital market this plan, he wondered? Could it afford to be wrong?

Despite all the reasons against it, Bell's strategy was formally approved by the Board of Directors in December 1978. "I took no active part in forming the strategy," Olsen admits. "But once it got going, it was my job to say, 'We're one company, this is the strategy. If you don't like it, get out.' " He proved once more why he has stayed so long on top of his company. He saw the new parade starting to march, and he simply got out in front and started waving his baton.

"Power doesn't come from telling people what to do; it comes from learning what goes on."

—*Ken Olsen*

21
Cracks in the Matrix

In FEBRUARY 1979, Gordon Bell quietly embarked on a side journey on the road toward a completed VAX strategy. He realized that DEC couldn't beat IBM simply by matching computing power. If DEC could hook its computers together across whole companies, however, it would gain a strategic advantage. DECnet software was already in place, but Bell needed a cabling mechanism to tie machines together. He and two DEC engineers, Bill Johnson and Sam Fuller, turned to Bob Metcalfe, a former Xerox employee who had invented a local-area networking protocol called Ethernet.

Bell liked Ethernet. He saw great technical merit in the network and, with Metcalfe, sought a way to create a new version of Ethernet without infringing on Xerox's patented one. It quickly became clear that rather than reinventing the wheel, it made sense for DEC to approach Xerox about jointly selling Ethernet.

Metcalfe treaded carefully. He had signed an agreement on leaving Xerox stating that he wouldn't reveal corporate secrets or gain personally from Ethernet. He wanted his invention to become an industry standard, but he had to work in low visibility or risk being sued by his former employer.

Metcalfe realized that one item was missing from Bell's plan: a semiconductor chip on which to base Ethernet. He approached Intel Corporation, a leading Silicon Valley chip maker. While avoiding direct involvement, he helped set up a trilateral meeting among DEC, Xerox, and Intel.

Bell knew that going with Ethernet was a gamble. Choosing a network for DEC before the industry had decided on a standard risked leaving the company racing fast on the wrong track. He kept the intricate plans under a thin cloak of secrecy. He updated the Operations Committee and Olsen frequently enough, but he put his dealings with Xerox and Intel near the bottom of his agenda so that no one would suspect their importance. In a year of consulting with DEC, Metcalfe never met Olsen. Yet he distinctly felt the man's presence. "In all the strategy meetings on Ethernet, you could feel Ken in the room, even though he wasn't there," Metcalfe says. "People would frequently say, 'Ken would never go for that,' or 'Let's keep Ken out of this.' He was there in many ways, but not physically."

The realization by Bell and his staff in 1979 of both the importance and difficulty of networking was a milestone in the VAX strategy. Metcalfe says today, "I believe the company's focusing on networking explains DEC's success and IBM's relative failure."

In May 1980, the unusual triumvirate of DEC, Xerox, and Intel announced its Ethernet plans to the world. Olsen was a skeptic, but he didn't try to stop the project. He did suggest changes in the cabling at the last minute, which infuriated Bell and the Ethernet engineers. In the long run, Olsen once again stepped out in front of the marchers. "A characteristic of many successful people is that they prefer being right over being consistent," says Metcalfe, a successful entrepreneur himself as the founder of 3Com, a local-area network vendor.

Resistance to the new VAX strategy continued. The European operation, for example, outright rejected the VAX, saying it didn't need such a system to increase its revenues.

Bell's VAX engineers worked outside the organizational turbulence stirred up within DEC by the move from many product architectures to one. Olsen tried to stem the mounting disharmony by restructuring the company—creating three umbrella groups over the existing product lines and putting one person in charge of each. To the vice presidents, it was a puzzling move, seemingly unrelated to the VAX strategy and the direction of the company. Then, just as he set up the new structure, Olsen changed his mind—he decided he didn't like partitioning the product lines into three. So he started fighting what he himself had pushed for.

Olsen was clearly angry at his group vice presidents in the late 1970s but was unable to articulate just what he wanted them to do differently or better. In an attempt to control the burgeoning company, the Operations Committee a year earlier had created the Office of the President, which included Olsen as president; Hindle as vice president, operations; and Knowles as vice president, corporate marketing. These positions were conceived as strategic roles but proved to be anything but that. For Knowles, in particular, being corporate marketing chief was an eighteen-month nightmare. He clashed with Olsen constantly over marketing and sales. He discovered that sales plans still weren't matching business plans, despite the use of formal charts to plot goals. For example, Europe could sell against one plan and submit an adjusted one later to Maynard. Worst of all, people were never fully measured against their proposals and agreed-on goals.

The matrix continued to undermine any attempt at cohesion. Memos and meetings proliferated. Olsen continued to flood his managers with electronic notes, sometimes two or three a day on the same subject. Successive memos might contradict a previous one. So the wise manager waited out a round of Olsen's messages before executing some action.

Olsen froze the salaries of his vice presidents, believing that they, not the company's rank and file, bore the responsibility for making things run smoothly. If there were problems, it was up to them to find the solutions. In the ranks of the managers, the consensus was that Olsen wanted the vice presidents to back off from the product lines and become portfolio managers. The product-line managers should be free to run their own show.

Some managers were bored in this setup. John Leng, like many of them, wanted to be an operational manager. He foresaw a major restructuring of the company coming in which many heads would roll. When a headhunter contacted him, he made up his mind to leave DEC.

He told his secretary on Friday to make an appointment for him to see Ken and only Ken. That meant specifically not including Win Hindle, the vice president of operations and Olsen's apparent second-in-command in 1979. Hindle sat in on virtually all of Olsen's meetings.

Though Leng knew how much Olsen disliked one-on-one encounters, he felt that this meeting called for it. He was going to announce that he was leaving DEC to become president of an office-automation company in Canada. His request for a private meeting was surely a tip-off, and it wasn't honored. When Leng walked into Olsen's office, Hindle—Olsen's buffer—was already there.

Leng had always felt a kinship to Olsen like many of those who grew up in the DEC family. Olsen was a demanding father figure, and Leng revered him despite the often difficult relationship. Leng wasn't relaxed around Olsen; in fact, he was plainly intimidated in some ways. But Leng felt a bond nonetheless, a desire to perform miracles for the man.

As one of Digital's top people in Europe in the 1960s, Leng had hosted Olsen and his family on their visits to England. It was the rare occasion when DEC executives socialized with the Olsens. From the start of his company, Olsen refrained from mixing with his employees after hours. He did not attend Ted Johnson's annual Christmas party, a tradition for executives. On many occasions, managers didn't invite Olsen to parties because they felt he would be uncomfortable in a crowd of drinkers—or the drinkers would feel awkward in front of Ken. As one manager remembers, "Ask people if they invited Ken, and they'd say, 'No, I didn't think he'd come.' "

In Olsen's office, Leng explained his decision to leave. Hindle tried to persuade him to stay. Olsen was cordial but did not attempt to change Leng's mind. People made their own choices, right or wrong, Olsen believed. It wasn't up to him to control their destinies. If they wanted to leave, if they could desert the family, then good luck to them. They just shouldn't expect to return if they failed.

The meeting ended quickly. Leng stood to go. Olsen wished him luck and made it clear that it was done. "If Ken had put his hand on my shoulder and said, 'John, we need you. We don't want you to leave,' I don't know what I would have done," Leng says. "I would have had to stay. It amazed me— he was that powerful an influence. I was probably disappointed a little that he didn't ask me, but I was relieved mostly."

Olsen couldn't afford sentimentality at the moment. His consternation at Leng and the other vice presidents sprang from the cracks he saw emerging in DEC's matrix. The structure that so perfectly fit a fast-growing young company was not holding up to the more formal demands of a mature member of the Fortune 500. Olsen did not downplay the shortcomings of matrix management. He and his officers acknowledged the inefficiencies to the press.

Wall Street analysts were looking behind Digital's 40 percent share of the minicomputer market and seeing mismanagement. The press looked closer, too. *Fortune* magazine's Bro Uttal compared DEC to Data General in the April 1979 issue, and DEC came up wanting. "DEC's organization, policies and management style are aimed at developing as many new products as possible. To achieve its long-term goal, DEC is willing to accept some internal disorder and sacrifice immediate profits," he wrote. "But in recent years, DEC has acquired an embarrassing reputation for being mismanaged." Data General, on the other hand, carried the reputation of an anything-for-profit company, the prototypical high-growth, high-tech company in America. Data General squeezed the margins to make the stockholders happy. DEC talked more about its customers than its stockholders. "We tell our stockholders that we take the long-term view," Olsen told Uttal. "Given that information, they can invest where they want to."

Much of the discontent was fomenting in Europe. DEC's overseas operations were floundering in the matrix. The European managers had a double dose of trouble to work through. Like other foreign managers of multinational companies, they waited for their marching orders from headquarters, a paralyzing method of operation. Olsen and his vice presidents couldn't see or understand the specific nature of the problems inherent in different European markets. Olsen viewed his foreign operations as entrepreneurial groups and expected them to take the lead. "When our group in England wanted to build a manufacturing facility, we said yes, and they built exactly what they had proposed,' " Olsen said. "Shortly afterwards they came back to complain: 'Other companies built more and are doing better. You didn't give us enough.' My answer was, 'You didn't ask for enough.' It took a long time for them to realize that when it was finally approved, their plan was their responsibility."

The Europeans, however, had enough trouble with cultural and international issues to try to cope with Olsen's subtle messages. Country managers had to react sensitively to local pressures while at the same time responding to confusing signals coming from corporate headquarters. As growth in Europe started to drop (it would bottom out at 7 percent in 1982), there were grumblings for autonomy. Olsen would not listen to the cries for independence for another three years.

The problems in Europe were only a fraction of the concerns at home. At the annual stockholders meeting in November of 1979, Olsen expressed his inner fears about DEC. "You're always scared you're not going to have the best products and not enough orders," he said, "so you have to design as if the whole world is after you. I don't know whether it's strategy or terror."

Olsen admitted that poor planning was at the root of backlogged orders that were reportedly costing DEC $50 million and several large accounts per quarter, though he suggested that customers were at fault as well for not ordering far enough in advance. He also said that a possible economic downturn worried him. Earlier recessions in 1970 and 1975 had caught DEC in "a cycle that went in the wrong direction of the economy." He vowed DEC's production cycles would never again be caught so out of line with the overall economic course.

Investors remained bullish. DEC hit $1.8 billion in revenues for fiscal 1979 and promised to increase its return on equity to 22 percent—the phenonemal level Data General was achieving—in the next two or three years. The company's performance face, however, masked Olsen's dissatisfaction. "Success is probably the worst problem for an entrepreneur," he says. "Someone who is successful finds it all too easy to believe he can do anything. He confuses responsibility with authority. He forgets that power doesn't come from telling people what to do; it comes from learning what goes on."

Olsen had cast DEC's future with VAX. But the new decade promised to launch another era, another challenge to stay on top. It was called personal computing.

"You will notice our sales force now wears dark suits, ties, and white shirts. They look like you can trust your whole company to them."

—*Ken Olsen*

22
Farewells

Bᴙ ʟᴀᴛᴇ 1979, Ted Johnson and Stan Olsen were floundering in the cultural revolution that was sweeping DEC. Both had been at the company since the beginning, Stan as the first official employee and Ted as the first salesman, badge number ten.

Johnson, a Michigan native with a Scandinavian background, felt great kinship and affection for Ken. Johnson brought needed talents to DEC. As a graduate of Cal Tech, he understood engineering and engineers; as a Harvard MBA, he intuitively grasped the right sales techniques for the newborn company. He had worked at Lincoln Labs as a technical assistant to learn about computers and pay his way through business school. After stints in California and Europe setting up DEC field offices, Johnson, at age thirty-three, took control of worldwide sales and service in 1965. He began to change the structure of the sales organization, creating networks of regional and district managers. He understood the need for technically competent salesmen, people who could speak the language of DEC's customers. He also knew enough to give them leeway to sell how they felt comfortable rather than by a

187

set of rigid corporate rules. "I didn't have any specific models, any cases from Harvard Business School," says Johnson. "I set it up as it seemed right. We had certain ways of doing things. We started off with very independent field offices, very unstructured and loosely coupled. We gave people very little direction in the early days."

Johnson was on the firing line. He fought to satisfy the needs of the product lines while combating Olsen's misgivings over sales. One thing they agreed on: the noncommissioned sales force. Johnson found that many salesmen who had been burned under a commission structure were happy to work under DEC's system. These people were not aiming for fast commissions in a few years and then moving on to another selling job. They were looking for a steady long-term career with steady long-term financial success. That's what DEC could offer. Johnson instituted the "DEC 100," an elite group of those who met their sales quotas each year. He gave out no bonuses for these high achievers—just recognition. "It fit my concept of human nature," he says. "We had a company built on the natural motivations of people. You give them the right environment, and the relationship between manager and salesman will grow stronger than ever."

Like the other vice presidents, Johnson was a frequent target of Olsen's tirades at Operations Committee and Woods meetings. But he was giving everything he had to DEC and to Olsen; he couldn't understand the anger thrown at him in return. Nonetheless, he worked harder. "There's something about Ken and his style that causes you to leap over fences to do things for him," Johnson says.

On the road, he thrived. He built a loyal sales staff; turnover was extremely low by industry standards. He was instrumental in building DEC's European operation. He traveled the country and the world visiting his people, making their day with a handshake and a good word. He estimates that by the late 1970s DEC was realizing about $850,000 per salesman in revenue.

Johnson still bristles at the "mythology" of the DEC salesman, that he wore a plastic pen holder and mismatched clothes, the classic techie outfit. Johnson was proud of the technical expertise of his people. If you are selling into a technical marketplace, he preached, and you know more than the next guy, you should get the sale. But as DEC pushed further into commercial markets, the challenge became more apparent: how could DEC's techies outsell IBM's business salesmen? In part, by looking like them. As Olsen observed in 1988, "You will notice our sales force now wears dark suits, ties, and white shirts. They look like you can trust your whole company to them."

At his apex, Johnson oversaw 15,000 people at DEC, including 3,300 salesmen. By 1978, however, the computer marketplace was changing too fast and DEC was too big to be slowed down in sales and service. The Operations Committee broke off the service organization from Johnson's control and put service and support chief Jack Shields in charge of it. Then Olsen dispatched Johnson to Europe to figure out how to reorganize operations there to allow more autonomy. Johnson came back with suggestions, but Olsen refused them all.

In 1980, Johnson flew to France for a summer-long management training course at the famed European business school, Insead. When he returned, he found that his position as head of sales had been handed over to Bill Long. Johnson was given Knowles's old job in the Office of the President, a corporate marketing function. Knowles had found that job confining and unfulfilling, and he fled back to Marlboro to become vice president of the technical group. "The door never came close to hitting me in the rear on that day," Knowles says. Not the least of the new job's appeal was that it was far enough away from the crushing encounters with Olsen in Maynard.

In the Office of the President, no product or functional line reported to Johnson. He became a high-placed, long-time executive without specific work to do. "Some people who were insiders suddenly were outsiders," he says of the late seventies, a time when many of DEC's old guard left the company. He stuck it out in typical DEC style, trying to become an insider again. Those suddenly on the outside had to figure out how to make themselves valuable. Or leave.

Olsen was in a quandary as to what to do. He told a corporate personnel manager, "You can't strip away people's dignity. You really have to be very careful about that." Olsen would not confront his managers one-on-one. He made his feelings plain in Operations Committee meetings, but there, the problems were not his—they belonged to the group. Olsen believed there was more dignity in allowing a person to find out for himself that he was no longer needed at DEC rather than telling him face to face. He preferred this self-discovery method to sitting down with the individual, explaining it was time for a change, throwing a farewell party, presenting a gold watch, and letting life go on, as in most corporations. Olsen would not fire anyone.

According to *Fortune*, "Olsen hounded Johnson relentlessly for two years, meanwhile whittling away at his responsibilities and encouraging underlings to make proposals of their own." Without a defined position, Johnson searched for something to do and a way to convince Olsen that he was needed again. He never found that way back to the center of Digital. In 1982, Johnson finally left the company "emotionally spent," according to *Fortune*.

For Stan Olsen, the separation from DEC was philosophically different but, in many ways, no less painful than Johnson's. The additional burden in Stan's case was that as Ken's brother, the relationship went on beyond the company.

In Merrimack by the late 1970s, Stan tried to drive DEC into commercial markets, with limited success. Measured against expectations, his DECmate was failing. Wang was walking away with the word-processing market. Some, like Knowles, blamed the failure on the decision to base the DECmate on the PDP-8, a technology nearly fifteen years old, instead of on the PDP-11 architecture. "Developing word processing on 1965 technology played clearly into Wang's strategy," Knowles says. Others felt the problem lay in the fact that low-end products couldn't get the funding they needed to succeed; all the big money was being spent on VAX development.

Olsen was particularly angry at the design and packaging of the DECmate, and he saw it all over DEC on secretaries' desks.

There were cables and connections pouring from the back. Olsen the packaging designer couldn't tolerate such sloppy engineering. He had a photograph taken and posted around the company. On it in big letters he asked, "Marketing or Engineering?" Then he pushed his brother Stan, the machine's proponent, to do better.

The failure to knock Wang out in word processing exacerbated an ill-conceived start-up of retail stores. DEC launched these small business centers in 1978 to present one-stop shopping for sophisticated office customers. Within five years, there were thirty Digital Business Centers; from 1983 to 1984, DEC doubled that number, even though they were failing as a vehicle for selling its low-end machines.

By 1980, personal-computer fever hit a high pitch. Stan Olsen believed that DEC could beat Apple in this business. He wanted to lead DEC's charge into the low end. He tried to coordinate companywide efforts to build a personal computer but ran head-on into his brother's resistance to PCs and his inherent distrust of marketing and advertising. Technical products couldn't be pitched like soap to customers, he felt. In looking at the market, Ken failed to see the ad-sensitive buyer of personal computers—the corporate professional who was tired of unmet promises coming from the data center and liked getting so much computing power right on his desk top.

Stan's failure to produce a winner in word processing made it tough for him to gain much ground internally as the one who should take the lead in personal computers. At DEC, the product lines with the best incomes always got the most resources. So with few funds generated by the DECmate, Stan was hard-pressed to create a PC. Knowles thought the Components Group, his former bailiwick, should take charge. Bell pushed for control out of his own central engineering.

Ken grew irritated that so much attention was being directed at PCs. And he was not pleased with the way Stan was handling his group. Stan had always been a favorite target at Operations Committee meetings, but in 1979 and 1980, Ken turned up the heat a notch.

Complicating the management structure, Ken created a

"Kitchen Cabinet," a small group of favored vice presidents who met quietly outside of Operations Committee meetings to work out issues that couldn't get settled in the larger group. Over the years, Ken summoned various groups of confidantes. In this period, the Kitchen Cabinet included Win Hindle, Jack Shields, and Jack Smith. Stan was excluded.

According to those who worked with him, Stan held neither Shields nor Smith in high regard. He considered Shields manipulative and untrustworthy. He viewed Smith as a yes-man, someone who wouldn't commit himself to a position until he knew Ken's view. And now Stan, who had been a trusted brother as well as employee since the first day of business, was getting shut out of the new inner circle.

Stan had been considering his options outside of DEC for a long time. His internal timetable specified staying at DEC for twenty-five years and then leaving while he was still young enough to build another career. Along the way he had invested heavily in real estate, and his DEC stock was worth millions. Stan tested the idea of leaving, but Ken gave back no clear signal of his wishes. He wasn't about to suggest that his brother should depart. In early 1981, Stan decided to take a year's leave of absence. "I thought, at age fifty, after twenty-five years at DEC, I should make a change," Stan says. "It was the appropriate time, and I thought Julius Marcus could take over. So I decided to go out on a boat for a while and figure out what I was going to do."

Ken told Stan he thought that decision was right. During the year's absence, communication between the brothers was minimal. Ken sent Stan books on sailing. He never urged his brother to return.

Perhaps if Ken had insisted, Stan would have changed his mind. But Stan knew before he left that Ken would not insist, that leaving for a year really meant leaving forever. Finally unburdened of DEC, Stan eagerly turned to the real estate business.

The brothers maintain a cordial but distant relationship. Ken, who had watched over Stan's activities at DEC for twenty-five years, stays clear now of his business. Stan is proud of the successes at DEC, but he yearns for a closer relationship to Ken. "We see each other from time to time," Stan says. "But I look forward to the day when he moves out and we can go off and fish together and we can relate like brothers and the business world doesn't get in the way."

"The personal computer will fall flat on its face in business."

—*Ken Olsen*

23
False Starts

As DAN BRICKLIN sat in his finance class at the Harvard Business School, the idea started coming to him. He had been making errors consistently on his assignment: three-year cash and balance sheet projections. He was relying on his trusty Texas Instruments calculator to handle the complex manipulation of numbers. But this little machine wasn't doing the job. As Bricklin stared at the blackboard over the next few days, an idea formed in his mind—a concept for computing these calculations more quickly and efficiently. He imagined an electronic spreadsheet.

Bricklin needed a machine to bring his idea to life. It was the spring of 1978, and personal computers were just hitting the market—to little response from the general public. Before going to Harvard for his MBA, Bricklin had spent three years at DEC as a programmer. He had worked on all of the company's major lines, the PDP-8, DEC10, and PDP-11. He'd seen the beginnings of the VAX architecture. He had a passion for DEC machines.

A few months before, Bricklin had attended DEC's annual stockholders meeting and noticed a product demonstrated called the PDT. This machine came from Knowles's terminal group. Knowles had long held the vision of DEC building a personal computer, but it was clear that Olsen didn't believe in such a machine. He had gone so far as to prohibit the use of the term *personal computer* within the company.

Yet, by any definition, the PDT was a personal computer. It coupled a computer terminal with built-in intelligence to a CRT screen and keyboard. It operated independently of a minicomputer or mainframe. The PDT was designed by the terminals section of the Components Group, which wasn't supposed to make computers at all. So Knowles, taking a cue from DEC history, had named the machine the Programmable Data Terminal and marketed it as an "intelligent terminal" so that the Operations Committee wouldn't see it as, in fact, a general-purpose personal computer.

The PDT was specifically designed for use by ADP, a DEC customer in New Jersey, which purchased several hundred of them. Bricklin decided that this computer would be the right one on which to build his electronic spreadsheet. He talked to former DEC colleagues to get the internal story on the PDT, but he didn't reveal to them what he planned to use the machine for. He was going to be the entrepreneur on this project. Then Bricklin contacted the local DEC sales representative, inquiring about buying a PDT. The salesman gave him product literature but no other attention. Digital dealt almost exclusively with corporate or scientific accounts. Confronted with a single interested party—and a student to boot—the salesman didn't find Bricklin worth pursuing.

Meanwhile, at the Harvard Business School, Bricklin borrowed an Apple II from fellow student Dan Fylstra to develop his idea into software. Bricklin called it Visicalc, short for visible calculator. He and partner Bob Frankston, along with Fylstra, published the software and wrote their names in computing history. With the advent of the electronic spreadsheet, personal computers suddenly found something important to do. Armed with Visicalc, the Apple II's sales took off, and the personal computer industry was essentially created.

At DEC, the opportunity to ride Visicalc into the PC market passed without much attention. "DEC didn't do anything wrong," Bricklin says. "The salesman just wasn't very aggres-

sive. I could have written Visicalc on the PDT, though."
Bricklin's experience symbolizes DEC's history in PCs—a
series of opportunities missed and wrong roads taken.

Throughout the 1970s, DEC's product lines fought over
development rights to PC-like machines. When he was in
charge of the PDP-11 group, Knowles had proposed the PC-
like DEC Datacenter as early as 1972. But chip technology
hadn't advanced far enough yet for it to be a true PC that ran
off its own microprocessor. David Ahl, a DEC engineer who
helped create the $7,900 Classic for the education market,
presented a plan to the Operations Committee in 1974 to sell a
downsized version of the PDP-8 as a stand-alone computer—
in essence a personal computer, though the term had not yet
come into use.

Ahl remembers that day—his birthday, May 17—very well.
Standing before Olsen, Hindle, Bell, Knowles, Dick Clayton,
and Stan Olsen, he asked for a $1 million budget to turn his
crude prototype into a working model of a self-contained
terminal computer. Traditionally, computers came in at least
three boxes—one containing the teletype for input-output,
one containing the CPU, and one the storage device. "I want
to put them into a single unit," Ahl told the committee, "a
stand-alone computer." He also proposed a price—$5,000—20
percent cheaper than the three pieces sold for separately.

The proposal divided the Operations Committee. "The
sales guys didn't think too much of it," Ahl says. "They saw it
as undermining their sales efforts on the bigger machines. But
the engineering guys were pretty enthusiastic." Hindle, then
in charge of the mainframe-size DEC10 line, opposed the idea
of a small, cheap machine. And Olsen asked, "Why would
anyone need a computer of their own?" Ahl could answer only
that it was his opinion from speaking to customers in the
education area that a significant market existed. He had called
upscale retailers, even hi-fi and electronics stores, but could
spark little interest without demonstrating a model of his idea.
He had no research, no field tests, no graphs or statistics to
show. That was why he was making this pitch—to get money
to explore what users wanted. Olsen said, "They can tie into a
DEC10, they can tie into anything else they want with a time-

sharing terminal. The world is going time-sharing. It's not going small, stand-alone computers."

"I was devastated," Ahl says. "I was hanging my career at DEC on this. I saw this machine as a start of a brand new product line." And he saw himself as the product manager. Two months later, he quit DEC to become AT&T's education marketing manager. Could DEC have successfully marketed a personal computer as early as 1974? As Gordon Bell says, "We had a lot of dreams like this, but it simply wasn't feasible yet at the right cost."

By 1980, DEC could no longer ignore the rising interest in these personal machines. There were more than a dozen PCs, generally called smart or intelligent terminals, in various stages of development around the company. These products were all outgrowths of specific customer requests, and each was being instituted by a different product group.

The product-line structure, which had worked so well to this point, was now becoming a tar pit, slowing down and smothering new ideas. The PDT that Knowles was trying to develop was talked to death, according to Bell. The product-line managers, who all had their own versions of PCs brewing, coveted that product space and wouldn't let Knowles sell it. "We spent countless hours deciding who could sell and get credit for it," Bell says. "Ken tried to get consensus in a world where that wasn't possible. It required a painful decision."

The product lines that were well-funded, like the terminals group, engineered their own machines. Others contracted with Bell's central engineering to build them. Bell was galled by the situation. He felt that his group was being forced to "act like whores," building anything anybody wanted as long as they paid for it. He sent a memo to Olsen, listing the various conflicting machines in development. He stressed the negative results of engineering being at the beck and call of the product lines. To Bell, this arrangement was a surefire disaster. He proposed a "golden rule" whereby engineering would have as much input into a computer as the product line.

Olsen responded swiftly. He sent a memo to the Group Vice Presidents committee, one of DEC's myriad management groups, saying: "I have long been dismayed as to why so many of our product-line products have been poor, and why it has been so hard to pin down responsibility for them. I think I now understand the problem, and I'll leave it with you and your committee to, with all haste, find the solution.

"Gordon Bell," Olsen wrote, "claims no responsibility for the low-end products which he contracts with the product lines. He says that they have to work with the 'Golden Rule' principle, and the product lines have the gold. They (central engineering) try in vain to encourage the product lines to do wise things, but the product lines don't understand, and insist on doing it their way . . . Gordon has a list of seven or eight personal, professional or specialized, smart or almost smart terminals which he thinks were incompetently done and un-necessary . . . and he claims he never believed in them and if we had not done them, we might have a had a computer that could take care of all the needs. I am frustrated by this statement and feel we have to change our system for doing things.

"The product lines, on the other side, claim they cannot be held responsible, because they claim they cannot get Engineering to do what they want, and when they do, it is always late. The result, from my point of view, is that I can't hold anyone responsible, and I think that is the ultimate of poor management. This has to be changed immediately." Olsen added parenthetically: "I am always fascinated to see that with the same product, on those days when the product is good, everybody claims responsibility, and those days when the product looks amateurish, late and uncompetitive, no one is responsible."

Despite Olsen's call for a solution, the problem didn't get resolved. And the personal computer itself was the main reason why. The enormous potential of these low-priced machines dazzled DEC's young engineers. It was a matter of corporate pride to them that DEC be on the leading edge of this new wave. Didn't DEC, after all, pioneer the concept of interactive computing, the very basis for personal computers? Wouldn't a desktop machine for the individual be the culmina-tion of Olsen's dream?

The answer, as the 1980s began, seemed to be a definitive

"no." Throughout the seventies, Olsen insisted that personal computing was a concept that had no basis in need or reality. No one, he believed, seriously required a computer at home. He viewed early PCs as toys, metal boxes that were bought so children could play video games at home rather than in game rooms.

Olsen seemed to be caught on the terms: in his mind, a personal computer equaled a home computer. In the business market, DEC already offered power to the desktop with its VT100 terminals hooked into PDP-11s and VAXes. Olsen's stubborn view—"The personal computer will fall flat on its face in business"—was, according to Ries and Trout's *Marketing Warfare*, "perhaps the biggest misjudgment in American business history since Henry Ford's failure to block General Motors' high-end flank. Ken Olsen is a computer genius, but even a genius can be wrong. As Fiorello LaGuardia once said, 'I don't make many mistakes, but when I make one, it's a beaut.' "

Olsen believed that a foray into this part of the market was straying from the task at hand. DEC's job was to build minicomputers, not home computers. "I've always said, if everyone else is in the business, there's no room for us," Olsen says. And though his motivations were not based on any crystal-ball wisdom about the future, Olsen's hesitancy would prove prescient within five years. Working on PCs would have deviated from Bell's VAX strategy. The technology to make a VAX-based personal computer did not exist at the time. According to the VAX strategy, no new machine should be developed outside the VAX framework.

Olsen's views on PCs changed abruptly in 1980. Bell pinpoints the catalyst of this change as an interview with a young female reporter from *Business Week*. She came armed with inside information about DEC's low-end efforts and questioned Olsen intensely about the company's lack of progress. "It challenged his manhood," says Bell. "Suddenly, we had to win in PCs." Others believe that Olsen hesitated because he was seeking a champion for the PC, someone he could count on to make it happen his way. That person just didn't emerge. So Olsen took on the task himself. "Once he made the switch and said we were going to do it, then (to Ken) nobody could beat us," observes Johnson. Olsen would later say that he was swayed into making "commodity computers" by the critics and DEC executives. Whatever the source of his motivation, he suddenly talked constantly about products a common person could use, easy enough for secretaries or even a minister at his Park Street church. His vision became known internally as "computers for clerks and clerics."

In the midst of the turmoil, Olsen was approached by one of DEC's most unlikely customers, Apple Computer. The infant Cupertino, California, personal-computer maker was growing rapidly and used a PDP-11 for billing and order entry. Michael Scott, Apple's president at the time, visited Ken Olsen in early 1980 to discuss whether Apple should order more PDP-11s or switch to VAX. The meeting was cordial, but there was a hint of discord in the air. Olsen couldn't hide his feeling that Apple was going to fail as a personal-computer supplier. And he believed that the upstart from California, personified by its brash founder, Steve Jobs, was more than a bit arrogant.

Scott ordered a second PDP-11, which Apple needed immediately to process orders because the first one was running out of capacity. But months went by and the machine didn't arrive in Cupertino. DEC was six months behind in filling orders for PDP-11s—and Apple was nearing paralysis in its order-processing system. Desperate to get some action from DEC, Scott sent Olsen a six-foot high, white-rose funeral wreath, with a rest-in-peace ribbon striped across the front. The accompanying note from Scott said: "This is what I think of DEC's delivery commitments." Apple's message was: "You are killing us with this endless delay."

The wreath clogged the front lobby of Building 12 in the Mill, the main entrance to Digital. Olsen entered that day through a back door and didn't see it. But his office was suddenly flooded with condolence calls from employees, who assumed there had been a death in the family.

A PDP-11 was in the air to San Francisco the next day with two DEC technicians on board to install it. But the machine flew out of the Mill untested. When turned on in Apple's computer room, the PDP-11 caught fire. Eventually, the machine was set right, and Apple remained a DEC customer.

Out of the episode, a legend emerged. It was Jobs, not Scott, who visited Olsen's Mill office, the story went. He put his boots up on Olsen's desk and told Ken that he was going to blow DEC out of the water in personal computers. He followed this arrogant display with a black funeral wreath sent to mock DEC's performance in PCs. Actually, Jobs never visited Olsen or the Mill.

In fact, there was much to question in DEC's PC plans. In July 1979, a young engineer named Avram Miller came from Israel to join the Central Engineering Group. Bell noticed early on this hard-driving and intelligent go-getter. Miller was invited to speak to the annual engineering meeting in Stratton Mountain, Vermont, in the summer of 1980. The meeting's major topic: what to do about the low end.

Miller made an impressive presentation to the 200 engineers gathered at Stratton Mountain on his views of the low-end dilemma. On returning to DEC, he was called to a Woods meeting in Bell's backyard in Lincoln. Unaware of Bell's intentions, Miller showed up and faced a grilling by a panel of DEC engineers. Bell was testing him, seeing if he could stand up to technical scrutiny. This interrogation surprised Miller, but a few days later, he found out what he was being tested for. Bell invited him back to his house for another meeting. Miller arrived as Olsen was struggling in the driveway carrying foam-core mock-ups of small computers. Inside, Bell and several other top-level DEC managers greeted Miller. He sensed that this meeting was going to be significant to his career.

Finally fed up with the low-end confusion, Olsen had decided that DEC should start from scratch to draw up a PC strategy. The group discussed hardware, software, design, and direction. The managers talked about integration of terminals and PCs and about the eventual path that the machines would take. Miller saw clearly how the project should go. He steered the discussion in that direction, but he already knew enough about DEC to realize that Olsen had to feel ownership of an idea or it would never fly. He was careful to ask for Ken's input and thoughts.

By the end of the day, the group was talked out. But there

had been no solution agreed upon. Miller sensed that it could be his call. It was a precipitous step for him to take. What he was about to do would either solidify him as a bona fide DEC hero, or it would be his ticket out the door.

He turned to Olsen. "Do you want this project to happen?"

"Yes," Olsen replied.

"I'll make it happen," Miller said. "But I'll only make it happen if I can manage it all. It's the only way to get it done."

"Fine," Olsen said. "I'll invite you to the Operations Committee and you can make your proposal."

Two days later, Hindle called Miller and asked him to the next meeting. So Miller stood before the committee and made his pitch. It was actually Olsen's vision, so he knew he was carrying a great deal of leverage. What he proposed eventually became the DEC Professional personal computer.

"I want to be program manager and I want a program office," Miller announced. "I want people there from manufacturing, service and from engineering, both hardware and software. This is how I want to do it, otherwise do it with someone else some other way."

The committee approved Miller and his plan. But he sensed even as he was leaving the room that most of the people in there thought he would fail and that perhaps a few hoped he would. Miller immediately dubbed the project KO. In memos it stood for Knock Out or Kick Off. But Miller's intention was clear: he wanted everyone to know that this was Ken Olsen's project. And indeed it was.

With a budget of $20 million, an unheard-of sum for a low-end project, Miller carried carte blanche around DEC. Bell sent out a memo on August 28, 1980, detailing the proposed project and its implications. "Ken would like to do this project in nine months," Bell wrote. "We will need maximum support from each group." Bell called the machine "an applications terminal and small system." He never used the words *personal computer*. On the list of people involved, he noted that Avram Miller was driving the overall project, and the packaging architect was Ken Olsen.

"The market will figure out which one is right."
                                        —Ken Olsen

24
The Three-Headed Monster

IN AUGUST 1981, IBM introduced its personal computer to the world. The company's choice of a name for it—the IBM Personal Computer, or IBM PC for short—showed IBM's presumption that its PC would become the generic machine for the masses. Philip "Don" Estridge had convinced IBM's hierarchy to let him go off to Boca Raton, Florida, and quickly build a personal computer to hold off Apple and the other contenders threatening to swallow this new market. IBM couldn't allow another market takeover to occur as it had in the mid-1960s when DEC quietly created—and then went on to dominate—the minicomputer business.

Miller immediately bought an IBM PC so he could examine firsthand what he was competing against. He took it into his office and called Ken to come and take a look. Olsen was excited. This was the first IBM PC brought into DEC. Together, with screwdrivers, they took the competition apart.

After seeing the inside of IBM's computer, Olsen looked at Miller and laughed, "If you ever built me something like this, you wouldn't be here anymore." Evaluating the machine as an engineer, Olsen saw junk—the inelegant engineering of a quickly constructed machine. If this was the best IBM could offer, he thought, Digital would sweep the market.

Olsen was misjudging how and why personal computers would be bought. His reaction sprang from the core of his beliefs about how computers should be built and used. It was fundamentally not within his psyche to accept something less than top quality. There was no point in creating a machine if you didn't make it the best possible way, with care and insight and elegance. Olsen's conviction flowed down through DEC to every layer of the organization. It was at the heart of "do the right thing." Every DEC employee understood this drive for perfection if they understood DEC at all.

Miller knew of Olsen's insistence on quality when he began formulating his KO project. Olsen demanded a product in nine months, and Miller said it couldn't be done—at least, not a quality product. He would need at least a year and more likely, eighteen months. To complicate matters, there was sentiment to develop two products—a low-end model built around a single processor version of the PDP-11 and a larger version with a more sophisticated chip set and greater functionality. As Miller started ramping up the project—planning, hiring, budgeting—it became clear that if he couldn't deliver one machine on Olsen's short timetable, he certainly wouldn't be able to deliver two. He didn't want to do the smaller machine anyway. It was slated to contain just 32K of memory, an abysmally small amount, not enough to run sophisticated business software. Olsen didn't understand the crucial part software would play in personal computers. In his view, the most important thing a computer company could deliver was well-engineered hardware. Software, he expected, would follow good hardware. He paid so little attention to software that some inside DEC said that he expected it to come from heaven. Olsen favored the small machine and was disappointed when Miller insisted both couldn't be done. Undeterred, Olsen went off to find someone else within DEC to build the other machine for him.

Early on in the KO project's life, Miller met with Olsen frequently, often spending half days together, discussing design and direction of the new machine. Miller began to understand the essence of Olsen behind the ambiguities. "When you were with Ken, you knew you were *with* somebody," Miller says. "He has this uncanny ability to get people to really want to do what he wants to make him happy. I once asked Jack Shields, 'Is it still like that for you?' And Shields said, 'Yeah, it's still like that for me.' "

Olsen talked quietly, but mostly he listened to Miller. Unlike his behavior in the Operations Committee meetings, Olsen seemed a different person in one-on-one situations. He asked many questions and spoke often of values. Though an engineer, Olsen deeply understood only packaging or design issues. He avoided discussing computer architectures, a subject he had long ago left to others. Miller often walked away not knowing what Olsen was alluding to in his offhand comments and parables. "He would have been much more effective if anybody could have figured out what he wanted," Miller says. "I'm not sure he knew what he wanted."

In fact, Olsen very definitely knew what he wanted in the design of the KO. Unlike the refrigerator-size minicomputers, which left little to the imagination for packaging designers, personal computers tantalized them with the possibilities of how a machine could look and feel and operate. For DEC, it was essentially unexplored territory. Olsen's personal involvement opened up an unlimited challenge for DEC's industrial designers. The clunky, uninspired boxes other PC-makers were turning out would never fly at DEC. Olsen foresaw sleek, stylized components that would enhance, rather than detract from, a work environment.

While Miller assembled his core team, Olsen dove into designing the monitor. He worked closely with engineer Dick Gonzales, who became Olsen's quasi-personal design consultant. Olsen worried particularly about the size and form of the monitor. He pushed for a wedge shape, which was, from an industrial design standpoint, a breakthrough. Packaging the necessary circuitry into the small, odd-shaped device was difficult. The quest was predicated on the belief that the monitor and keyboard should complement the desktop rather than conflict with it. Olsen questioned his designers closely: should there be a handle on the bottom? How would the machine sit on the desk? How could glare on the screen be minimized? He frequently used the word *elegant* to describe what he was after.

Olsen argued that a light filter should be built over the screen. The designers said that a filter was too susceptible to fingerprints. Against their recommendations, Olsen specified that filters should be included. He suggested a spray can of window cleaner be shipped with each system. "They can wipe away the fingerprints, but they can't wipe away the glare," he said. And so, DEC shipped window cleaner with each personal computer.

As reported in the *New England Business* magazine, Olsen told designers to build a floor stand for the PC so that the CPU could fit out of the way, under the typical office desk. When the prototype was presented to him, Olsen had second thoughts. What would happen to the unit under the desk? People would kick it, of course. "So they're going to put it at the end of their desks," he reasoned. "Then they're going to sit on it." He demonstrated. As the bulky Olsen sat, the box creaked. And the designers went back to their drawing boards to strengthen the unit. The reworked floor stand later won a design award at the Hannover Fair in West Germany.

Olsen's involvement in the project was a mixed blessing for Miller. The stamp of approval afforded him more freedom and influence than someone so new to the company would ever have achieved so quickly. But it also created agonizing delays and costly retrofits caused by Olsen's unbending views on packaging. Olsen rarely stated what he did or did not want done. Miller found out that Olsen was displeased with the initial monitor design through Gonzales, who was prototyping a different one. Miller had already spent months and hundreds of thousands of dollars on the first monitor, and this change of direction upset him. But he was also a realist. "I knew I was going to end up building his monitor," Miller says.

As the KO project continued, Miller was forced to "fire" Olsen from the team. He could see that Olsen's style of redesigning and reworking the packaging might never end. "Ken just didn't understand how difficult it was to get things done," Miller says. "I once complained to him how long it took to get something out of the model shop and he would say, 'I don't know what you guys are complaining about. I put something in there yesterday and got it out today.' " Miller eventually told Olsen that the monitor was finished, thanked him, and said he didn't have to come to the meetings anymore. Olsen accepted the status report and left, disappointed that he was not needed anymore.

Despite his mandate, Miller ran into resistance from various quarters. There was no consensus on how the low end should be structured organizationally or strategically. Even though Miller was operating with Operations Committee approval, the low end remained volatile—unexplored territory in DEC's matrix. Unlike the existing product lines, the KO project was an illegitimate child, which had sprung up quickly, without roots in any other machine and with an enormous amount of funding—all ingredients for attracting envy and jealousy in DEC's structure.

Miller could see that getting consensus on how to proceed would be impossible. There were too many competing voices advising how sophisticated the machine should be, what ports it should have, how it should look, how it should be sold. So he and his fledgling group set their own course. At DEC, where open debate was presumed, Miller committed heresy. Knowles, now overseeing DEC's technical development and marketing, expressed his opinion in a quick memo to Miller. "I am saddened by your gross insensitivity. How many times have we discussed this, Avram? Zero times. And you have cast a major project in concrete without interfacing with the PDP-11 strategists. Dumb at best."

Miller, passionate and undaunted, was convinced that he had a mission in the low end. Before IBM announced its PC, he was motivated by a different competitor—the Japanese. He believed that allowing Japan to control PCs would be disastrous for DEC and the country. He also saw IBM formulating a strategy to control the mainframe and desktop markets and push DEC out of the middle. This squeeze play had to be stopped. Avram became an evangelist, preaching that DEC understood display technology and interactive computing better than anyone; therefore, it had to lead the market. DEC now controlled 38 percent of the minicomputer business; it would soon own an equal amount of the personal computer business, Miller predicted, a market that would reach $5 billion in a few short years. "We have to be number one," he told his people. "If you are not number one, you can't control things, and that's no fun."

When IBM announced its machine in August of 1981, shock waves rocked DEC. How could IBM have developed the machine so quickly? Except for the Winchester hard disk drive and the line cord, DEC designed and built every piece of its machine. DEC tooled the sheet metal and plastics for all the components, manufactured the floppy disks, developed the microprocessor. Under the constraint to "build it here," it was a minor miracle that the machine came to market as fast as it did—in eighteen months.

Under Estridge's guidance, IBM sourced out 80 percent of its PC. IBM bought the operating system, MS-DOS, from a then small software company in Bellevue, Washington, called Microsoft. IBM turned to a host of third-party suppliers and to the Far East for disk drives, monitors, and add-in boards. IBM assembled the purchased pieces in nine months—the same timetable Olsen had originally demanded. IBM's PC and DEC's Pro would have hit the market at the same time. In retrospect, Miller believes that DEC's best strategy would have been to do what IBM did: get a product out quickly, build market acceptance, and then plunge ahead with a higher quality follow-on. But now it was too late for second-guessing. IBM was out to market first; DEC was playing catch-up. And anyway, Miller doesn't believe either Olsen or Bell would have allowed DEC to produce a quick and dirty machine. It wouldn't have been the "right thing to do."

Miller pressed on. KO—renamed CT, for Computer Terminal—would go far beyond the IBM PC's capabilities. IBM's personal computer was designed to be just that—personal, a stand-alone device for the individual. DEC was building a machine to network to other DEC systems. It included features that, in hindsight, were years ahead of the competition, such as a high-resolution, bit-mapped display and a multitasking operating system. It had a proprietary operating system based on the PDP-11, which allowed it to hook cleanly into networks of DEC computers.

Meanwhile, Olsen found a champion for a smaller version PC. In June 1980, a talented and aggressive young Southerner named Barry James Folsom had joined DEC as senior engineering manager of the Terminal Products Group in Marlboro. He brought with him some innovative ideas about building intelligent terminals, which he showed to the Operations Committee. In late 1981, Folsom started designing the smaller, less complex machine at the request of Olsen and Bell. It was simply an insurance policy against IBM because besides CP/M, an early and popular PC operating system, it could run MS-DOS, the same operating system IBM had chosen for its PC.

While Miller was marshaling the company's resources on the CT project and Folsom was designing the Rainbow on a shoestring budget, Dick Loveland began developing the follow-on to the DECmate in the word processing group. DEC still believed the stand-alone word processing market was there for the taking. Much to his chagrin, Miller didn't even learn of the two other low-end projects until well after they were launched. He had thought he was carrying the company's banner in the personal computer battle. Suddenly, he had unwanted company in the field. This situation was not unusual at DEC. Olsen often set up competing product-development groups believing, as he said, that "Competition vastly improves a product. History keeps proving that when we allow healthy competition, we get better products."

But to Miller, this competition was not healthy. He and Folsom butted heads, arguing over the merits of their approaches and fighting for resources both internally and outside Digital, sometimes going so far as to undermine each other's efforts in the crucial software development community. The word spread outside DEC to third-party developers—the Miller and Folsom groups each were claiming to have the resources of the company behind them.

To Folsom, the battles were frustrating but useful. "Even though you are being grilled by everyone, you are going through trial by fire with friends before it's trial by fire in the marketplace," he says. "You may go away angry, but after a few days, you start to think about it and it hones you. The give and take, people grinding away at you, actually leads to a much better product."

And somehow, despite his warnings that DEC was making a mistake in its approach to the PC market, Andy Knowles found himself in overall charge of the low end. Knowles saw trouble for himself in taking this job. He knew the pain of being in Olsen's proximity from his experience in the Office of the President two years earlier. All of a sudden, he was in the middle of Ken's favorite activity—the low end.

Shields had originally been tabbed within DEC to take charge of the PC business, but he didn't want any part of it. He felt that the company should stay out of the low end and stick to VAXes. At dinner one night in late 1981, Shields convinced Knowles that his experience as a marketer and his work selling LSI-11s made him the person for the job. And so Knowles reluctantly accepted. He saw a possible big seller in the CT that Miller's group was developing, even if he didn't like Miller's methods. In late 1981, no clear-cut winner had emerged in the PC market, despite IBM's August entry. DEC appeared to have as good a shot as anyone. Success here, Knowles believed, would cement his status and power within DEC.

Folsom and Loveland were riding the coattails of Miller's CT, using all the essential packaging and manufacturing models that he had paid for and sweated over. Olsen still considered the CT DEC's personal computer; the other two were back-up machines, "just in case." Miller complained about sharing resources. "It was a total disaster," he says. "Nothing worse could have happened. We managed to split all the engineering activities, all the third-party software activities, manufacturing, everything. I ended up without any word processing software, for instance. I couldn't go outside to get it, and I couldn't get the DEC group to do it because they were busy doing it for DECmate."

Conversely, Folsom found out that he couldn't get Visicalc, by now a bestselling software program, written for the Rainbow because, he believes, Miller told Visicorp that the Rainbow was an underfunded, unapproved machine that would likely not see the light of day.

Even the product's name ran into trouble. Convergent Technologies, the company founded by former DEC engineer Allen Michels, put out a model called the CT, so Miller had to choose another name. The Operations Committee voted to call the machine the Professional 350. Word leaked out about the change, and in months, the market was flooded with machines named the Professional from Wang, Texas Instruments, and others.

The names followed a pattern. Xerox, for example, code-named its personal computer the Worm because it would eat the Apple. Folsom named one of his PC efforts the Robin to eat the Worm. The Rainbow was code-named Cat, to eat the Robin. Unbelievably, the official naming process of the Rainbow lasted four months. Olsen periodically put different names to an Operations Committee vote; if he didn't like the results, he arranged a new vote a few weeks later. The Operations Committee actually wanted to call Folsom's machine CP/M, after its primary operating system. Folsom vehemently argued against that name. He called his friend Bill Gates, the wunderkind chairman of Microsoft, and asked him to lobby for his operating system—MS-DOS.

Gates met with Olsen in Maynard in late 1981 and convinced him that CP/M had not wrapped up the PC market. MS-DOS, Gates insisted, might well become the industry standard since IBM was embracing it. Olsen accepted Gates's argument and crossed CP/M off the list of possible names. That move saved DEC the enormous embarrassment of tying its PC to an operating system that would soon become extinct.

Folsom championed the name Rainbow. He thought it made

the machine seem friendly and accessible. When he approached Olsen, Ken laughed. "Barry, that's the first mistake that I know you've made," he said. "I know you make lots of mistakes, but that's the first one I know about. There's no way you are going to call it Rainbow." After four months of debate, Olsen finally gave up trying to decide what to call Folsom's machine. "Name it whatever you want," he told him, and Folsom chose Rainbow.

By early 1982, time was running short. The new target date to introduce the personal computers was set for May, just in time to make a splashy market entrance at the huge National Computer Conference in June. The development teams for all three personal computers were working at a crushing pace— seven days a week for months on end. As the announcement approached, Miller called in a corporate psychiatrist to help his tense group cope with the stress. "I've been here almost eighteen full minutes listening to you," the psychiatrist said, "and I'm exhausted."

Knowles, who could see the chaos of the low end, tried to coordinate the impending introductions of the three new machines. At Saturday meetings, he gathered the principal managers involved to sort out the marketing efforts.

Miller hoped someone like Knowles could stop what seemed to be inevitable. But a meeting with Ken sealed their fate. Olsen called in Miller, Folsom, and Loveland to discuss the three-headed monster—DEC's low-end strategy. He said, "You know, I'd make it easy on everybody if I said just one of these products will come out. But I'm not going to do it, because they do different things, and the market will figure out who is right."

"The market figured out who was right," Miller says, "and it was IBM."

*"This architecture should last and propagate
forever."*

—*Ken Olsen*

25
The Big Bang

Ken Olsen appeared visibly excited. May 10, 1982, on a brightly lit stage in a downtown Boston auditorium, he stood facing an audience of journalists and consultants, grinning broadly. In his big right hand, he balanced the monitor of one of DEC's new personal computers. "This has been by far the largest investment in people, in manpower, that we've ever presented in any announcement," Olsen declared. "This set of products has created more enthusiasm, more excitement in the company than I've ever seen before."

Uncharacteristically, Olsen became a showman. He suddenly embraced the term *personal computer*.

"Twenty-five years ago this month," he said, "we visited Boston many times raising money to start a new company, a company to make personal computers. We didn't call them personal computers then. But we said they had to be fast enough to interact with people, inexpensive and small enough so that people would be allowed to interact with them. And that's what we've been doing ever since."

DEC broadcast the announcement via satellite to London and Toronto. The media caught the feeling and believed DEC had the winner it claimed. Olsen bragged that the three machines—the Professional (models 325 and 350), the Rainbow 100, and the DECmate II—had "an architecture that should last and propagate forever."

Olsen spent much of the announcement boasting about the superior design of the systems—how clean and utilitarian they were; how they fit perfectly on an executive's desk; how they could be used in the bathroom or while "sitting in a hammock." He ended the announcement by stating, "My reaction is only one: I'd hate to compete with these machines."

According to *Computerworld* newspaper, "Analysts were generally impressed with all the systems, finding them extremely competitive with the IBM PC in both functionality and price."

As Miller watched anxiously, no one questioned why DEC was bringing out three different PCs simultaneously—three machines incompatible with each other. This oversight by analysts reflected the basic misunderstanding of personal computers in 1982; it was not just Olsen who misjudged the market so completely. Throughout the rest of that year, however, lessons were quickly learned.

The PC market flowed according to its own currents. Traditional truths about interactive computers that Olsen had learned in the minicomputer business didn't apply to this market. Customers didn't care about the elegant styling or the ambitious functionality of the Pro. They didn't care about the revolutionary wedge-shaped monitor that had occupied Olsen for months. Corporate customers cared about only two things: price and application software. DEC didn't offer any advantage in the former and was severely limited in the latter.

But the fatal error for DEC was allowing IBM to preempt the marketplace uncontested for a full year. IBM's typewriters had already earned the company trust in the office. With a headstart in PCs, IBM established its name as the standard setter in the low end. Dozens of companies were introducing PCs by mid-1982—in fact, four were unveiled the same week as DEC's announcement. But none could compete against IBM in reputation for value and support.

The major blow to DEC's chances came from an unlikely source—a former teacher of transcendental meditation named Mitch Kapor. In January 1983, his new company, Lotus Development Corporation, shipped a break-through software program designed specifically for the IBM PC. The program, called Lotus 1-2-3, integrated spreadsheet, word processing, and graphics capabilities that took users far beyond the popular Visicalc. The timing was perfect for IBM. Business people who needed a reason to buy a PC found it in 1-2-3. IBM itself was astonished at the response. Few in IBM's Armonk headquarters believed that Estridge's Boca Raton experiment would succeed, certainly not sell hundreds of thousands of PCs in the first year. Once the potential was realized, IBM used Charlie Chaplin's Little Tramp image to spread the IBM PC across the business world.

Olsen did not foresee IBM's market sweep when he confidently introduced Digital's PC trio in May of 1982. On that morning, he believed that DEC would dominate the corporate low-end market. The only thing he feared was not being able to manufacture the Pros and Rainbows and DECmates fast enough to meet customer demand.

The gala announcement hid the facts. Only fifty working models of the Pro had been built. The supply of vital third-party software barely existed. Technical problems plagued the assembly line. DEC couldn't ship machines in volume until nearly a year after the announcement, giving IBM another twelve months to rule the market.

Beyond the technical delays, arguments raged within DEC about marketing and advertising the new products. Olsen scoffed at IBM's Charlie Chaplin campaign even as it sold millions of machines. He didn't believe that serious business users were swayed by the Little Tramp. They would certainly choose DEC's elegant, technically superior products, presented without the cute advertising. "People will pay more for a PC from us because we designed it better for an office, for people who sit in front of it eight to ten hours per day," Olsen said. He distrusted both television advertising and retail sales, but DEC ended up doing both. His marketers bought air time on the 1983 Super Bowl to promote "computers for professionals by professionals." And they signed agreements with Computerland and other outlets to sell the machines retail.

Olsen used a parable to express his dissatisfaction over the marketing efforts in the low end. He titled the memo "Big Bangs and Marketing Plans" and distributed it to Miller, Folsom, and a list of managers involved in the personal computer introduction. He wrote in February 1982: "During the Civil War, the North and the South faced each other in trenches outside of Fredericksburg for months on end; nothing seemed to happen. No one was winning, and no one was losing. The Pennsylvania coal miners in the Northern trenches had the idea of tunneling under the Southern lines and planting massive amounts of explosives and blowing up the Southern entrenchments.

"This was favorably received by the Northern headquarters and the project was started. It worked beautifully. When they set the explosives off, they blew an enormous hole in the Southern line. The Northern soldiers ran over the top, ran into the hole and rejoiced in their success. The Southern soldiers crawled over the side of the hole and shot every one of the Northern soldiers who were dancing around the hole.

"It was an enormous success. They forgot one thing. They never planned what they were going to do after they made the hole."

Then Olsen made his point: "Marketing at Digital has deteriorated to a low ebb. We still make great big bangs we call product introductions. The more money we have, the bigger the bangs are. We do very poorly in planning the whole military operation. One bang, unless it is a nuclear bomb, does not make a military success.

"A military campaign and a marketing campaign take an enormous amount of detail, every piece of which has to be planned, organized, staffed and carried out with precision. Napoleon himself worried about details. He gave a prize to the one who invented margarine so his soldiers could have it when far away from home. He also had developed for his army the first canned foods. Most military men are only interested in the big bang, but very few have the successes Napoleon had. If we are going to be successful at the low end, in the office and in all our other projects, we are going to have to define marketing as being a much more detailed, thorough set of plans and operations than just our massive announcements.

"People think I have been against advertising our word processing. That is not true at all. I don't want to advertise when it is impossible for many to buy our products. First you make it easy for people to buy, and you make sure all the details are taken care of so they can buy and can be talked into buying, and then you carry out the advertising program."

While Olsen was absorbed in personal computers, DEC was bounding ahead on other fronts. The company had shipped its 200,000th computer system in 1980 when it hit the $2 billion mark in revenues. Now just two years later, DEC was nearing $4 billion in sales, had shipped its 360,000th computer, and employed 67,000 workers. It ranked 137th on the Fortune 500 list. But on the underside of this growth, there were problems. The demand for the new VAXes was not being met by manufacturing. Customers complained about the protracted delays, but DEC just could not make products fast enough. The follow-ons to the VAX 11/780 and the DEC10/20 were in turmoil, engineering efforts gone awry. DEC's retail stores were misdirected and losing money. And start-up costs for the PC development, running upwards of $100 million, had cut deeply into profitability. DEC was forced to freeze hiring and salaries in October of 1982. For the first fiscal quarter of 1983, DEC announced a drop in earnings of 36 percent, its first profit dip in seven years. And the Operations Committee formed a task force to study yet another reorganization.

In 1982, Digital reached a milestone—its twenty-fifth birthday. Olsen wasn't going to allow anything to mar his achievement. He had prodded and encouraged, angered and cajoled his way through a quarter century at the helm of his company. In September, Olsen was invited to speak to the Newcomen Society in North America, an organization that fosters the study of business and industrial history. Thomas Newcomen was the British inventor whose steam engine helped drive the

Industrial Revolution. The occasion honored Olsen and Digital's founding.

General Doriot introduced Olsen to the gathering in Boston. "You know," he said, beaming, "Newcomen was a lucky man. If Ken Olsen had been alive in 1712, he would have designed a better engine and today this would be called the Olsen Society." In his self-effacing way, Doriot summed up his role in Digital's history. "I am just a director," he said, "and that means I am just a slave to Ken—no question about that. When you have a strong president, your directors should be very peaceful, very quiet and very fortunate, and I try to be just that."

As Olsen looked out from the podium, he could see the faces of the many people who had played a role in DEC's history. Seated near the front was his brother, Stan, along with Harlan Anderson. Anderson—Digital's cofounder—hadn't seen or spoken to Ken since he had left DEC in 1966, sixteen years before. Anderson thought it appropriate that he be on hand for the company's birthday. He listened with interest as Olsen recounted Digital's history, an account that didn't include much about him.

"We had a number of ideas that were quite unique at the time but are rather normal now," Olsen said. "First of all, in those days there was a belief that making a profit was bad. That sounds strange now, but at the time it really was true. Companies would hire an engineer and say 'We're hiring you for the good of science; we're going to hire you to develop yourself professionally.' Secretly they hoped he'd help them make a profit, but they wouldn't say that to the engineer." Olsen always unabashedly told engineers that DEC was out to make a profit.

He finished his Newcomen speech by extolling the virtues of office automation. "Computers are making work more interesting, making it more fun, making it more satisfying. That's the business we're in. We're having more fun at it than ever before, and there is no end in sight," he claimed.

Fun was not quite the operative word of the day at DEC in 1982. If Olsen was having fun, he was having it alone. His vice presidents and managers were tangled up in a product-line structure whose rationale had disappeared. It was no longer necessary to sell dozens of different products to individual markets. Increasingly, general-purpose machines could cover the specific needs of an entire organization.

DEC's product-line managers fought each other for responsibility as the territory decreased. Dedicated people such as Kaufmann, Leng, Stan Olsen, Irwin Jacobs, and others had already left. Shields was emerging as the man with Olsen's ear. He had convinced Olsen that Bill Long shouldn't be running sales, and soon the sales and service organizations were reunited—this time under Shields's control. Long, another twenty-year veteran, left the company as well.

DEC's internal electronic mail network hummed with rumors and innuendo. Haggard and stressed, Miller often climbed out of bed at 4 A.M. and flipped on his VT100 terminal to check his electronic mailbox. Many managers used terminals at home hooked by phone lines into DEC VAXes. The conflicts started reaching electronically into people's homes at all hours. "People would get up and send nasty notes all night long," Miller says. "You had to read your mail before you went to work because they would send copies to everybody and everybody else would send copies and maybe a thousand people would see some cheap shot before you even got to the office."

The lack of cohesion in the personal-computer effort was taking its toll throughout the company. The topic dominated Operations Committee meetings. Digital was not used to failure—and that's just what the PCs were bringing to the company. 1983 had all the makings of the year of living dangerously.

"What we do today, tomorrow sounds old."

—Ken Olsen

26
Banned in Maynard

O<small>N THE OCCASION</small> of its twenty-fifth birthday, Digital decided to make a movie. At the behest of the Operations Committee, public relations chief Dick Berube hired filmmaker Marc Porat to capture the culture and spirit of DEC.

In January 1983, the film was completed. But it was never shown to DEC employees as intended. Just a few who appeared on camera ever saw the finished work. To DEC management, it is the film that was never made or simply a bad movie that didn't deserve being shown.

Unofficial copies of the forty-five-minute celebration of DEC's first quarter century still exist. Actually, the "bad movie" looks like any slickly produced documentary. But by the time it was finished, the film became a chronicle of a disaster rather than of triumph. It exemplified the confusion that rocked Digital during the early 1980s.

After hiring the filmmaker in 1981, the public relations group couldn't decide what the focus of the film should be and so sent Porat to talk to Avram Miller. Miller was at first reluctant to participate. But Porat persuaded him that the creation of the Pro was a good journalist's story around which to build the film. Miller finally agreed to let the filmmaker follow him around the Mill for the year leading up to the introduction of the Pro in May 1982. No one questioned the filmmaker's narrow focus on one PC, despite the original intention of profiling the whole company. And anyway, if DEC hit it big in personal computers, this film would testify to the company's future as well as celebrate its past.

The result was DEC's celluloid version of *The Soul of a New Machine*—the story of a machine and the people developing it. The film opens fittingly enough with eighty-four-year-old General Doriot expounding on his favorite themes: success, failure, and mediocrity. Then the scene shifts to Houston, site of the National Computer Conference, and the narrator declares 1982 the year of the PC. "The stakes are huge," he says, "and Digital Equipment Corporation wants to be a major player." But time is running out—the old clock in the Mill tower is ticking away. IBM and the Japanese are racing ahead in this lucrative market, and DEC has to work fast to stake its claim.

After introducing Miller and his team, the film cuts to Olsen sitting alone in his office wearing an old flannel shirt. "It was clear we had to make a major commitment to personal computers," he says. "We have experience in that area which no one else has. We understand how it fits into business life better than others. We just had to do it; we had an obligation."

Despite Olsen's backing, Miller faces considerable obstacles maneuvering through the matrix, including the DEC culture, which revolves around meetings and consensus. Sensing low morale at one point, Miller gives a pep talk. "I want us to believe we can make it, 'cause once you do, you'll find ways to make it. Once you believe you cannot," he tells his troops, "you'll fail absolutely." The film sounds the theme of DEC's passion for excellence. Engineers, including Bell, discuss design, programming, engineering, and the commitment to perfection. Attention to detail is identified as the main ingredient of success.

Michael Weinstein, the marketing manager for the machine,

talks on camera about the spirit of the team. "The people who started the CT (Pro) were the bandits and brigands of DEC," he says. "They were willing to go out to new territory, take the risks, like pioneers on a wagon train. There's a certain idealism. Unless you have an overwhelming commitment, coupled with idealism and some form of egotism, then you don't do it."

From his office again, Olsen grows philosophical: "Probably the biggest danger, the biggest weakness, comes from a few years of success. It blinds us. It blinds anyone. Pride—probably the biggest human weakness."

The culmination comes in Houston. DEC's gleaming Pro, Rainbow, and DECmate are on display, proclaimed by the narrator as "the hit of the show, a tremendous success." Miller and Weinstein crisscross the exhibition floor, checking out the competition. Weinstein says with obvious satisfaction, "I'm amazed that the big guys did not do better." In their hotel room after the conference, the pair is pleased with DEC's showing. "I'm really underwhelmed by the competition," says Miller. "I really expected something more."

"If this was supposed to be a war, then this is depressing," Weinstein adds. "We are the only people in the world out there with a third-generation system. We're the only player."

"I only did this to say, 'I own the marketplace. We're number one.' " Miller concludes. "There's no other reason to do it."

After a noisy celebration at Gilley's, the famed Texas dance hall, the film ends with a panoramic view of the Mill and Olsen's voice: "Right now, there are several tremendously creative projects going on. The PC is one of them. Now we go on to others, and in each one, there's a danger—that we're not bright enough, danger that we don't see it correctly, danger that somebody else does it earlier or better. But then life is filled with danger. What we do today, tomorrow sounds old. Tomorrow there'll be a new challenge."

Digital's twenty-fifth-birthday film was completed at an embarrassing time for the company to be celebrating. Late to market and with little software to make it run, the Pro immediately stalled. As 1983 unfolded, it was the Rainbow that began selling beyond expectations—though still not much beyond DEC's installed customer base.

Miller, the star of the show, knew he was going to flee DEC as soon as the Pro was completed—and before the film was edited and ready to be shown. The constant battle to marshal internal support for his personal computer against DEC's other machines mired him in bad feeling. He wanted out. He told the filmmaker to hurry; he knew it would sabotage the entire film if its star left before the film was finished.

Despite his misgivings about taking charge of the overall PC strategy, Knowles had realized that once he picked up the baton, he had to conduct the orchestra. "They had illusions of grandeur in the original plan," he says, referring to the KO project set up by Miller. "I wasn't part of the original plan, but I got stuck with it, and I got blamed for it."

The project obviously required input and cooperation from product groups, functions and resources that had never been pulled together in this way before. The product lines were territories jealously defended by their guardian managers. Knowles, in a race against time, invaded them to grab the resources, manpower, and influence he needed to make DEC's late entries competitive in the PC market. There was no time to solicit consensus or even cooperation.

Knowles found himself battling Olsen and other managers over pricing, volume, and design. He saw the production and sales estimates for the three machines—initially set at a total of 250,000 units—as far too optimistic. He tried to scale down the numbers to a more realistic level, perhaps 100,000 units. When he visited DEC's Boston and Westfield assembly lines, where keyboards and power supplies were produced, the plant managers told him they were still building 250,000 of each component. "Our forecast is less than 100,000," Knowles said. "We've been told to build 250,000," came the reply. Knowles couldn't pinpoint who was ordering the high volumes, but it was clearly from high up in the Operations Committee, and he was furious. "If you guys are going to build them, you can eat them," he told manufacturing.

Olsen reacted angrily to Knowles's methods. He believed

that his low-end vice president was out to build an empire for himself within the company, perhaps even try to take over the top spot. "After Kaufmann," says one former manager, "Olsen moved on to be paranoid about Knowles taking over his job." Olsen remembered the Anderson and Kaufmann incidents and distrusted anyone who grew too powerful at DEC.

At the same time, DEC's business slowed. The matrix was bloated with too many people and resources in places where they weren't needed. The personnel department held secret meetings about the unwritten no-layoff policy. Should and, more important, could DEC continue the tradition of no layoffs under these circumstances?

Knowles required lots of people. Many parts of the company were overstaffed. Instead of continuing his raiding, which was generating bitterness and anger within DEC, or hiring new people for the three low-end projects, why not pull together the excess from around the company? And if Olsen didn't like his methods, here was a chance for the Operations Committee to officially approve a better one. It seemed logical to Knowles, but it was a bold move. Not everyone bought into the idea of DEC's making personal computers in the first place. Getting the Operations Committee to approve such a plan—even where there was overstaffing—was sure to be a tough sell.

Knowles's group brought its restructuring plan for the low end to the Operations Committee. As a staff person explained the strategy, Olsen interrupted, firing with both barrels. He pounded the table and exclaimed, "I am NOT going to put all the company's resources into this one basket. I am not going to the shareholders and tell them that I am gambling with their money this way!" The target of Olsen's attack was obviously Knowles. The staff people were asked to leave the meeting, and the discussion eventually ended without resolution. But clearly, Knowles's plan to draw resources from around the company was dead.

In February of 1983, Knowles went to Olsen and resigned. He said that he would stay until the end of the fiscal year (June

30) because it would hurt DEC's image for the vice president in charge of the PCs to resign several months before they shipped. Coincidentally, Miller reached his decision to leave in early 1983 as well. Knowles had appointed Joel Schwartz as product-line manager of the Pro, a spot that Miller, as developer of the machine, believed should be his.

Miller also realized that his visible move to take charge of the company's PC had backfired. He was now viewed jealously as Olsen's boy. In order to dispel that notion, Olsen told Miller that he was going to verbally attack him in an upcoming meeting. Olsen did just that, but rather than help Miller's image, it opened the floodgates of the managers' anger at Miller. For Avram, it was a discouraging exclamation point to his short career at DEC.

Miller saw himself as operating his own business within DEC. He envisioned building a family of compatible workstations and terminals that could be part of a network running VAX/VMS software. He thought DEC could beat IBM in the corporate marketplace and forego retail sales. But being passed over for product-line manager of the Pro made Miller realize he might never run a business at DEC. He wanted eventually to be a general manager. But, he realized, there was only one general manager at DEC, and that was Olsen.

With Miller gone in March 1983 and the Pro stuck at the starting gate for lack of operating software, the twenty-fifth-birthday film was quietly set aside. Plans to circulate it around DEC for viewing, and possibly even showing on the local PBS outlet in Boston, were shelved. In time, DEC officials no longer acknowledged that the film existed.

The year was shaping up to be a nightmare for Olsen even beyond the walls of DEC. In midsummer, a Green Beret demolitions expert stationed at nearby Fort Devens hand-printed a note to Olsen requesting an eighteen-month interest-free "loan" of $1.25 million. The letter writer claimed to be a member of a paramilitary group "performing still-classified dirty work in Southeast Asia, Africa, Central and South America." According to *Computerworld*, the letter said the group was soliciting "loans" from some of the "wealthiest people in

the country" and threatened a "demonstration of the serious-
ness in this matter." The letter concluded by saying that
Olsen's failure to accede to demands would mean "he will die
and we will move on to someone else."

Olsen called the FBI. Two days later, two telephone poles
near Olsen's home exploded. A second note followed with
instructions for delivering the money. The FBI staked out the
proposed pick-up site and apprehended U.S. Army Staff
Sargeant Marc McDonnell as the extortionist.

The harrowing experience set the tone for the entire year.
For Olsen and DEC, 1983 represented a lesson in corporate
reality. Whereas the world had found it difficult to believe
anything bad about DEC before, it was now believing all
things bad about DEC. The business press was changing
through the late 1970s and early 1980s, and not just in its
attitude toward Digital. Reporters came into a CEO's office
with an aggressive posture, predisposed not to believe what
they heard.

Olsen stepped onto the firing line in May 1983, when
Business Week published a cover story by Boston Bureau Chief
Emily Smith that exposed in intimate detail DEC's turmoil.
Years of record growth and profits had painted DEC as a
model of corporate success. Just a year earlier, *In Search of
Excellence* lavished praise on Olsen's strategies and style. Even
as late as January 1983, *Fortune* magazine published a survey
of 6,000 American business executives rating the most ad-
mired companies in the United States; DEC finished seventh.
But now the internal problems were impossible to hide, and
the press swarmed over the company. Olsen reacted with
shock and disappointment. He was not ready for the pointed
questions. He took the interviews and resulting articles as
personal attacks. He believed that some, like Smith, came in
with new reporting techniques: they already had their story
lines firmed up and were merely looking for Olsen to confirm
that there was indeed trouble. He believed that no matter what
he said, the story would be the same.

Unlike some corporate leaders able to deflect such inquiries,
Olsen couldn't hold back his emotions. He lashed out at some

reporters. He declared their questions out of line and unwarranted. He said they didn't know what they were talking about.

As public relations chief, Berube sat in on the interviews and was himself stunned at the "meanness" of some of the questions. Smith, he says, was always distrusted at DEC. During an interview in 1981, she described trouble in DEC's low end to Olsen and cited unnamed sources inside the company to back up her story. Olsen lost his corporate cool. This was too much—the suggestion that someone inside Digital was revealing family problems to the press. And even more galling, here was a young female reporter with the nerve to challenge his assessment of Digital's PC strategy. His face reddening, his voice rising, he railed about the stupidity of the press, and soon the interview was over. Of Olsen's behavior, Smith says, "It was the most outlandish I'd encountered."

In her 1983 article, Smith detailed DEC's marketing and management troubles, particularly in the low end. She pointed out the political battles that caused Stan to leave and termed Knowles "a vicious infighter" who had fought Stan to get the low end for himself. The story infuriated Olsen, Knowles, and many other executives, both those named and unnamed. Berube called the editor of *Business Week* to complain about the treatment. DEC pulled its advertising for several weeks. But *Business Week* stood by the article.

Smith's story initiated nearly two years of bad press for DEC. Reporters hovered around Maynard, each looking for his or her own angle on the decline and fall of the Olsen empire.

"Good entrepreneurs can't delegate anything."
                                    —*Ken Olsen*

27
Gunfight at the KO Corral

"E NTREPRENEURS," OLSEN SAID in 1984, "don't make good businessmen." In many ways, Olsen had thrown off the label *entrepreneur* years before. He became the general manager of DEC, the unifying spirit at the center that held the confusing whole together.

But the center was not holding in the early 1980s. Conflict management, which worked so well in the 1970s as an outgrowth of the product-line matrix, no longer fit a company nearing $5 billion in annual revenues. The problems became evident first in Europe. A joint visit there by Shields and Smith in 1981 revealed the initial rumblings about the need for a restructuring. In Maynard, the mounting problems with the personal computers and the high-end VAX showed that product development was in jeopardy at the top and bottom of DEC's computer line.

There was a hard decision to be made, and Olsen made it: the product lines had to go. And so he set in motion another reorganization, the third in the company's history. In July 1982, Olsen consolidated manufacturing and engineering. In January 1983, he melded together twelve product groups into three regional management centers and reassigned 200 of the headquarters staff into the field. He disbanded the Office of the President. And in March, he replaced the powerful thirteen-member Operations Committee with three committees in charge of product strategy, marketing and sales, and management.

It was time to spread decision-making among a larger number of people. Olsen added thirty middle managers and line executives, creating a new operations core in the company. Above it all, he set up an Executive Committee with just himself, Hindle, Shields, and Smith as its charter members.

The reorganization jarred the company. Power and responsibility were shifting across dozens of individuals and groups. The transition would be painful. In 1966, when the company had changed from a functional to a product-line structure, key players left, including the cofounder. And now, the switch back to a functional organization—"one company, one strategy, one message"—would take its toll again.

Stripped of their profit and loss responsibility, the product-line managers suddenly found themselves without power. The change occurred in the middle of a feverish period of venture capitalism in the computer business. The former entrepreneurs within DEC found that they could be entrepreneurs again, but outside the company this time. As a result of the shake-up, DEC soon lost a nucleus of vice presidents, including Julius Marcus, Andy Knowles, Robert Puffer, Dick Clayton, Larry Portner, and Roger Cady. Still more executives, such as Stan Olsen, Ted Johnson, John Leng, and Si Lyle, left just before the reorganization. From the middle ranks of the product lines, more than fifty managers fled the company. One former executive called it "the gunfight at the KO Corral."

Olsen was bewildered at how quickly the players raced to the exits. He felt betrayed. Hindle sums up the sentiment of those who stayed: "We just don't like people that left when the going got hard." Later, Olsen came to terms with—or rationalized—what had happened. "The entrepreneurial groups were losing some of their effectiveness partly because they were successful and rich," he says, "and the measurements that made them successful after a while were neutralized. You can't measure a group the same way for too many years because after a while the measurements start to become more important than the good of the company. Good entrepreneurs can't delegate anything," he says. "It's just contradictory to their nature. So when I said, 'We're going to be one company and all work together,' that was the ultimate blow to their entrepreneurial spirit. People said, 'If Ken doesn't appreciate me to the point where I have to work with other people, obviously he doesn't know how good and important I am.' And they had to leave."

Olsen lumped together all who left into one box marked "defector." The reorganization did generally dilute power, but each vice president resigned for a reason specific to his own situation. Despite the lure of venture capital, most of the top executives say they would have preferred to stay in their DEC family. They felt that it was Olsen who created the environment that forced them to look elsewhere.

Olsen was stunned by the remarks he read in the press attributed to his former employees. One manager called the PC situation "a four-ring circus." Another, speaking about late deliveries of DEC products, said, "They have an incredible ability to screw up product schedules." Olsen responded, "When the senior people left the company, I don't think any of them ever said bad things to the press. But some of the people who lost out at the more junior level don't know enough to keep their mouths shut, and the press often doesn't know enough . . . you shouldn't talk to people who either left angry or who didn't make it here, who failed here or were let go. The press should be more sensitive."

Marcus watched his office-automation group be restructured, resulting in less personal control. "I did not leave because of Ken," he says. "I felt I couldn't be effective in the environment anymore. The environment fostered in me a sense of entrepreneurial behavior and freedom, a sense of responsibility and can-doism that generated an enormous amount of energy. I felt a direct sense of responsibility, and I seemed to buy what Ken Olsen said, 'Hey, this is your problem, you make it happen.' I was generally able to run around the company and make it happen. I left because it became difficult to have an open meeting in which you could speak your piece. And that was a shame."

Marcus exemplifies the deep feelings and emotions that run through the hearts of those who left. "I would venture to say there were 10,000 people there who I might have known by name, or certainly what their jobs were if I didn't recognize their name," he says. "Leaving a company like that, that you've helped to build, is a very difficult thing. My badge is sitting here on my desk encased in plastic. When I was leaving, I mentioned to Ken that it was hard to leave my badge. He told someone to find a way to give it to me, and they sent it to me in plastic."

Stan Olsen believes that Ken feels a personal sadness about everyone who leaves, but he can't show it. "He has to say, 'OK, that period is over, that person is over, we've got to forge ahead.'" About his own departure, Stan says, "I fully expect everybody to forget about me. They've got a big job ahead, and they've got to work with what they've got and who they've got."

John Sims, vice president of personnel, handled the departures of many key players. "I wasn't shaken for a minute," he insists, "because in every one of those situations, the foundation didn't change. We had some heated exchanges, but they were all treated with honesty and respect for the most part. If anything, I came out of that period with a hell of a lot more reinforcement of our philosophy and way of dealing with people."

Over four years, DEC lost sixteen vice presidents and uncounted lower-level engineers and managers because of the reorganization. The group, in total, represented some of the most talented individuals in the computer business, and they took their skills with them to both new and established competitors, such as Data General, Sun Microsystems, Apollo, Prime, and others throughout the industry.

Olsen doesn't believe those who defected came to much in

their new careers. "It's embarrassing to me, but they haven't done well," he says. "It's one of the things I can't brag about. We don't have a good yield of people who are successful after they leave."

Many believe that Olsen's refusal to let anyone else try his hand as a general manager at DEC results in the mediocre track record of ex-employees. Another factor is that the former managers had honed their talents and styles within DEC's unique framework; outside of DEC, their skills and experience seem out of place. The departures were like divorces for most of these men, the breaking apart of a lifelong relationship.

People who defect to another company often find themselves written out of DEC's history. One man controls the corporate past as much as the present, and Olsen will airbrush people out of the picture as he sees it.

"Ken's view of history will always be different than a lot of other people's," says a former vice president. "Like most leaders, he has the capability to rewrite history. Whether it is accurate or not is something else. But he should realize that the people who left loved him and had tremendous loyalty; and if they were frustrated, it was because he wouldn't let them help him solve the problems. Many of us felt that if we had gotten together in a room and he said, 'This is the problem, guys, you come back with a solution,' we would have done it, just like that. We were problem solvers. And the fluidity and teamwork in that company were just something to behold."

"We will never compete on price."

—*Ken Olsen*

28
Black Tuesday

Dᴜʀɪɴɢ ᴛʜᴇ sᴜᴍᴍᴇʀ of 1983, Olsen decided to boost company spirit. The executive exodus now under way and the mounting negative press were causing unease in the company. Olsen wanted a public demonstration of strength.

He called it DECtown. Digital rented the largest conference facility in Boston, set up displays of technology, and flew in employees from around the world to see what their company was developing. As an afterthought to this morale-building event, Olsen allowed press and analysts come into the exhibition on the last day.

Coordination was spare in this hastily pulled together show. As so often happened, each group did its own thing, setting up its products without coordination with other groups. But the end result was impressive enough to the rank and file. DEC displayed its product lines working in simulated professional environments. Sixteen unannounced products were previewed to demonstrate that the company was forging ahead, despite increasing criticism that DEC was slow to react to market opportunities.

The late follow-on to the VAX 11/780 was particularly troublesome since DEC had already fallen behind competitors like Data General and Prime. And IBM stepped up the pressure by reducing prices of its small mainframe and targeting it as an alternative to the VAX. Olsen's answer to critics: "Our response time will be slow—we plan it that way and it will always be that way. We don't produce TV-quality computers. We are in the business of making serious computers."

In his suite at a downtown hotel before opening DECtown, Olsen reviewed the press materials that had been quickly prepared. He didn't approve them, but he didn't disapprove them. He asked Joe Nahil, his public relations manager, to explain what would happen on Monday when the press and industry analysts arrived. Nahil said that, of course, the unannounced products would be pulled off the floor. "Who made that decision?" Olsen snapped. "I didn't make that decision. Why are you doing that?" Nahil and the marketing people in the room explained the legal reasons that prohibited leaving those unannounced products on display. Olsen didn't want to hear it. He insisted that the products stay on the floor. He gave no reason, and it was unclear to the marketers and public relations people whether Olsen was testing how they would handle the situation or just didn't care about the havoc he would create.

Confusion reigned when reporters and analysts arrived at DECtown. No pricing or target ship dates had been set and no marketing plans firmed up. No one from DEC knew how to answer the insistent questions about new products. "There might be some out there, but you'll have to find them," journalists were told. When a reporter did find a new product, like the widely anticipated Microvax, DEC personnel were at a loss as to describe what it was, what it cost, or when it would be shipped.

Bizarre confrontations ensued. Two reporters spotted Olsen moving through the crowd and approached him. They asked if what they had seen was indeed Microvax—the machine that had been the subject of much speculation in the trade papers already. Before he could comment, several DEC marketing people jumped in, distracted the reporters, and hustled Olsen away.

After lunch, reporters were denied reentry to the exhibition without being told why. The press, Olsen assumed, couldn't say anything worse about DEC than what had already been said. But there Olsen was wrong. The pandemonium for a day at DECtown foreshadowed even more chaos that would unfold in the next two months.

Despite the best intentions of DECtown, all was not well within Digital. The situation was not immediately apparent to Olsen. Underneath the old layers of management, he found a new group of managers ready for their turn at the top. The exodus, he says, "was the best thing that ever happened to DEC. Jay Forrester once said , 'You're either going to have too many managers or too few managers; you're never going to hit it exactly right, so plan to have more managers than you can use and let some of the others go to the rest of the industry.' Having more qualified managers has always been our goal. The corollary says you're never going to be as good as people think you are. So our goal is always to be better than people think we are."

The reorganization redefined not only formal reporting structures but also the informal way things got done. According to a report in *Business Week*, "Insiders claim that the corporate overhaul destroyed a delicate web of alliances that allowed people to get their jobs done. And battles broke out among managers over who was going to shoulder new responsibilities." Initially, the reorganization created more chaos than the structure it replaced. Says one DEC manager who survived the shuffle, "My network disappeared. You didn't know who was going to be on the other end of this number you used to call."

New administrative systems weren't put in place quickly enough. Forecasting, order processing, and production scheduling were in turmoil. Customers often received incorrect shipments or no shipments at all. So many orders were improperly logged that DEC suddenly found itself with a serious drop in earnings for July, August, and September 1983, the first fiscal quarter of 1984. And one night as Olsen turned out the light to go to sleep, his wife, Aulikki, asked, "How can you lose orders?"

The administrative snafu caught DEC by surprise. A week before announcing its quarterly earnings in October, the company advised Wall Street analysts to expect lower than projected numbers. No reason was given. When DEC revealed the figures, the news was even worse than had been hinted: earnings dropped 72 percent from a year earlier. The next day, October 18—DEC's "Black Tuesday"—the stock plunged twenty-one points.

The investment community watched in shock as the stock continued to fall. Five shareholders filed lawsuits against the company. The Securities and Exchange Commission investigated the sale of large portions of stock by three DEC vice presidents within a month prior to the earnings announcement. According to Stephen Smith, an analyst at Paine Webber in New York, Wall Street felt betrayed that it was not warned of the severity of the financial problems. DEC was dropped from most buy lists, and analysts and press began to disparage the company—and Olsen. "The mood on the Street was that DEC was done for, that this was the end," says Smith. Industry analyst Ted Withington told *Computerworld*, "I'm not too surprised at what has happened. We've been saying for some time that DEC has been getting technologically fat and lazy."

Olsen opened the company's annual meeting in November by saying, "I never thought I'd have to come up here and explain why we goofed up. It is hard to explain how a computer company can get into administration problems. Our sales pitch is that we will usually save you from these."

Inside DEC, the 70,000 employees were confused and stunned by the sudden turn of events. At many levels, work just flowed on, untouched by the chaos at the higher levels. But some employees echoed the fears of Wall Street. "Personally, I thought Ken had lost it," says one former employee. "You always hear about these entrepreneurs who can manage a company up to a certain size, and then they lose control and don't have the skills to run a really large company. I thought, here's an engineer who is losing control of the company."

Whereas DEC employees had once heard only praise and envy when they told others where they worked, they were now hearing barbs and criticism, people parroting what they read in the newspapers. The attacks stirred the family loyalty. "There were people around who had been through cutbacks before," says a former employee. "They said, 'You just have to hunker down; you'll have these cutbacks, but they'll go away.' "

As the news sank in over the next month, some longtime customers began to consider switching vendors. But generally, DEC's loyal customer base stayed solid. Even for a moderate-sized computing operation, changing vendors is no simple feat. The investment in existing systems is too large and the technological switch too complex to permit quick decisions about changing vendors.

But the bad earnings report did hurt DEC's bid for new accounts. Sales and marketing operations were so confused that potential customers couldn't get straight answers on even basic questions. Some waited weeks to get calls back from DEC; others were quoted different prices on the same systems from different sales people. DEC lost out on a bid for a $40 million office automation contract from E. F. Hutton because the marketing effort was chaotic.

Behind the financial downturn, DEC's three-legged personal computer strategy was toppling. An internal memo from DEC financial analyst Ken Swanton written in July 1983 encapsulated the depressing news: the Pro, which was intended to generate 90 percent of the profit, was a bust. In the original plan, DEC intended to ship 55,000 Pros in 1983 and 215,000 in 1984. The revised estimates specified 13,000 in 1983; and 60,000 in 1984. Profits were forecast at $13 million in 1983, $302 million in 1984. The new plan: $78 million loss in 1983, $46 million loss in 1984.

The original PC plan, the memo continued, "assumed that the Pro would be an outstanding success upon its introduction. Its operating system and key third-party application software packages were expected to be clearly superior to other PCs in ease of use, performance and functionality. In reality, the Pro was only a month late, but its performance and applications software were nowhere near expectation and remain that way today."

The Rainbow and, to a lesser extent, the DECmateII were actually exceeding forecasts. The Pro had been expected largely to replace the two other machines by 1984. But it was the Rainbow that people kept buying. Suddenly, Folsom was the fair-haired boy. The company shipped 23,000 Rainbows in 1983, but that number still represented a one-year's loss of $26 million. "Financially," Swanton wrote, "it's unpleasant to think about where we would be now if we had focused even more on the Pro, as some suggested, and did not have today's Rainbow and DECmate products."

But Swanton and many others at DEC still weren't seeing the complete misdirection of DEC's PC strategy. His recalculations forecast a $50 million profit from the Rainbow in 1984. The memo insisted that the potential of an enhanced Pro model, due out soon, was considerable. "Don't underestimate the financial attractiveness of today's PC plan," he wrote. "By the end of fiscal year 1984, Digital will have invested close to $900 million in the business, including all cumulative losses from fiscal year '76 to '83, all assets and the cost of tying up all that capital. I estimate that Digital's PC business will be worth approximately $2 billion at the end of FY84. Investing $900 million to generate $2 billion in value is always a very good deal."

In fact, that $900 million investment is about how much DEC lost in sticking to its Pro-Rainbow-DECmate strategy. By the end of 1984, Digital's PC strategy was worth essentially zero.

What went wrong came down to the marketing of three totally different machines. "We should not have brought them all to market," DEC vice president Jack Smith says. "There's nothing wrong with having either a competitive approach or a back-up approach to any area of computing. The mistake you make is when you decide to bring all approaches to market because you don't want to turn one off. It confused the market; but more importantly, we confused ourselves."

DEC added to its own confusion by jumping into the retail market with a bizarre marketing plan. The DECmate was sold only through Digital Business Centers, which were geared to sophisticated business users, while the Pros and Rainbows were sold through Computerland. DEC also contracted with Hamilton/Avnet stores to act as an authorized DEC dealer, so a shopper could see that sticker in three different places. But the customer couldn't always buy the machine he wanted. As *Fortune* magazine put it, "Consumers would go into a Digital Business Center looking for a Rainbow. Alas, they were told, we don't have Rainbows here, but you can find them at Computerland. So the customer would go to Computerland where the dealer would sell them an IBM PC." *Fortune* concluded, "Olsen, holding tight to DEC tradition that any decision worth making is worth making ten times . . . thought out a retail strategy that proved in practice to be so chaotic it's a wonder anyone knows where to find DEC's personal computers."

Olsen argued against going into this retail business but was talked into it. "When we finished with (our personal computer), it was a beautiful machine. Everybody else's was ugly," he told *Computerworld*. "People within the company said, 'Gee, that's beautiful, we ought to sell it retail.' And that was a mistake. People in retail care nothing about subtleties, nothing about the reflection on the CRT, nothing about beauty. All they care about is price, and we will never compete on price. So we lost our shirt in that market."

On the outside, DEC battled Computerland and other retail outlets about how best to sell its computers. On the inside, Folsom ran into obstacles creating a retail image for his product. After struggling for months to get permission to name his PC the Rainbow, he had to fight for another year through the matrix to get rainbow colors and scripted lettering on his marketing materials. Folsom sent Olsen a blunt memo: "Ken, we have three choices: 1) Let's fight IBM. 2) Let's handcuff ourselves. Or 3) Get out of the PC business. I'm tired after two and a half years of number 2. It's 1 or 3 for me. We can't fight both DEC and IBM. I want to fight IBM. Please let us."

The plea came too late. Quickly, Pros and Rainbows started disappearing from shelves as retailers grew disgusted by the lack of customer interest and the difficulty of dealing with DEC. Stores that kept a few models on hand often turned customers away from them. "I remember going to Computerland and watching some guy ask the salesman about the DEC machine," says Michael Weinstein, the Pro's marketing manager. "The salesman said, 'That's a real neat car, but it ain't got no gas.' "

But most of all, DEC got outmarketed by IBM. Though a few diehard Rainbow supporters believe that DEC could have captured a major portion of the PC market had it been introduced earlier, most analysts and many DEC executives believe the company really didn't stand a chance in the low end. IBM launched its massive, mulitmillion dollar ad campaign featuring the Charlie Chaplin look-alike. And it curried the cooperation of third-party developers to arm its machine with applications software. Whereas DEC sold a total of 300,000 PCs, mostly Rainbows to existing customers, IBM turned out more than a million machines per year, bringing in billions of dollars in revenue. The IBM PC gave life to a new and untapped segment of the computer industry.

Digital tried its hand at television advertising, running a series of expensive ads. Olsen said in *Fortune* magazine, "I tell my marketing people that the main reason they like to advertise is so their mothers-in-law in Idaho will know they're doing their jobs." DEC marketers bought ads for the 1983 Super Bowl. Olsen moaned. "One minute of advertising in that game would pay for 600,000 handbooks" to explain DEC products, he said.

Soon all non-IBM compatible PCs except for Apple's populist machines fell by the wayside. Clonemakers started popping up around the world, turning the PC business into a commodity marketplace. "A thousand people have introduced personal computers," Olsen summed up the industry in a memo dated October 1983. "Almost all of them are doing exactly the same thing, following the same leaders and designing the same application notes. Most of them have a generation of engineers who know little about circuits and transmission lines, power supplies, motors, Maxwell's equations, materials or physics and electrical engineering in general. Most of them have never decided what unique contribution they will make, except to say that they want to do the same thing someone else did. And, like the new mayor of Boston, they have blind faith that they cannot help but be better than the previous mayor, but can't tell why."

Folsom and others had expected that building the Rainbow with MS-DOS capability would allow it to run all IBM software. That was not the case. Small technical differences in the two machines resulted in wide operating incompatibilities. And if it couldn't run IBM-compatible software, the Rainbow wasn't much use to the businessman.

In late 1983, Olsen had met with Mitch Kapor, creator of Lotus 1-2-3, the software package fueling tremendous PC sales. Folsom was negotiating to get Kapor's company to write 1-2-3 for the Rainbow. He flew Kapor into Maynard via DEC helicopter in hopes that the young software visionary could convince Olsen that the growing PC boom wasn't a fad. Instead, Olsen spent the hour extolling the virtues of DEC's VT100—how superior a terminal tied to a VAX was to a PC. Finally, Kapor interrupted. "No one gives a damn about that," he said. "People want to get the work done, and there's over a million people out there who verify that it gets it done on PCs." The meeting ended on a cordial note, and 1-2-3 eventually came out on the Rainbow. But Kapor had done little to change Olsen's deep-seated views. "I have a great deal of respect for Ken Olsen," says Kapor today. "He seemed to be an extremely savvy, dedicated, passionate engineer. But we were coming from different worlds. The rules of the game are different for personal computers, and that's a challenge DEC still hasn't met. I hope they do."

By 1984, DEC found itself without the insurance policy it had counted on, and thus it was effectively out of the PC business, though it continued to sell Rainbows and DECmate

IIs. The personal computer steadily grew in importance in corporations, and DEC's failure in this market would haunt it through the rest of the decade.

Olsen looked for a place to pin the blame. Knowles, who had made his play and lost, got stuck. As he departed, Knowles sent a bitter memo to Smith and Hindle documenting his participation in the low end. "I understand I am being scapegoated," he wrote. Then he added a quotation: "Tradition is an important help to history, but its statements should be carefully scrutinized before we rely on them." Bell says, "Ken had a wonderful ability to rationalize history where he was blameless. I believe leaders must have a critical ability: either one must be able to completely rationalize a past, which is independent of their own poor judgment, or must understand the past in a completely honest way and then build on it. Ken operated in the former mode and was able to revise history."

As the smoke began to clear, Olsen took to the offensive against personal computers, the very machines he had dismissed as toys in the late seventies and then praised so highly in 1982. Sure, millions of PCs were being brought into corporations, he now said, but it wasn't clear what they would do. Charlie Chaplin wasn't going to run your business for you. In November of 1984, Olsen told the *Boston Globe*, "We have little to contribute in personal computers." He described them as "cheap, shortlived and not very accurate machines." Back in Maynard, Folsom's group read these demoralizing words as they labored still to market the Rainbow.

But Olsen was finally right on target in assessing DEC's role in the low end. Expectations had run high that the company would be a major player in PCs. In hindsight, failing there may be the best thing that ever happened to the company. The lesson was costly—almost $1 billion. And the timing was atrocious—DEC was reorganizing its structure and losing sixteen executives from its vice presidential ranks. But by failing, Olsen refocused his attention on the much more important VAX strategy and the company's new message: networking.

"Entrepreneurs are not the people who come naturally to the conclusion that they have more to learn."

—Ken Olsen

29
Breaking the Faith

IN EARLY 1983, Gordon Bell penned a memo that assessed the status of his VAX strategy in the five years since he had conceived of it. "We're really making it, but it's two years away, and there's still lots to do." The foundation piece—the VAX supermini—was only the center of the wheel. The spokes had to be added one by one. And each addition was a painful, complex process.

The first step: get the company and Olsen to understand the underlying philosophy. Bell saw VAX as a family of machines with a 1,000 times cost/performance range, meaning that someday, at its zenith, the biggest VAX would cost 1,000 times as much as the smallest. But it would be even more. VAX would become a way of computing life, the basis for tying an entire organization together. The key was networking—that was the fuel that would turn DEC's smoldering present into a blazing future.

Olsen expressed skepticism at first. He didn't see the changes to the world of computing as Bell envisioned them. But Olsen also had the wisdom to listen to his engineers, people like Bell, Strecker, and Demmer, and they convinced him that DEC's future lay in the VAX strategy. Once converted, Olsen turned into a zealot. And he liked the challenge. The computers DEC made in the sixties and seventies were relatively simple engineering achievements by his measure. "The harder job is to make bigger, more complex computers," he says. VAX fit that description. And beyond a single VAX machine was networking. "Networks to cover a whole corporation are very complex, very difficult and take massive discipline," he says.

Getting computers to communicate in a fluid and useful manner was a bold concept going into the 1980s. DEC had made tremendous strides already with its pioneering DECnet software introduced in the mid-1970s. Computer makers such as IBM had traditionally treated communications capabilities as just an add-on. Its SNA protocol emulated the company's view of computing: the IBM mainframe was the master, other computers were the slaves. DEC's vision, along with fortuitous timing, made communications an integral part of the strategy. DECnet came into being in 1975, simultaneous with the creation of the first VAX and its VMS operating system. DEC viewed computers as peers; each machine, and thus each user, should have equal access to the network. DECnet capabilities could be designed directly into the operating system, giving DEC computers a significant advantage over its competitors.

In February 1980, when DECnet Phase III arrived, DEC led the pack in communications capabilities. But like a marching band with no parade behind it, DEC was too far out in front of the marketplace. Though the press used networking as a buzzword, customers didn't understand the benefits that could be derived from it. IBM's style still reigned: different machines and different architectures were spread around a corporation to suit the individual needs of individual parts of the company. But Bell's computing model from 1978—the three-tiered concept of distributed processing—was gaining momentum, and its success hinged on networking.

Bell also saw that in the real world of corporate computing, most customers brought more than one brand of machine in-house. Vendors were creating a situation that computer users could only shudder at. Imagine a recording industry in which companies make records that only play on their own machines. If you want to play a different kind of record, you must buy another record player. Out of just such a disjointed marketplace the computer industry developed. In the multivendor environment of the early 1980s, machines from different manufacturers could not even share information, let alone work together. The vendor that could design a machine to communicate with the competitor's machine could gain a major weapon for its marketing arsenal.

Bell took the first step with his quiet but bold move in 1979 to endorse and embrace Ethernet. By jumping in with Xerox and Intel, DEC chose its wiring scheme before IBM showed its hand. In the computing industry, IBM very often set the standard. But Bell was confident. He saw Ethernet's potential in his grand scheme and believed that DEC could help drive this networking format into a standard. Bell always backed standards. He believed a company should either set the standard or follow it, but definitely not get caught somewhere in between. Bell preferred to compete on the basis of product quality rather than locking people in with proprietary standards.

Because of its complexity and unknown future, Bell kept Ethernet development low-key. "DEC, Xerox, and Intel pulling off Ethernet was a major coup," Bell says. "I attribute it to the marketing people and Ken really not knowing what was going on."

The creation of Ethernet was long and complex. Several vendors wanted to get in on the design process, but Bell refused them. "I'd get hate calls," he says. "Olivetti would call and say, 'Let us in on the design.' I would say, 'No, people all over DEC want in, and I've got four of the best people in the world on it. Even that might be too much.' " Bell always resisted design by committee. In a memo to the Digital engineering community headed "Building Great Products" he wrote, "Committees do not design! They are never held responsible, nor are they rewarded or punished. Committees can review." Bell concluded, "No matter how large the project, it must be led from a 'single head.' We often make two errors in leadership: having no clear technical leader/problem resolver, and abdicating to a committee."

Among the sensitive parts of Ethernet's development was creating the communications and interconnect capabilities. Bernie Lacroute and Dave Rodgers were working on those areas when Olsen involved himself in the cabling design. His fascination with packaging came to the fore once again, and he suggested changes to the cables. His insistence on trying various options caused delays and consternation among the engineers. Fighting the boss as well as complex technical problems was extremely frustrating.

Both Lacroute and Rodgers left DEC shortly afterward. Lacroute tired of the ongoing tension between Olsen and Bell over engineering direction and product development. As DEC grew bigger, it took longer to get a machine out the door, and Lacroute wanted to see his ideas turned into products quickly. He joined the California start-up Sun Microsystems, a workstation supplier that would eventually become a serious challenger to DEC. "We lost a super guy when we lost Bernie," says Bell. "Sun would not have been a competitor without him."

Bell feared that the free-flowing venture capital was costing DEC many of its top engineers, the kind of superstars who would come back to haunt DEC as competitors. In 1980, he demanded and won vice-presidential-level stock options for several of his key people, which essentially shackled them in golden handcuffs. "I set it up so that they would be giving up $1 million if they left DEC," Bell says.

The development of Ethernet fit in as just one part of the puzzle. Filling out the VAX family was another. Though networking might become important later, in the short run, customers clamored for more variations of the VAX, from the low to the high end. The company introduced two new machines by 1982, the VAX-11/750 and the VAX-11/730, filling in the middle range.

But Bell realized that customers would soon start requiring more power at the high end. In anticipation of this demand, he had initiated the Venus project in 1979 to provide performance beyond the current top-of-the-line 11/780. Concurrently, DEC set out to build a follow-on to the non-VAX architecture DEC10/20, a new and more powerful 36-bit machine code-named Jupiter. Both Venus and Jupiter were being built under DEC's large systems group in Marlboro. And these machines exemplified everything that had gone wrong with the product-line structure.

On May 13, 1981, a day Bell calls Black Friday, he sat down with 100 engineers in Marlboro to review the status of Venus and Jupiter. He circled the room soliciting opinions. The predominant sentiment: Venus might be a few months late. Otherwise, the engineers expressed little concern. Bell exploded. He couldn't believe how polite they were. The Venus wasn't just late, it was a disaster, "the worst project I have ever seen," he says.

The project had run out of control, and the matrix was at fault. A "process manager," as Bell describes him, had been put in charge of both Venus and Jupiter, products he didn't technically understand. The functional groups overwhelmed him with their demands for budgets, salary reviews, human resource plans, and schedules. He answered their requests and ignored the underlying technology of the product. The project leader, Bell says, simply didn't know what was going on with either the Venus or Jupiter projects. "It was a simple case of incompetence," Bell declares, "incompetence on the part of engineers. And I was responsible."

After getting little sleep over the weekend, a glum Bell reported to the Operations Committee on Monday that the follow-on to the 11/780 might never work. He calculated that each day the Venus was late, DEC lost $1 million.

It seemed to Olsen that Bell was losing control of his engineering organization. Olsen dispatched him to fix the Venus and Jupiter problems. Bell essentially moved to Marlboro for the next six months to redirect the projects. For two days he interviewed all the engineers and studied the design. Bell lopped off the two top layers of management and put Bob Glorioso, a rising star in engineering, in charge. Computer-aided design was just coming into vogue, allowing designers to simulate what a machine would do before time and expense went into actually building it. Bell set up a group to apply simulation tools to Venus. Finally, the project was on the right track.

But Jupiter took much longer to sort out. The very existence of a follow-on machine to the 36-bit DEC10 line stirred up contention for several years at DEC. An entirely different architecture at the high end simply didn't fit into the overall VAX strategy. Bell pushed the DEC10 group to come up with a means of migrating its customers to VAX. The 10 marketing group produced a button in response: "Birds migrate, customers don't."

In fact, the DEC10 group worked almost as a separate little company—an anomaly at DEC. The customers were as fiercely loyal to the machine as the engineers who built it. Attempts to kill it off within DEC, VAX strategy or not, were fought off.

So Jupiter lived, and the user base eagerly awaited it. Like Venus, however, the engineering development was a disaster. With the hardware built and partially running, the Jupiter developers made a crucial error. They decided to forgo simulation and build the machine from the design table. That approach failed to uncover serious technical roadblocks.

Against all better judgment, Bell listened to the pleas of the Jupiter group for more time to straighten out the mess. They would get Jupiter working soon, the engineers promised. Bell felt that DEC was just torturing its customers and wanted to be done with it, but the 10 group persisted. Olsen also resisted killing the machine. He didn't want to leave any DEC customers in the lurch.

In the spring of 1983, after eighteen months more of fruitless effort by Jupiter engineers, Bell reviewed the project once again and saw that it was hopeless. The project leader had taken ill, and the development team begged for the chance to start over again. Bell refused. Enough was enough. Olsen agreed—finally, and reluctantly—to cut off Jupiter development.

DEC dreaded telling its customers about the decision. Smith and several other managers concluded that the right thing to do was redirect customers to the VAX. A DECUS meeting approached in May. "Let's send Win," the group decided. So Hindle, the past champion of the DEC10, was sent off to the St. Louis meeting as the bearer of bad news.

"Was it difficult?" Smith says. "It wasn't just difficult, it was awful." Customers were "really, really pissed off." Expecting the announcement of the Jupiter, customers heard instead that all DEC10/20 development was being killed. DECUS president Goldsmith became the first customer affected by the decision. "I won approval to buy my third DEC20 at 9 A.M." he says, "and at 10:30 I got a call from an engineer at DEC saying, 'On Friday it will be announced that the Jupiter doesn't exist.' "

At the DECUS symposium, the atmosphere was grim. Rose Ann Giordano, manager of DEC's Large Computer Group, told owners of DEC10s and 20s that DEC would provide integration tools to allow their software to run on VAXes. She stressed that DEC was offering "integration" and not "conversion" packages. "We are not asking users to convert; we don't believe that most people will convert," Giordano said.

The anger was palpable—and not just from customers. The engineer who called Goldsmith quit on the spot. But DEC didn't back down. Olsen knew it was the painful, but right, thing to do. Moving customers toward VAX now was better than leading them to a technological dead end. "If we had known the problems it would cause, we might have looked for another solution," Olsen admitted to *Computerworld* years later. "But this was the only thing to do. We told our customers, 'IBM kills machines all the time.' And they said, 'Yes, but we didn't expect you to do it to us.' "

So the ingredients for disaster were complete at Digital: a failing PC strategy; Venus two years late; loyal DEC10 customers alienated; and in the midst of it all, a reorganization that exposed the very guts of the company. There was irony in what this period taught Olsen. "Entrepreneurs are not the people who come naturally to the conclusion that they have more to learn," he says, referring to the product-line managers who fled the company in the middle of DEC's travail. "They are not naturally people who delegate; above all, entrepreneurs are not naturally people who will cooperate with others."

In the midst of the chaos, Olsen recognized the beauty of the VAX plan and saw his mission. "It was done without any help from me," he says about the strategy. "It was done by our engineering management, and then, once we had decided to be one company with one message, they didn't follow it. It was with a passion they didn't follow it. The same people who did this magnificent, absolutely ingenious piece of planning didn't follow it." Olsen decided that it was time for him to skip consensus building. "I learned to be heavy-handed," he says. "That was probably way overdue." His role became clear to him: "My part was to say, 'We have a plan, it's accepted, now everybody is going to follow it.' " Olsen's implication to DEC engineers was clear: "If you don't like our plan, go somewhere else."

And they did. "To my dismay," Olsen says, "almost all my vice presidents went somewhere else. I can't explain why. It bothered me no end. But the lesson is clear. Working together is not natural. And for an entrepreneur who has been successful for many years, it is a most serious affront to his genius. I said to our people, 'We have one company, one strategy, one message,' and pressed it home."

"We're not his kind of company anymore."
—Ken Olsen

30
Exit the VAXmaker

THE STRESS WAS getting to Gordon Bell. In the reorganization of 1982, DEC joined engineering with manufacturing. Bell now shared authority with Jack Smith. Bell naturally felt his role, along with his ability to cope with the continuing engineering crises, diminishing.

As he raced to correct the high-end problems, Bell heard the suddenly ubiquitous question: where is Venus? Customers cried for the VAX follow-on. Competitors exploited the opportunity to bite into DEC's market. As delays appeared in the low end as well, the feeling grew—DEC, it seemed, could no longer get products out the door.

Yet the VAX strategy—Bell's monolithic idea—was proceeding along well enough. The powerful Venus, though delayed, was at least on track to completion. And the networking scheme was in place.

Bell began thinking about leaving. He couldn't thrive without a challenge, and the VAX was now becoming a process, just carrying out the plan. The creation was over. More important, stress was wearing Bell down. He felt at times as if he were carrying both engineering and Olsen. "Running engineering was never that hard for me," Bell says. "It was doing it with Ken on my back that made life pretty miserable, because I simply didn't respect his engineering judgment on anything except packages."

The combative, but synergistic, relationship that Bell and Olsen had shared for the past decade was collapsing. Bell believes Olsen grew frightened of him because he understood the details behind "every nook and cranny of engineering." Bell says, "I used to keep management on their toes by simply being able to challenge any manager to know more than I did about a project." Olsen, by putting Smith in a co-leadership role with Bell, apparently intended to see engineering run as a process rather than as a content-oriented job.

Bell was losing control. Small incidents incited his anger. Sometimes he threw erasers at people during discussions. Meetings often ended with his engineers confused and angry. It is ironic that, without realizing it, Bell took on the methods he saw in Olsen—"management by ridicule."

In December of 1982, the first pangs of angina throbbed inside Bell, but he refused to see a doctor. "Even though I thought I was impervious to the pressure and stress of DEC and could dish it out as well as take it," Bell says, "my body told me that apparently wasn't true." He noted the attacks on a piece of paper and kept it in his wallet. In January, Henry Burkhardt, a former DEC engineer, and Ken Fisher, ex-president of Prime Computer, contacted Bell about cofounding a new company called Encore Computer. They asked Bell to head up engineering.

In early 1983, Bell wrote a long piece for an internal newsletter about the history of engineering at Digital. It was intended as his farewell letter to the company, even though he hadn't made his final decision about joining Burkhardt and Fisher. The thought of actually leaving DEC seemed impossible. He had given his creative being to the company. His soul and passion coursed through DEC's machines.

In early March 1983, Bell and his wife, Gwen, left on a ski trip to Snowmass, Colorado. The Bells met up with several of DEC's top engineers and their wives. On Saturday morning, they skied for three hours and that night joined the group for an evening of food, wine, and laughter. Bell, who hadn't felt well all weekend, carried mattresses up and down stairs as the group arranged sleeping quarters. Gwen told him, "You're crazy exerting this kind of energy at this altitude on the first day."

On Sunday morning, Bell woke with chest pains. But after his morning coffee, he felt better. He went upstairs to the bathroom but collapsed before getting there. From the next room, Julius Marcus's wife, Kay, heard Bell fall and called for help. In the midst of a major coronary attack, Bell lay unconscious on his bed. Then he stopped breathing. Bob Puffer, a DEC vice president and an emergency medical technician in his spare time, was eating breakfast downstairs. He raced up to Gordon and performed CPR for twelve minutes while the others called for an ambulance. Puffer brought Bell back to life.

But Bell was not out of danger. He slipped in and out of a coma until the following afternoon as the local hospital sought to stabilize him. Then a helicopter transported him to a Denver hospital where it became clear that he needed immediate bypass surgery. The doctors feared that the attack had damaged his brain. Bell did suffer some amnesia after the operation—he lost memory of a week of his life—but his brain remained intact. Each day Bell's doctor checked his mind with basic questions. On Thursday morning, four days after the heart attack, the doctor asked, "Who is the President of the U.S.?" Bell, so apolitical that he never voted, replied, "I don't remember, and it really doesn't matter!"

Back in Maynard, Bell's collapse shook the company. Engineers called Mary Jane Forbes constantly to find out news of his condition. Many cried as they spoke to her. Olsen also seemed shaken, but he kept his emotions inside. He directed the company's resources to help in any way possible. And Olsen spoke to Bell by phone nearly every day. When Bell was well enough, Olsen sent a corporate jet to Denver to fly him back to Boston.

DEC withheld the news from the press. It wasn't clear

immediately whether there would be any long-term impairment to Bell, and there seemed little need to alarm customers or the investment community. After several months of recuperation, Bell returned to the Mill. But to his colleagues, it was not the same old Gordon. The fire was gone.

Bell stopped his combative, frontal attacks on engineering issues. He still emotionally engaged himself in company issues and the VAX strategy in particular. But he no longer showed the will to fight the constant, wearying battles. With Smith running engineering as Gordon's equal and Olsen very much controlling the corporate direction, Bell felt overwhelmed. Neither Olsen nor Smith understood the architectural complexities of computers. And DEC's decision-making process was slowing down as the company grew.

Bell contemplated another sabbatical, this time at Stanford. But he finally decided to go with Burkhardt and Fisher to launch Encore. He sent Olsen a message along with the resignation, asking if he would like to discuss it. Olsen was getting ready to leave on a canoeing trip, his annual escape from DEC, and he replied that he did not have time right then. That response sealed the decision. "I would have stayed had he asked me," Bell says. Olsen would not ask people to stay once they decided to go, not even the architect of virtually all of Digital's computer lines. He was particularly upset that Bell would join up with Burkhardt, one of the renegade trio who started Data General fifteen years before.

Hindle, Smith, and General Doriot spent hours trying to change Bell's mind. "General Doriot told me, 'Don't feel discriminated against, he (Olsen) treats us all bad,' " says Bell. But he had lost the final vestige of motivation to put up with the stress anymore.

Bell walked away from Digital in midsummer of 1983. "Gordon's leaving set everybody back," says Folsom. "Ken was expecting a lot of things from Gordon that he couldn't do in the time frame he was given. Everyone was devastated that he was leaving. I think Ken was, too. Ken would say both good and bad things about Gordon after he left. But I think Ken personally really misses Gordon."

Whether Olsen misses Bell or not, he does not see Digital as the right place for him anymore. "It's not his kind of world anymore," Olsen told *Computerworld*. "It used to be a lot of disconnected projects. Now we're organized and scheduled and planned. He couldn't tolerate it. He's fun, exciting, charismatic, but he doesn't fit into a disciplined, organized environment. We're not his kind of company anymore."

31
Town and Company

O<small>N</small> APRIL 19, 1983, Maynard threw a twenty-fifth birthday party for Digital on the night of the town's own 112th anniversary of incorporation. It was the second largest celebration Maynard had ever held, just shy of the Centennial, in 1971. A huge crowd for Maynard, 500 people, gathered at Alphonse's Powder Mill Restaurant, now the Elks Lodge, to honor the company and its founder. The townspeople who mingled with him in the donut shop or newspaper store came to pay their respects to the man they knew as "Ken," Digital's president.

The town fathers planned to do more than just praise Olsen that night. In the revitalization of downtown, they saw a way to commemorate his achievement beyond the single birthday celebration. They decided to designate the crossroads nearest the Mill, at the corner of Main Street and Walnut, "Ken Olsen Plaza" and recreate a bandstand there. In the 1920s, the town's Poles, Finns, and other ethnic groups played their national music on warm summer nights at the old bandstand. A scaled-down model would preserve that bit of Maynard's heritage.

After the roast-beef dinner, the selectman unveiled the plan

256

to a surprised Olsen and his DEC colleagues. As everyone cheered, he politely smiled. The next day, he sent word through his public relations man, Dick Berube, that he would prefer the town not name anything in his honor. The party was very nice, he said; a plaza was too much.

The selectman respected Olsen's humility. Still, the town fathers intended to go ahead with the bandstand part of the project and solicit Olsen's approval again when it was done. But the state denied funding, judging the area's history not significant enough.

To the people of Maynard, though, thirty years of DEC history has been very significant. The town and company share an unusual relationship in American business. Most corporations are headquartered in or very near large cities, housed in glass and steel towers rising into the sky. DEC, a multinational titan, is centered in the second smallest town in Massachusetts, a community with fewer than 10,000 people squeezed into 5.25 square miles an hour's drive west of Boston. The only access routes—Routes 27, 117, and 62—are two-lane country roads that wind lazily through the outlying rural communities. The only quick way into town is by helicopter—Digital helicopter.

DEC's world headquarters sits in obscurity on Main Street. A pedestrian walking down the sidewalk past the post office could look across the street and not realize that there is the front door to the country's thirty-eighth largest industrial corporation. The entrance is now a smoked-glass enclosed atrium, with exposed brick and handmade wooden furniture. This lobby is a concession by Olsen to his marketing people. Until 1985, the main entrance was a single glass door that led into a tiny waiting area with one black vinyl sofa. Olsen's office was just steps away, down the hall to the right.

Olsen didn't purposely set out to hide on the banks of the Assabet River. He just never considered moving away once he set up shop in the Mill. He could drive from home in Lincoln to Maynard in fifteen minutes. Most of his employees enjoyed similar accessible commutes, far from the maddening traffic of Boston.

As DEC grew, Olsen kept a purposely low-key relationship with the town. He believes that more important than taxes (DEC pays about one-fifth of the town's total levy), a responsible company provides good jobs close to where people live and raise their families. To Olsen, stable employment is Digital's most important contribution to Maynard.

In the past several years, young professional couples have begun moving to town, attracted by some of the lowest housing costs west of Boston. They find in Maynard a tight-knit community of blue-collar families, third-and fourth-generation residents who maintain Maynard's character essentially as it was. If there is a certain detachment between DEC and Maynard, that is just fine with the townspeople.

Not much seems to have changed since 1957. Dreary and ragged at the edges, Main Street is lined with double-decker houses in need of paint, a barber shop, beauty parlors, a True Value hardware store, the Faucetorium, and a smattering of coffee shops and pizza parlors reminiscent of another time. The parking meters in front of Woolworth's still take a nickel and, except for traffic jams when the giant DEC facilities let out, cars generally cruise by slowly and infrequently.

DEC executives don't generally choose to live in Maynard. They find large backyards and stately houses in such wealthy surrounding communities as Sudbury, Concord, and Acton, often just across the border from Maynard. This snub doesn't bother Maynard hometowners. They take their opinion of the company from its president, and Olsen is a regular guy whom they've seen drive through town in a Ford and buy tools in the Maynard Hardware Supply.

He is rich, but he doesn't act rich, an attitude that the people of Maynard appreciate. They remember that during the great blizzard of 1978, when the entire Commonwealth was shut down for a week, Olsen ordered all workers paid full salaries. They remember the story of Olsen himself defying the driving ban and somehow maneuvering his Ford Pinto through the deep snow to try to get to the Mill. There was work to be done. He berated a Maynard policeman who stopped him but later apologized for his outburst.

In earlier years, Olsen maintained an open-door policy. Townspeople felt free to bring to him problems about parking on Main Street, pollution in the Assabet, or employment at the Mill. The policy became impractical as the company grew rapidly in the 1970s, so Olsen appointed Berube as liaison to the town, a role he played until he left DEC in February 1987. "We called the process *deinstitutionalization*," Berube says. "We didn't want the folks in the town to feel as if they were dealing with this big thing called The Company. But I had to make them understand that they couldn't talk to Ken all the time."

Olsen believes that a balance must be kept between company and town. As DEC passed the $4, $5, and $6 billion revenue marks, it became to Maynard like an elephant sitting on the head of a pin. It took great effort not to overwhelm the town with corporate largesse, influence, or political views. And conversely, the town shouldn't see Digital as its benefactor, doling out unlimited funds for any project that the selectmen could conceive.

According to Michael Gianotis, administrative assistant to the board of selectman and the town's liaison to DEC, the corporate philosophy of moderation is appreciated. "A lot of companies try to be flashy or showy as to what they do," he says. "Every time they make a donation, you've got to have cameras and reporters around. DEC understands the community's needs, but they do things low key. They don't try to be all-encompassing. There are donations made that never get in the press."

"It doesn't feel like some monolith looking over your shoulder, Big Brother watching you," says Anne Flood, a town selectman. "They are not making decisions for us. They respect our board's requirements."

At the twenty-fifth birthday, Maynard estimated that Digital had given $2 million worth of cash and products to the town during its lifetime. In the mid-1980s, DEC contributed half the cost of a $150,000 VAX system to upgrade the town's computer operations. DEC paid for much-needed lights at the high school football field. For the $2.5 million town renovation project, DEC gave $40,000 of the $125,000 Maynard itself had to pay. Berube says that Maynard asked the company to cover all of its costs on the project. DEC refused. "We won't give you everything because we want to ensure that you are emotionally involved with the process of getting it done and share the sense of urgency," Berube told the planners. "We had to be tough with the town," he says.

In 1979, a group in local government considered anti-DEC assessed the company excessive taxes. Unconcerned about being perceived as a corporate Goliath, DEC sued the town. The lawsuit created ill will, but after some haggling and the departure of several members of the tax board, the suit was settled out of court in DEC's favor.

One puzzling part of Olsen's hands-off attitude toward the town sits directly across the street from DEC's main entrance. It is Florida Court—a name that belies the look of this block-long tenement, a row of decaying, low-income houses. Only recently have two private developers come in with plans to fix up the area as part of the town's overall renovation being completed in 1988.

DEC stayed out of the situation. Olsen's tenets on the town-company relationship and his puritan beliefs told him that buying or renovating Florida Court was simply not DEC's business. "He just views himself as a resident and a taxpayer," Berube says. Says one town official, "It is strange that it's across the street from world headquarters; but until three years ago, there was a big train trestle that blocked the view. You just didn't see it. I couldn't imagine IBM allowing that, though." The town never associated DEC with Florida Court as part of the problem or solution. Complaints today from residents center on the traffic that clogs the major intersections at rush hours.

DEC takes great pains to keep a low-key profile while at the same time beneficially influencing both other cities and other countries. When Stan Olsen took his group to New Hampshire in 1975, it was a timely coupling for the state and the company. DEC quickly grew to become the Granite State's largest employer. Julius Marcus assumed responsibility for DEC's corporate citizenship in New Hampshire when Stan left the company. Marcus minimized DEC's visibility. "That way, you avoid being the target for the community in both bad and good things," he says. "I can tell you that most people like bad news rather than good news; most people will spread bad rumors before they spread good ones. So what you want to do is lay low. DEC wants to be a good public member, but it doesn't want to be any more important than anybody else."

DEC has traditionally kept its corporate giving low-key. It donates millions of dollars in cash and equipment each year to Freedom House, the NAACP, public television (including sponsorship of "The Infinite Voyage" and "Evening at Pops"), the Kennedy Center for the Performing Arts, Boston Museum of Fine Arts, Massachusetts General Hospital, and the AIDS Action Committee, as well as numerous other educational, health-care, and arts organizations in local communities where it operates. In 1987 alone, DEC donated $22 million in cash and equipment worldwide. The philosophy is simple: "We see corporate giving as an investment in the future of both the company and the community," reads DEC's corporate contributions report. "We believe that the continued well-being of one is directly linked to the continued well-being of the other."

Mostly because of Olsen's reverence for education, DEC heavily supports universities, particularly ones with strong research and engineering departments, such as MIT, Carnegie-Mellon, and Purdue, and local school systems with cash and generous equipment grants. "If we ever needed to teach people to continue learning, it is now!" he wrote in 1983. "Learning," he said, "has to be continuous and forever."

Olsen worries about engineering education in particular. "When we all used slide rules, we always knew the significance of the precision of our measurements. You always had to keep in mind how many digits were significant and where the decimal point was. All of a sudden that has disappeared. The calculator relieves the student of the need to understand mathematical functions. They'll be fine as long as the battery holds out."

DEC joined IBM in a landmark of cooperation at MIT in the early 1980s. Project Athena ties together various machines of the two companies with the goal of exploring computers as a medium for teaching and learning. DEC contributed $25 million, its largest single gift ever.

In 1979, the company established a minority education program to increase the number of minority students interested in the technical sciences. In 1981, DEC followed with a women's advisory committee to support organizations helping to develop qualified women for jobs in high technology.

For Olsen, charitable donations are given with clear signals. DEC expects the recipient to do something positive with the grant—take the gift and grow with it. In that way, the gift is returned. That is why much of the grant money goes to educational and cultural institutions, which can provide something positive and proactive with the funds. Olsen's puritan ethic leaves little room for giving something for nothing.

"We built a plant in Springfield in the old Armory that George Washington built," he said, referring to Pete Kaufmann's initiatives in the late 1960s. "It was a depressed area where there were a few problems. Good people, but a depressed area. Our approach was not to say, 'We're do-gooders from Boston who are going to help you poor people.' We said, 'We're going to hire you if you're good and fire you if you're bad.' We gave people responsibility, and the results were just beautiful. We also did it without publicity."

"I'm not paid to be pleased with anything."
                                    —Ken Olsen

32
The Long Road Back

THE YEAR 1983 was pivotal for DEC and the
entire information industry. *Time* magazine dubbed the computer "Machine of the Year" in place of its usual "Man of the
Year" designation. Entrepreneurs were flocking to the industry, primarily to start personal-computer companies. The
excitement of computers began to reach out beyond the
borders of data centers into schools, homes, and businesses.
And AT&T was in its final year as a government-regulated
communications monopoly. On January 1, 1984, deregulation
would dissolve Ma Bell.

Arch McGill, a feisty, former IBM marketing whiz, took
over American Bell, the subsidiary of AT&T set up to allow
the telephone company to move gradually into the competitive
computer market. In preparing for deregulation, he realized
that AT&T couldn't easily break into the crowded and high-
powered computer business alone. McGill envisioned a perfect union: AT&T and DEC.

Acquisition of—or merger with—DEC would give AT&T
immediate access to an experienced, entrenched computer
industry player. As DEC's largest customer, AT&T knew its

263

proposed target well. PDP-11s and VAXes ran much of the business already. The familiarity between the two companies would provide a jump start to a relationship.

McGill decided to play matchmaker behind the scenes. He introduced several DEC managers and then Olsen himself to senior AT&T executives, including James Olson, who later became chairman. Olsen and Olson began a series of discussions about bringing the two companies together. It tore at Ken Olsen's heartfelt belief in going it alone, but there were clear advantages to a merger. On their own, the future of both companies seemed uncertain. AT&T was heading into the unknown waters of deregulation; DEC had just lost its executive core and was struggling to stay competitive at both the high and low ends. But together, with the resources of a $40 billion company, AT&T-DEC could stand up to IBM.

What happened in the negotiations is known only to the few participants—and they won't acknowledge publicly that talks even occurred. But sources say that the two companies came within weeks of signing a deal. AT&T would acquire Ken Olsen's Digital for $5 billion. But at the climactic meeting, Olsen insisted on retaining his management team in place. AT&T demanded full control, including the power to fire or shift DEC executives to different positions. Olsen said no, and the deal fell through. "I thought I came up with a super stroke, and for some reason it didn't work," says McGill. It wouldn't be the last time DEC heard from AT&T.

Rumors raged throughout the year and into 1984 about an impending merger or takeover. In public Olsen gave no credence to the stories. AT&T held discussions with several other companies and, within days of deregulation, purchased a 25 percent stake in the Italian firm Olivetti for assistance in getting into the personal computer business.

Olsen faced the press and analysts many times during 1984, the year of DEC's chagrin. On October 31, he stepped down from a helicopter at the spacious Marlboro facilities and strode into one of the manufacturing buildings. Inside, in a warehouse room filled with VAXes in shipping crates, the journalists, financial analysts, and consultants waited. The lights were dim; on the walls and ceilings, spotlights beamed through cardboard cutouts projecting the figure "8600" in huge block numbers.

Olsen seemed distracted and withdrawn, considering the magnitude of the announcement. Today he would unveil the long-awaited Venus, now called the VAX8600. When he introduced DEC's new product, he called it the VAX6800 instead of 8600 and then quickly yielded the podium to his marketing people.

It had been a rough two years. Olsen had suffered a stream of criticism since early in 1983. In the November 5, 1984, *Business Week*, in fact, he was once again scored for failing to understand the changing computer marketplace. "He has put DEC in a defensive posture that could ultimately relegate the company to an also-ran status in the industry," the article stated.

The DEC-roasting in the media and on Wall Street spread. Olsen, who had always been folksy and disarmingly candid with the press, grew surly and distrustful. His public relations people became cautious and less accommodating. They looked for hidden agendas from reporters and reflexively assumed a defensive posture . Joe Nahil, the DEC public relations manager, regularly tried to brief Olsen prior to interviews—was the reporter amiable, bright, arrogant or looking to make a name for himself on DEC's troubles? Even in these difficult times, Olsen paid little attention. When he allowed himself to be briefed at all, a phone call would inevitably interrupt, or he'd get up in the middle of the session and head to a meeting. His remarks in public settings were, as usual, off the cuff. Despite his unwillingness to better learn how to take on the press, Olsen angered quickly at the resulting bad publicity.

Olsen knew that while he may have deserved some of the criticism, the picture was not nearly as dismal as it was painted. He had taken an aircraft carrier and turned it around—no easy manuever, and it left a big wake. Things were going to be different, he believed, and it wouldn't be long before others saw his company as he did. Olsen had no intention of letting DEC become an also-ran. It became clear to him that all the chest thumping in the world was not going to change opinions. The press and analysts wanted to see new machines, new software, and lots of new customers before they would write that DEC was back on target.

And if there was a catalyst for the change in attitude toward DEC, it was the announcement made that day of the VAX8600. DEC packed Venus with more than four times as much power as its top-of-the-line machine. The 8600 marked the beginning of the second generation of VAX machines, a milepost in the superhighway of Bell's strategy. The 8600 burst through the ceiling of computing power that had bottlenecked DEC customers, who had waited five years for a more powerful VAX. And it proved that DEC could turn out products once more, machines that, unlike its personal computers, flowed from a coherent development and marketing plan.

At DEC's annual meeting the next day, Olsen seemed more buoyant. The embarrassing problems of a year ago, he noted, had disappeared. DEC's revenues and profits were once again heading up—sharply, in fact. Digital had become a $6 billion giant, with 85,000 employees and 660 offices in forty-seven countries. And it reached eighty-fourth on the Fortune 500 list.

At the 8600 announcement, an analyst had asked whether DEC was now ready to go after IBM. Olsen answered: "What do you think we've been doing for the past two years?" A day later at the annual meeting, he responded to the same question differently: "Obviously, no," he said. "IBM is eight times bigger than we are. It is mathematically impossible for us to overtake IBM." DEC's simple objective, he said, was defensive—to prevent IBM from making inroads into DEC's customer base. "IBM has no reason to worry about us," he claimed. Olsen's apparently casual attitude toward competing against IBM harkened back to the old rule he lived by—don't kick the tiger. On the positive side, press and analysts now viewed DEC as pitted against one of the world's most respected companies. Though it would take months for the industry to see it, the story of Digital was changing.

Olsen had somehow survived the kind of adversity that left

most entrepreneurs littered beside the highway. Business wisdom dictated that it was time for him to step down in the early 1980s and choose a strong, new corporate medicine man to heal his company. *Fortune* magazine posed the problem: "DEC's troubles raise a difficult management question faced at many corporations that started small, grew fast and became giants: Are the engineering and entrepreneurial skills displayed in abundance by the man who founded the company the kind of skills needed to keep it growing in a changed competitive environment?"

Olsen proved the answer can be yes. He realized after months and years of sharp attacks on his company and his leadership that the only response that meant anything was to succeed. Some former vice presidents attribute much of Olsen's achievement to luck and timing. But the past two years proved that opinion wrong. Olsen's survival sprang from assertive leadership in the midst of a crisis and adherence to the VAX strategy that he recognized to be right for Digital, even though he had no part in its creation.

Olsen learned from the errors and misjudgments of his earlier years. He still believed that his people should accept responsibility and do the right thing. But now he needed to take a firmer hand in shaping the way things were going to be. The man who "captained one of the loosest ships in corporate America," as *Business Week* phrased it, became a "leader and enforcer," as he described himself. Olsen added discipline to the list of corporate commandments.

"Our message to American business is: If you allow everyone in your organization to run off in a different direction, you are never going to communicate and never accomplish what you can with modern computing," Olsen says. "But if you get going in the same direction, that really allows creativity and productivity. We both preach that message and say, 'It sure did help us.'

"You have to give people a lot of freedom in order to keep them," he adds. "But people are only going to be productive and contribute to the common good if you have a disciplined approach. Let people have to reinvent all the unimportant red-

tape things and they never get around to making a contribution."

Though Olsen hadn't planned to precipitate the mass exodus from DEC in the early eighties, he did little to stop it. New
players jumped into the power positions underneath him,
driving the company's engine. Analysts criticized DEC for its
excessive inbreeding, promoting only from within. But Olsen
showed flexibility by looking outside to fill a critical position.
The corporate financial officer, Al Bertocchi, had stepped
down. On the advice of Digital director Philip Caldwell, a
former president of Ford, Olsen hired James Osterhoff as new
financial chief. It seemed a strange choice to some. Osterhoff
came from a shrinking business in Ford's tractor division.
According to the *Wall Street Journal*, DEC insiders expressed
surprise that the company found its new financial officer in a
backwater division of a smokestack industry. But Dorothy
Rowe, a DEC director, told the *Journal*, "Ford Motor Company is probably the best training school in the world for
financial managers."

Another strike against Osterhoff: outsiders historically
hadn't done well at DEC. Only two on the Executive Committee ever worked for any other company. The academic or
practical experience earned elsewhere never counted for much
in Maynard. Two of the most powerful executives—Shields
and Smith—didn't finish college. Osterhoff noted DEC's
iconoclastic style when he first joined it in late 1984. "It's a
different system from what you learn in business school," he
told *Business Week*, citing the blurry reporting channels, which
hindered financial controls. "The structure reflects its
founder." Osterhoff arrived as DEC was overhauling this
structure once again, and he instituted needed reforms, such
as insisting that operating expenses fall in line with revenues.
The old attitude of "a decentralized structure has to live with
its inefficiencies" no longer excused waste.

Osterhoff became a behind-the-scenes hero in DEC's turnaround, implementing tight fiscal policy. He symbolized
Olsen's ability to change when necessary, to find an answer
when one was demanded, whether or not it fit with tradition.

Under Olsen's puritanical hand, DEC always maintained a strong cash position and avoided debt as a means of financing growth. The company's cash reserves rivaled a small bank, with well over $1 billion stashed away in the early 1980s. The conservative philosophy dictated seeking financing through new stock issues rather than through borrowing. In 1982, Olsen said, "Growth is nothing to be proud of. Our double A credit rating—that's something to be proud of." Osterhoff personally resists DEC's long tradition of stock offerings, fearing the dilution of shareholders' value. But he has upheld Olsen's insistence on a strong cash position.

Financial stability did not alone guarantee survival. With the advent of the 8600, DEC once again established product superiority over its minicomputer rivals. Throughout the chaotic 1982-1983 period, DEC engineers had painstakingly pushed through the pieces of the VAX strategy. The business press didn't pay much attention, preferring to belabor the PC failures. In May 1983, the company had unveiled the VAX-cluster, a means of hooking VAXes together in a proprietary local-area network. This capability laid the foundation for giving customers mainframe power using DEC minicomputers. In October of 1983, the company announced the Microvax I, the low end of the VAX line, and shipped it in late 1984. A revolutionary single-chip version—the Microvax II—appeared in 1985. DEC shipped its 25,000th VAX computer in April 1984 and preached the wonders of Ethernet.

Most important, DEC quietly built links to other vendors' equipment, such as Wang Labs and IBM, an effort that would eventually make DEC's product line the most attractive in the market. DEC salespeople loved to show off this networking prowess to potential customers. In the Littleton, Massachusetts, facility, DEC hooked up its various minis to an IBM 4381 mainframe—a machine that could communicate to few other IBM computers. "We connect better to IBM products than IBM does," boasted DEC's vice president of marketing.

In Merrimack, New Hampshire, Julius Marcus pieced together an innovative plan to take DEC into corporate accounts through the office. He utilized competitive analysts, a first at

DEC, and formulated a strategy to first knock off Wang and then go after IBM. According to Marcus, the plan was simple: don't try to outadvertise the competitors; simply play up the storehouse of technological resources that DEC had in its arsenal.

His carefully orchestrated maneuvering began to have an impact. DEC landed a series of important commercial accounts in companies like Banker's Trust, Avon, and DuPont. Marcus, a victim of the reorganization, would not be around to see his plan flower.

On New Year's Eve 1984, Ken Olsen sat with a *Computerworld* reporter in a quiet and nearly deserted Mill. He spoke softly, sometimes barely audible. When asked if he was happy with the early signs of a turnaround, he grinned. "I'm not paid to be pleased with anything," he said. "It's like raising children. If you're confident, you're sure to be doing a poor job. You always have to worry about it, study it. Just spending money on it is not the answer."

"Can I pull us through a few years of good times
without running into the same old trouble?"
—Ken Olsen

33
Freedom and Discipline

ACCORDING TO EGYPTIAN mythology, the
phoenix consumed itself with fire and then rose, renewed,
from its ashes. For Ken Olsen, 1985 brought renewal. In his
mind, DEC had never been consumed by fire. There had been
plenty of heat and even smoke, but things had never been
quite as bad as everyone seemed to make it.

Inside DEC, the flames subsided. But those on the front
line—the engineers and managers who had seen the transformation—knew that there had indeed been fire. And many had
gotten burned.

As he had done in the mid-1960s in creating the minicomputer, Olsen now stood ready to fill a vast market need that
IBM had overlooked. This time it wasn't a single computer
product but a concept—networking. Corporations were catching on to a new vision: computers could do much more than
back-room accounting and financial services. In the Information Age, the key was strategic advantage. Whole industries—
airlines, banks, brokerage houses, insurance companies, and
many more—reshaped themselves around their access to computing resources. Information replaced goods and services as

271

the new-age commodity. Those companies who created the right flow of information in their offices and factory floors, the right access, the right uses, would lead their industries.

Waiting for the technology—and vendors—to catch up to their needs frustrated users. DEC was the first to offer them a solution—VAX and DECnet.

The first report of DEC's rebound came in *Computerworld*. A February 1985 article stated, "As 1985 unfolds, Digital Equipment Corporation has quietly positioned itself to have an exceptional year." A few analysts, such as Marty Gruhn, vice president of the Sierra Group in Tempe, Arizona, began touting DEC's prospects in early 1985. Her consulting clients responded, "Why should we be interested in them? Their sales people wear plastic pen protectors and speak English as a second language."

"By October 1985, my phone was ringing off the hook," says Gruhn. "Everybody was screaming, 'What do you have on DEC?' " Peter Lowber, a senior market analyst at Boston's Yankee Group, declared at the time, "Across the board, DEC's product offerings are stronger than any other vendor, including IBM."

Sales took off. DEC shipped every 8600 it could make, and orders backed up. In May the company introduced the Microvax II, with its revolutionary VAX-on-a-chip design. This powerful desktop computer took DEC into the escalating workstation war against companies like Apollo and Sun. Armed with VAX software, the Microvax II became an instant bestseller. DEC shipped 2,000 of them by August.

The office strategy, now led by Bob Hughes, a ten-year IBM veteran, and the Merrimack group, took hold. Positive reviews sent sales of office systems soaring. DEC, generally considered a stumbling also-ran in the office, suddenly found itself among the top three and climbing.

After a string of five quarters of declining earnings, DEC finally showed a gain again in 1984. By the first fiscal quarter of 1985, revenues jumped 41 percent to $1.51 billion, and profits leaped to $144.2 million compared to the dismal quarter of a year before. DEC started posting quarter after quarter of dramatic growth. The company hit $6.7 billion for fiscal 1985 and moved up to number sixty-five on the Fortune 500 list. It was a stunning turnaround, made all the more remarkable by an industrywide slump that choked the fast pace of companies like Wang, Data General, and Hewlett-Packard. IBM, more than seven times bigger than DEC in 1985, had the farthest to fall. Customers clamored for departmental solutions that Big Blue had not developed. IBM caught itself in the very web that Bell had predicted eight years before: it built different products to handle different computing problems. No one at IBM planned to make the products communicate to each other. The company—always known as the "safe buy" among users—had boxed in thousands of customers with incompatible architectures, operating systems, applications software, and machines.

The Microvax II introduction marked the beginning of nonstop announcements over the next eighteen months. Ten VAX computers were unveiled, from bottom to top of the line. And every machine was hooked together by a golden thread of connectivity.

Inside DEC, debate raged between marketing and engineering over the soul of the company. Shields long ago decided that DEC had to turn away from acting like an engineering organization and become a marketing company. Commercial accounts—IBM's stronghold—would respond only to top-notch marketing and sales. Olsen still viewed marketing as the follow-on to quality products. The ultimate marketer, Olsen says, sells "a product that the customer doesn't need or want. When people say we're not marketing oriented, they really mean that. In that area, I will always be naive in the eyes of most of the world."

DEC's marketing prowess—or lack of it—became the press's new focus. DEC doesn't understand marketing, reporters wrote, and therefore can't hope to compete with IBM. Inside DEC, marketers such as Shields and Hughes sought the compromise that would keep Olsen satisfied while silencing the critics. Olsen never approved of television advertising, and his fears were borne out trying to sell PCs that way. He would not be talked into another TV campaign. Yet Shields knew that the time was right for DEC to make a big marketing splash, to let the world hear about this once-obscure computing company. But how to grab that attention was not yet clear.

Success selling VAXes was tempered by the constant question: Can DEC keep it up? Olsen asked himself the same question. "The best things you learn are during the tough times," he says. "We got into all the trouble we were in by having too many years of good times. The question is: Can I pull us through a few years of good times without running into the same old trouble? That's humbling."

Olsen searched for novel ways to keep DEC on track. He called together twenty-four of his top executives and told them to get ready for a day at the warehouse assembling Digital computers. They were allowed to study and even order needed parts. When they arrived, the executives were handed screwdrivers and pliers and set to work. Olsen assigned five different customer problems to each executive. The task was to figure out network-based DEC solutions using the same tools a customer would have available. Olsen talked through the day about the importance of understanding customer problems. Besides getting hands-on experience for the first time in years, the executives received the clear message that Olsen would no longer tolerate empire builders or entrepreneurs seeking personal glory. Everybody now worked together—or they didn't work at Digital.

As the employee head count approached 100,000, the necessity for tighter control became clear to the Executive Committee—but control in the DEC sense, meaning harmony with the existing culture. As Jack Smith put it in 1986: "Discipline allows freedom. The quickest way to let freedom deteriorate is to allow people to do whatever the hell they want to do. Invariably they are going to do something you don't want and you will have to say, 'Don't do that.' And they'll say, 'What happened to all this freedom?' " DEC created boundaries and let workers operate freely within them. "They know what the rules are," Smith says. "They know they can operate aggressively and with total freedom within those rules."

DEC's experiments in the Enfield, Connecticut, plant embodied this new tenet of freedom within limits. The employees themselves managed this manufacturing facility, a kind of grass-roots manufacturing. The concept was simple: create employee autonomy and produce a profitable product. Employees designed their own processes and structure and implemented their own reward systems. "Running a plant, you see lots of things that could be done differently," plant manager Bruce Dillingham told the *Training and Development Journal.* "In applying technology all the time, we forget about the people. That's what triggered me, all that potential in the people." Work teams of twelve to eighteen, a mixture of men and women of all ages, races, and backgrounds, were given autonomy to work out methods for building and testing the product, an electronic module for one of DEC's computers. Enfield workers doubled the production of modules with half the people and half the space.

In Maynard, the reorganization helped unearth a problem at the core of the company, an outdated manufacturing system. DEC didn't have a workforce skilled enough to implement a new automated manufacturing plan. In shifting from a single-product assembly-line system run mostly by direct labor to a highly automated system, DEC faced the problem of what to do with all these workers. Rather than lay off existing employees and search for new talent, DEC chose to retrain. Former materials planners—detail-oriented, creative, willing to practice a new skill—were found to be good programmers. Supervisors were trained to design the manufacturing process of future products.

DEC offered each employee up to twelve months of retraining and so developed more than 4,000 new manufacturing employees without hiring from outside. Many who didn't want to make the transition to the new manufacturing system moved into sales. About 600 left the company.

Olsen searched for a way to continue the tradition of an open, democratic environment built around his unifying vision. In a long memo titled "Business Management III," Olsen summed up the new perspective: "There is no room for sloppy management or secrecy in an organization which is so inter-dependent and which has to cooperate at so many levels," he wrote. "Strategies must be reviewed and modified as competition develops, particularly with the aggressiveness of IBM. They have set about to copy many of our traditional ways of doing business, while we have lost many of them.

"In those areas in which we have been most successful," he continued, "we have had simple open plans which were reviewed and criticized and argued by much of the company. This interchange, struggle and travail of decision-making is what made many of our products great. Our original strategy said that we cannot do everything, we cannot exploit every technology, and we worked hard to pick those areas which are most important to us and which would give us a unique position in the market. And we would not follow everybody into everything. We were often publicly ridiculed because we were not doing everything that everyone felt we should do. We now have to be sure that fear of public ridicule does not force us into trying to do everything, with the result of doing nothing well, or uniquely.

"My theory of management is very simple: The boss or a committee cannot know enough to make a strategy or to make a product or to make a plan. Their job is to approve plans, integrate plans, add wisdom to plans and make sure they form a Corporate plan and strategy."

Olsen's lecture by memo clearly challenged those managers who considered themselves naturals at routine executive tasks such as writing proposals. "People often feel," he wrote, "that driving a car, making budgets and making plans are skills that they are born with, and their macho image of themselves is destroyed if they ever have to admit that there is something they can learn about driving, budgeting or proposing."

He laid out a list of do's and don'ts for proposing ideas. On the "Don't" side:

1. "Don't be dishonest in the slightest way. Don't mislead, don't oversell, don't avoid facts or data. Individuals will never trust you even though they will not publicly raise the issue."

2. "Never say there is unanimous agreement with other groups unless it is absolutely true. Be sure to present other points of view."
3. "Never intimidate the committee or the boss, and never intimidate other groups to agree with your proposals so that you have a unanimous presentation."

On the "Do" list:

1. "Make simple, straightforward proposals that require little risk until the ideas and the competence of the people are proven."
2. "Assume that commitments over a certain value have to go to the top committee of the corporation and those over another value have to go to the Board of Directors. And assume that it is not only polite, but wise to get them on board with the idea well before they are asked to make a decision."
3. "Remember that ideas that make us unique can give us a unique position more easily than ideas that say we should now do what IBM did two or three years ago."
4. "Above all, remember that our future is dependent on good ideas, original ideas, unique ideas and people who think them out so that we can be successful with them."

DEC's unique idea—networking-compatible midrange computers—carried the company into the mid-1980s as the predominant systems challenger to IBM. Analysts who had lined up to disparage the company just months before were now heaping praise on the strategy. In 1986, Olsen unveiled a new marketing campaign: "Digital Has It Now." No one could miss the message's meaning—IBM didn't have it now. Ken Olsen was suddenly called the brilliant strategist who, despite his supposed lack of marketing savvy and slick corporate demeanor, was once again the master of minis, the darling of Wall Street.

*"Every time we have done the same as everyone
else, we have failed."*

—Ken Olsen

34
The End of the Rainbow

IN EARLY 1985, AT&T came courting again.
Olivetti chairman Carlo di Benedetti, AT&T's partner in
personal computers, revived the idea of taking over DEC.
Inside AT&T's corporate office, Morris Tanenbaum, executive
vice president for finance and planning, along with John
Segall, senior vice president for corporate strategy and development, took up the quest.

After researching merger possibilities, the corporate staff
advocated the acquisition of DEC for all of the reasons given in
1983. The most powerful argument: an AT&T-DEC alliance
could match IBM in resources and image. DEC's stock early in
1985 hovered in a low enough price range (about $80 per
share) to make a takeover financially feasible. AT&T's computer systems division, however, balked. That part of AT&T
looked at DEC and saw basic product incompatibility—their
respective computers didn't work together. Besides the mismatch of technology, the two companies lacked complemen-
tary strengths. Both were strong technically and weak in
marketing or sales. And research revealed that DEC was a
high-cost manufacturer, just like AT&T.

As AT&T wrestled with takeover possibilities throughout 1985, DEC continued its furious climb in revenues and earnings. Toward the end of the year, its stock traded above $130—more than fifty points higher than when AT&T began contemplating its target. DEC was now worth too much to be bought outright by AT&T. Suddenly, the acquisition plan turned into a merger offer. And the new questions centered on which Olsen/Olson—Ken or James—would run the show.

During its months of deliberations, AT&T did not approach Ken Olsen or anyone else in DEC management to test reactions. "That is sort of vintage AT&T," says a former executive. "They do all this internal work and never raise their head into the outside world."

A week before the sponsors of the merger were to put their plan formally before AT&T chairman Charles Brown, he flew to Florida to discuss the deal informally with Ken Olsen. According to a former AT&T insider, Brown sketched out the proposal for AT&T and Digital to merge. Olsen reportedly replied, "Over my dead body. It's a terrible idea. We don't want to be acquired by you, and we don't want to merge with you." After twenty-eight years of going it alone, Olsen was not going to give up his company now. AT&T discarded a hostile takeover as financially impractical and finally gave up altogether linking with DEC.

Despite the categorical refusal by Olsen, the AT&T-DEC merger rumors persisted throughout the year. He paid little attention. A booming business kept him more than occupied. While the midrange VAXes were being gobbled up as fast as they could be produced, Olsen turned his attention to a lingering and painful question: what about the low end?

By 1985, DEC had halted production of the Professional PC in its Westfield, Massachusetts, plant. The machine couldn't even die a quiet death. The *New York Times* learned of the production shutdown of a Digital personal computer and assumed that it was the manufacturing of the Rainbow that was being stopped. Actually, DEC had shifted Rainbow production to the Far East. The *Times* didn't understand that when DEC spoke about PCs, it meant the Pro, despite the fact that the Rainbow was the only one of the original three low-end machines selling in any quantity. Barry James Folsom was floored. His machine, which had survived lack of funding, lack of faith, and lack of marketing effort, was now being declared dead in the *New York Times*. Folsom remembers, "It was like reading that your child has died."

The low end was becoming DEC's Death Valley. Olsen acted as catalyst and obstacle at the same time. He very much wanted a solution to the personal computer question; but he refused to accept that IBM owned the industry standard. DEC, he believed, would win in this market by doing what it had always done: create a unique solution.

DEC had pursued this uniqueness strategy from the onset of its PC plans. In a November 1983 memo, Olsen made clear the philosophical direction the company's developers should take: "It has been the tradition at Digital to always look for a different and unique approach to a product," he wrote. "It seems to me that every time we have done the same as everyone else, we have failed, and we have only had successes when we have been unique and different."

In another memo, he described the kind of proposal he wanted brought to the Executive Committee. "A plan for the low end should be simple and straightforward and should be made by someone standing up without charts," he wrote. "These questions may be considered red tape that slow down young people who are out to save the Company, but these are questions that I have to live with long after the young people are gone."

Even while praising DEC for its financial turnaround, analysts kept insisting that the company needed a competitive low-end computer. Folsom, the last holdover from the Pro-Rainbow-DECmate debacle, finally saw PC reality and won approval for DEC to build a true IBM-compatible machine. Once again, Olsen involved himself in the packaging design, delaying getting the new machine off the drawing board. Folsom knew that each day DEC went without a marketable personal computer cost the company thousands of dollars and entry into new customer accounts. He suggested that DEC buy out and market as its own a low-price clone from a third-party vendor. It wasn't the best solution, but at least DEC would get into the PC-compatible game. But Olsen rejected the cheap, Far East import brought to him—the packaging wasn't elegant enough.

In late 1984, Jeff Kalb was given responsibility for the low end. Kalb can't quite figure out how he ended up with that unenviable assignment. He was happy enough as group manager of semiconductor operations. But slowly he was handed more and more responsibility for low-end products until he ended up with control.

Kalb had witnessed the first PC go-round. He joined DEC in 1981 during the creation of the Pro and six months later made a presentation to the Operations Committee listing the reasons it wouldn't succeed. Olsen's response: "If you have an only child, you have to learn to love it."

During his first year as part of DEC's semiconductor group, Kalb envisioned opening up the Microvax's proprietary chip—then in development—to third-party software builders. He hoped that it would become the industry standard in workstations, much as the IBM PC became the standard in personal computers. Kalb theorizes today that workstation companies like Sun and Apollo would never have existed if DEC had tried this bold move. As a recent addition to DEC, he searched for someone to champion his radical idea. Kalb's group asked Andy Knowles, then head of the low end, to lead the effort. Battle-scarred already, Knowles replied, "No way, I can't do it again. There's too much pain associated with it." Kalb never found a willing leader, and the idea simply died.

Olsen was clearly unhappy with the course of DEC's low-end machines. In January 1985, Kalb sent a memo to Folsom and members of the Executive Committee that effectively killed the Rainbow 25, DEC's latest attempt at IBM PC compatibility, and set the company on still another path—developing a new personal computer to be called VAXmate. It would be much more than IBM PC-compatible. The VAX-mate would be an elegant desktop machine incorporating the best of DEC's networking capabilities, including a connection to Ethernet. VAXmate would get the highest corporate priority in order to minimize time-to-market, considered the crucial element of success. Kalb suggested that the first units should be ready for shipment in six months, by July. "While this may seem like an impossible task, we should only accept defeat if and when every alternative has been exhausted," he wrote.

Folsom said good-bye to DEC in March. He could see that with its current strategy, the company was not going to wrest market share from IBM in personal computers. Sun Microsystems had been courting Folsom for a year and a half, and finally Folsom said yes. Unlike the departure scenes of some of his predecessors, Folsom left Olsen on cordial terms. "Ken sort of viewed me as a son," says Folsom, reflecting a frequent sentiment among DEC's younger managers over the years. "Someone once told me, 'Barry, for a period of time, you were what he wanted his son to be.' "

Olsen claimed to have learned a lesson during DEC's initial venture into the PC marketplace. But his decisions proved otherwise. He only reluctantly accepted IBM PC compatibility as a necessity and still believed that corporate users wanted the elegant packaging he pushed Digital to design into desktop machines.

Problems cropped up trying to implement the VAXmate design. The beautifully sculpted machine ran without a fan, thus eliminating the bothersome whirring noise common to other PCs. But without the fan, the machine ran too hot. And fitting components into the sleek design caused nightmares for manufacturing. Delay followed delay, and news of the machine leaked to the trade press six months before it was announced. *Computerworld* ran a product sketch and listed the VAXmate's specifications.

Developing the VAXmate tried the patience of Kalb's engineering team, just as it had the other personal computer makers. He learned firsthand what those before him had discovered about the low end at DEC. "It is extremely painful to carry through a new idea," he says. "You can do it once or twice, and then you don't want to do it anymore."

More important, too many people inside DEC had been burned by supporting low-end machines. Marketing and sales didn't want anything to do with the VAXmate. Says Kalb, "It was the kind of thing where people said, 'If I don't get out in front of it, I won't be the one on the end of the spear.' "

In the end, VAXmate fell victim to what remained of the matrix structure. The machine became the focal point of a tug-of-war between the networking and office systems groups and Kalb's small-systems team. Arguments raged over how the computer would be positioned: as a stand-alone PC or as a machine geared solely to the networked office environment?

The VAXmate finally appeared in September 1986. Unlike DEC's other low-end introductions over the years, the VAXmate announcement was kept low-key, part of a series of new products providing IBM PC connectivity to the VAX environment. VAXmate arrived too late—a year later than Kalb originally proposed. It also carried a high $5,000 price tag for functionality that was clearly not in demand from personal computer users. VAXmate reflected Olsen's philosophy of competing on features, never on price. DEC could barely sell VAXmate into its own strong accounts. Most had already bought the PCs they needed—from IBM.

Though corporate America consumed millions of PCs, Olsen refused to accept their special value. At a conference in Boston in November 1987, he said, "Five years ago, people said you fill your organizations with personal computers and magic will happen. And people bought them by the thousands. It probably caused the computer industry recession because they all put their money in that and it didn't do what they wanted. Personal computers did wonderful things for people personally, but they didn't work together for the organization." Olsen liked to blame the media for hyping PCs. "One thing the press will never understand is personal computers," he says.

Kalb saw that people in the low end spent most of their time writing new plans or justifying existing ones. The company's unwillingness to adapt to market demands became more than he could handle. He also wanted a chance to be a general manager, and like others before him, he realized that Olsen alone filled that position.

Kalb thought about his decision for several months and then

announced his resignation in the spring of 1987. Although not on par with Bell's departure, Kalb's leaving rippled through the organization. Olsen broke from his usual posture on resigning executives and asked him to stay. He had seen Kalb as an emerging star of the engineering organization. But Kalb couldn't be dissuaded. Tired, burned out, and seeking a new challenge, he moved back to his native California.

By early 1987, DEC stopped talking publicly about the VAXmate. When pressed, executives call the machine a success because it met, they claim, projected sales figures. But in fact, the machine is yet another disappointment in the low end. Olsen said in November 1987, "We never intended it to be a big seller." By early 1988, DEC had already started work on still another PC, known internally as Personal VAX. "This will be DEC's third trip to the desktop altar," says consultant Marty Gruhn. "It's amazing a company like that cannot introduce an acceptable desktop product."

"We're planning to be one of those who survive."
—Ken Olsen

35
Front Page

T HE APRIL 3, 1986, page-one story in the *Wall Street Journal* epitomizes Ken Olsen's ascendence to business superstardom. The article pointed out that "Mr. Olsen is still firmly in charge at Digital—the largest U.S. manufacturer still headed by its founder. Moreover, he and Digital are back in favor on Wall Street and are increasingly feared by competitors." But the *Journal*, which prides itself on accuracy, accompanied the story of Ken Olsen with a picture of James Olson, the new chairman of AT&T.

Olsen cared little about his obscurity. He preferred the stable solitude of the shadows to the unsteady glare of the spotlight. He was bemused by the sudden change in the perception of him. The same analysts who had called for his resignation were now analyzing his genius. He understood the fickleness of the media and sought no vindication. The swiftness of the turnaround only solidified Olsen's belief that things had never been as bad as they were made out to be. He realized that many young business writers had gotten caught up in the excitement of personal computers, and he hadn't been able to explain to them DEC's different view of computing. "If I couldn't explain it to them, I can't really blame them for not grasping it," he says. Deep down, Olsen knew that the reorganization of the company had cut DEC open, and the press was just reporting what it saw.

Computerworld declared 1986 "The Year of DEC." Industry analysts were predicting that the VAX strategy would propel the company into a twenty-four-month joy ride. The competition would have to scramble to catch up. DEC stock continued to rise by five- and eight-point leaps, and in the spring of 1986, it reached $180 per share and split two for one.

In February, DEC transformed the parking garage of Boston's Hynes Auditorium into a glitzy computer exposition called DECworld. Jack Shields assigned Bob Hughes to spend five million of DEC's dollars on a marketing gamble—a single-company computer conference. Twenty thousand customers and potential customers were flown in to see hands-on demonstrations of just what DEC was selling. The parking garage became a pseudocorporation—an entire "business" full of VAXes hooked together with Ethernet.

Unlike DECtown three years before, DECworld was a coherent, focused demonstration of technology. DEC filled the exhibition floor with trained employees who could explain, in business terms, the value of networking. Potential customers could see what DEC could do for them by sitting at CRTs in simulated retail, banking, insurance, manufacturing, educational, and medical environments. The decision to put on DECworld in lieu of television advertising showed new DEC marketing thinking. Hundreds of millions of dollars in orders flowed in, and the show renewed interest and excitement in the company.

Inside DEC, the executives still worried, how long can it last? William Hanson, vice president of manufacturing, told the *New York Times*, "We talk about it every day. We can't believe our own snake oil. But this is more than just temporary—we're riding a new wave."

According to Win Hindle, the prosperity inspired great introspection. "You get overconfident; you think you can't make a mistake," he says. "When you think you know everything, you're in the worst position to make decisions because you think you're infallible. And we worry about that, and we'll worry about that even more in the next year or so. As long as we're on top of the heap, we have to worry about staying there. Ken has an ability to go into the organization and pick up something that he senses is wrong and get it examined so we can fix it. That ability to reach out to all parts of the Digital organization is a trademark of his."

Olsen saw an industry in transition. "The nature of the computer business has changed," he said. "You used to have a lot of people who could make computers. Those who worked harder and moved faster could make them faster. It's just like it was with automobile makers or airplane manufacturers. There used to be many, now there are just a few left. That has to happen in the computer industry. I won't say to whom or when. We're planning to be one of those that survive."

Suddenly, Olsen's self-imposed challenge on a cold Poughkeepsie night in 1953 was becoming real. He was beating IBM at its own game—commercial computing. Some inside DEC believe that Olsen has stayed at the helm of DEC so long to prove that his view of computing is correct—and make IBM pay for its arrogance. Says one former vice president, "With financial security clearly there and his own place in computing history fairly safeguarded, I believe he's out to settle an old score with IBM." The chance had finally come.

The press had actually begun comparing DEC to IBM in the midseventies. But the battle then was no contest, just a fantasy dreamed up to make good copy. Now DEC was actually taking territory. In 1986, Carol Muratore, a security analyst with Morgan Stanley, calculated that DEC had captured $2 billion worth of office systems from IBM customers in the past year. DEC was "IBM's most serious challenger in 20 years," she said in *Fortune*.

For years Olsen had cautioned his managers not to position DEC against IBM. In the early 1980s, IBM was growing at the rate of one DEC every single year! The wisest course in competing against a company eight times your size seemed to be to deny that you are competing. Olsen himself often referred to Big Blue in interviews, but his remarks varied depending on his mood. Sometimes he'd say nothing to stir up controversy, claiming that DEC was too small for IBM to worry about. Other times, he'd speak bluntly about his rival. In a 1986 *Wall Street Journal* article, he went so far as to tell a somewhat risque joke about IBM's technique of announcing new technology long before it delivers. "A woman, married to an IBM salesman, complains that her marriage is unconsummated," Olsen said. "For three years, he sat on the foot of the bed telling me how great it was going to be." DEC, Olsen says, "won't stoop to announce products that we don't have ready yet."

After sidestepping IBM for three decades, Olsen was lacing up the gloves. In the office market, DEC decided it was no longer becoming to compete against Wang, a company sitting on a powder keg of troubles. DEC knew it would soon pass this neighborhood rival. The new target was IBM. "To our mind, IBM didn't have a presence in office automation," says a former public relations employee. "But the way it always works with IBM, they say, 'We're in the business,' and lo and behold, everyone else starts saying they're number one."

The press characterized the battle as DEC's products vs. IBM's marketing. DEC was painted as a stodgy, dull organization—a reflection of its founder—without much flair for selling itself. DECworld started to deflate that argument.

DEC never professed to be the marketing force of IBM. In Olsen's mind, DEC was doing well enough pitching its message in its own way. "Secretly, I think we've done really clever marketing," he said in 1984. "The marketing we've done may not be obvious to people. We write down everything we know about our products. We don't try to hide things or overexaggerate. That's a technique of marketing that may not be good for the soap industry, but it's good for technical people."

By 1986, Olsen learned a lesson in marketing from Shields and Hughes. He began to realize that factual brochures alone did not sell products. The catchphrase at DEC became "listen to our customers." The old unstated presumption—that DEC engineers knew better than the customers what the customers needed—had to be put aside.

Olsen let Shields lead the way. With him aggressively driving the business, DEC began to beef up the sales force, hiring by the thousands and redeploying 5,000 from manufacturing. Shields set up massive training courses in networking and VAX computing to get knowledgeable salesmen out into the field quickly. Many of those hired came from IBM, as well as other vendors mired in the computer industry slump. They brought with them a more stylish, businesslike selling approach that was new to DEC. And they came with a taste for commission sales. Olsen and DEC finally compromised, instituting a commission-like bonus for the top 20 percent sales performers. The new marketing target—the upper-level corporate decision maker.

Hughes instituted an industry marketing plan that moved the company even further away from the original product-line philosophy. DEC would now sell into specific industries with customized applications and solutions built around the VAX line. "The marketing group vice presidents decided that instead of letting sales reps invent company strategy daily for their customers, we'd put it together for them right up front," he says. "We grouped all five million businesses into sixty industries and then organized those around three sectors—government, services, and basic industry marketing." This integrated marketing plan aimed at doubling market share. The new setup took DEC into markets where it had traditionally been weak, such as financial services, and strengthened its presence where it was strong, such as education.

As DEC sold more directly—and profitably—into corporate accounts without a middleman, it allowed its OEM business, which used to account for more than 50 percent of sales, to sag. Suddenly, the name Digital Equipment Corporation, which had been only vaguely recognizable in the executive suites of the Fortune 500, became a respected corporate identity.

Meanwhile, IBM continued to stagnate. The company tried desperately to find a way out of the hole that it had dug itself into with incompatible designs and operating systems. While DEC was connecting IBM PCs into the VAX environment, IBM was floundering at getting its PCs to hook to its own minicomputers, let alone anyone else's. John Akers, the former fighter pilot now heading IBM, presided over a string of quarters in which profits dropped. The number reached five in a row by late 1987, clearly IBM's worst performance since the Great Depression. In all, net income plunged from $6.5 billion in 1985 to $4.7 billion in 1986, and IBM tightened its belt from Armonk to Japan. The company trimmed its work-force by 15,000 and redeployed 11,000 employees to sales and service in 1987. Still, at $51 billion in revenues in 1987, IBM remained the fourth largest industrial company in the Fortune 500—and the most profitable. By 1987, DEC had mush-roomed to $9.3 billion in revenues and broke the $1 billion mark in profits for the first time. Though the difference was still staggering, DEC suddenly was one-fifth the size of IBM and growing stronger.

IBM began to leak word of a "VAX killer," a new midrange system called the 9370 that would supposedly win back the hearts and minds of customers considering DEC solutions. IBM officials publicly acknowledged that the war was no longer IBM vs. AT&T, or IBM vs. the Japanese. The scorecard read "IBM vs. DEC."

IBM showed its muscle by landing a $400 million office-automation contract right under the eyes of Olsen in the summer of 1986. Ford chose IBM despite Olsen's presence on the board of directors and DEC's strong bid for the job. His response: "Most people are dependent on their MIS [manage-ment information systems] groups, and the MIS groups are dependent on IBM. We tell our friends it's a mistake because MIS is not the group that knows the most about how a company runs." At the same time Olsen was dismissing the role of MIS, DEC's marketers were trying to sell to this powerful group that had been IBM loyalists for so long.

Olsen stayed out in front at all major DEC announcements, preaching his networking message. He was the star of the show at the European version of DECworld in the south of France in September of 1986. It was called DECville. Thousands of overseas customers and journalists poured into Cannes for the exhibition. Europe now generated nearly 50 percent of DEC's revenue, and DECville, like its American counterpart, was a smash.

So hot was the company that the press hardly mentioned the ship DEC anchored off the coast to house its employees in Cannes. The only large cruise ship DEC could secure as an offshore hotel was named the *Achille Lauro,* the vessel just hijacked by Arab terrorists. Using the *Achille Lauro* would have surely brought reams of ridicule from the press three years earlier. But DECville went off without a hitch.

Because of terrorist gangs reportedly operating in France, Israeli frogmen patrolled the waters near the ship on twenty-four-hour duty. American and European bodyguards watched over Olsen. He detested that kind of attention. While a limousine waited to escort him back to his hotel one day, Olsen slipped out the side door of the convention center and strolled back to his hotel unwatched.

In late October came the high-water mark. *Fortune* put Olsen on the cover and deemed him America's most successful entrepreneur. The magazine said, "A few, like Teledyne's Henry Singleton or Wal-Mart founder Sam Walton, have done better for their shareholders or made themselves richer than Olsen. But none has created as mighty or important an industrial enterprise as DEC. And on that basis, *Fortune* considers him the greatest success."

Olsen didn't make it easy for *Fortune.* At first he refused to be photographed. He didn't want to appear on the cover, saying that it was time for other DEC executives to get some attention. But *Fortune* persuaded him. The magazine hired a French photographer to take the picture in Cannes. The man didn't understand Ken Olsen. There would be no posing and hours of shooting. The photographer had a half hour.

Fortune editors judged the photographs unusable and called Olsen again in Maynard. They suggested that new pictures be taken in a more relaxed environment. Olsen said that the most likely place he'd be found—other than at work—was in his canoe. So with his canoe strapped to his car—a familiar sight at DEC—Olsen and the *Fortune* photographer set off for the nearby Sudbury River.

Wearing a lumberjack shirt and an old fishing hat on the magazine cover, Olsen looks more like a suburban gardener than a business sensation. In an odd moment of spontaneity, he posed standing up in his canoe for a picture accompanying the article. The photographs surprised some of his employees. Few had seen him dressed like that. But as one employee put it, "Ken is Ken." There he was, the rumpled plaid shirt with an open button seemingly burst by his paunch, old work pants, and a pair of thick-soled boots. Grasping the paddle with his name stenciled on it like a kid off to camp, he stood unsteadily, grinning awkwardly at the camera. The moment of glory.

At the company's annual meeting a week later, Olsen took the podium and said, "Before I start, let me assure you that I'm not that stupid. I know you're not supposed to stand up in a canoe."

With the issue on the newsstands, Olsen stopped into a book store in Maynard. The shop, in honor of its local celebrity, put stacks of the magazine on its counter. Spotting Olsen, the store manager rushed over to congratulate him. "What do you think?" the man asked.

"Well," Olsen replied, embarrassed. "My mother didn't like the picture."

"When the message finally gets across, we're going to need all the cash we can get to handle the growth."

—*Ken Olsen*

36
Riding Out the Good Times

ENTERING 1987, DEC'S surge continued. But in order to boldly challenge IBM, DEC had to be ready to endure the harshest scrutiny of its existence. Not surprising, this attention caused noticeable changes to those inside DEC. The once offbeat engineering haven was now smack in the mainstream of American business.

While some old-timers suffered the stress of the metamorphosis, Jack Shields felt in his element. "He, more than any other single individual, represents the new DEC," says analyst Stephen Smith of Paine Webber. Shields's aggressive style ruffled many DEC executives both past and present; but most agree that if you are going to jump into the icy waters with IBM, you need a sharklike mentality. Shields liked to inspire his sales troops by telling them the projected date that DEC would surpass IBM in revenues: July 2007. Thinking the idea would spark the sales force, the company went so far as to print up invitations: "We're going to have a party!" the note said. "If our current growth rates continue (and they will), and if IBM's current growth continues (and they will be hard-pressed to do that), we will pass them in revenue and certainly in profit by July 10, 2007. More details to follow." DEC sent the invitations to certain customers and analysts—and they were shocked by the premature boast. The marketing campaign was quickly pulled.

Many in DEC realized the danger of arrogance—or even just appearing that way. Shields sent a long memo to his salespeople, urging them to head off that view of DEC in the minds of the public and press before it could take hold. "I wanted to make sure that each of you were sensitive to the fact that some of our customers and consultants have been quoted in the press as perceiving us to be arrogant and complacent," he said. "We must change this perception quickly. When even one customer holds this view, we have no choice but to reflect on the behavior we all exhibit on a daily basis."

The memo praised the staff for a winning attitude but cautioned that the very things that made the sales force strong could lead to a negative image. Shields laid out the key elements to avoiding a bad reputation:

- "It is okay to say 'I do not know the answer' as long as you get back to the customer in a prompt manner with the answer."

- "It is not appropriate to disparage competition. We should be careful to stress the advantages of our way of doing computing and never the negatives of our competitors."

- "One of the cardinal rules of a successful sales organization is to never argue with the customer. The customer is always right. Nothing leads to the perception of complacency and arrogance more than arguing with the customer, particularly over trivial technical matters."

- "For the first time ever, you are calling on some people who have made nothing but IBM decisions for decades. Be cautious that no matter how conservative and eloquent your presentation, you are indeed challenging the prior decisions of this management team."

Shields concluded by repeating that arrogance and complacency, rather than the competition, were the factors that stood between "us and our goals."

DEC and Olsen spent much of 1987 trying to remain humble. But in the light of unparalleled success, it was a difficult task.

As the sales numbers rolled in each quarter, analysts and the press soaked DEC in positive reviews. Fiscal 1986 had been a record year, with a 38 percent increase in profits in a slump-ridden industry. In the fourth quarter alone, DEC racked up a 138 percent increase in profits over the same quarter a year earlier.

In September, the thrilling year reached its apex. Digital grabbed the attention of the business world in a way that no company has ever done. It invited nearly 50,000 customers, reporters, and employees to the next installment of DECworld, the most extravagant edition of this DEC-only exposition. The massive show required $30 million to $40 million dollars, a year's planning, and a fifth of the company's work force to fuel its nine-day run at the World Trade Center in Boston. Outside the expo, the world's largest cruise ship stretched along the dock—a floating DEC hotel. The *QE II* testified to how big Digital had become.

The company, so tight-lipped about every dollar during the previous show eighteen months before, announced that this DECworld investment might result in upward of $1 billion worth of orders. Later Digital raised its estimate to nearly $2 billion. Shields announced that DEC now sold 1,000 computers per week and would soon ship its 100,000th VAX.

Olsen rode the crest of Digital's wave. At the kickoff press conference for DECworld at Anthony's Pier Four Restaurant, he no longer defended past actions. He was bold. He acted even a little antagonistic toward IBM. Despite his own admonition about staying humble during the good times, he appeared, uncharacteristically, almost arrogant.

The company, for example, used DECworld to unveil its next-generation Microvax. A reporter asked Olsen whether this machine was DEC's answer to IBM's 9370, the much heralded "VAX killer." "We never thought the 9370 needed an answer," he replied. Another asked what Olsen planned to do with the $2.2 billion in cash lying in DEC's coffers. "When the message finally gets across, we're going to need all the cash we can get to handle the growth," he said. Presumptuous or not, he appeared to be right.

The reviews were unanimous: "Digital is the talk of the industry," wrote analyst Jean Orr of Drexel Burnham Lambert. "Competitors are comparing themselves to Digital at least as much as IBM these days; in many cases, the comparison with IBM is more favorable. We believe that Digital will grow 20 percent per year over the next five years."

The awards for excellence, which had vanished in 1984, reappeared. *Electronic Business* magazine surveyed 1,400 industry executives and 1,000 securities analysts. They voted DEC the top computer maker for the industrial market. "Under reasonably heavy criticism, they followed their own path. And they've been right," the publication stated.

At DEC, there was great irony in the offspring of success. Employees began to hear what they had thought impossible: that their company was becoming like IBM. Having met the ultimate enemy, the company was actually taking on its characteristics.

Olsen unwittingly set the tone himself. He spoke out with his usual candor about such issues as industry standards and product directions, but now he was a highly visible industry spokesman, and his words were carefully scrutinized. Negative comments about General Motors's attempt to create a manufacturing automation standard made business and trade journal headlines and cast Olsen as brazen. Analysts were surprised that Olsen would argue over technology in public with GM, a major DEC customer.

DEC made certain IBM-like moves, such as closing the architecture on its BI-Bus, the latest connection to VAX machines. This action prevented third-party vendors from writing software for the newest VAXes without obtaining licenses. When questioned about this change in policy at a press conference, Olsen replied, "We paid millions to develop this technology, and we're not going to just give it away."

DEC decided to deal only with large accounts. Smaller customers—those buying under $500,000 a year in products and services—were turned away to a value-added reseller. DEC tightened its margins and took charge in the larger accounts, taking business from its traditional partners, the OEMs. In general, DEC made it clear to the OEMs and value-added resellers that the salad days were over.

Despite the GM flap, Olsen didn't hesitate to air his pet peeves publicly. He used a major computer seminar in November as a forum to denigrate two of the most popular personal computer applications: spreadsheets and graphics. "Graphics are terrible," he railed. "They are the second worst contribution to society after spreadsheets. Spreadsheets will go down in history as the worst thing that ever happened to business. If you start a business and can't remember every line of your P & L statement when you are lying in bed at night, then you've got too many lines. If you're running your business on a spreadsheet and you're stuck in traffic and can't remember that spreadsheet, you're in trouble. That P & L statement has to be yours. And a spreadsheet will take it away from you."

In one of the stranger moves during this period of intense competition with DEC, IBM offered to supply vital semiconductor chip technology to its rival. The reason: reportedly to fend off increasing American industrial dependence on Japanese suppliers. According to the book *Trading Places: How We Allowed Japan to Take the Lead*, by Clyde Prestowitz, IBM approached DEC in mid-1987 offering "to transfer certain key technologies. At first, DEC suspected a trick," Prestowitz wrote. "Then it realized the objective was to prevent DEC from falling even further into Japanese hands."

DEC would not officially comment on the matter, though Olsen acknowledged that the two companies offered each other technology from time to time. The fierceness of the DEC-IBM rivalry made this intriguing story front-page news in the *New York Times*.

Also making headlines was the suddenly cozy relationship

between DEC and Apple. During the summer of 1987, Olsen took a rest from DEC at his vacation home in Maine, near the Canadian border. There he heard from a summer neighbor down east near Penobscot Bay—Apple chairman John Sculley. Sculley called Olsen, and the two began talking about bringing their companies closer together. Apple had been seeking ways to sell its Macintosh computers into corporate environments, and it too faced the massive market presence of IBM. Customers of both DEC and Apple found a commonality in the two environments, a certain sense that both of these "outsiders" sought to free the computer world from the shackles of IBM.

In January 1988, in meetings on both coasts, Olsen and Sculley appeared together to announce a DEC-Apple agreement to integrate Macintoshes into VAX networks. Though the talk fell far short of a merger of any kind, the pact showed how far Olsen had come in realizing the marketing ramifications of combating IBM. It put him in the position of endorsing the Mac as a desktop machine, a graphic admission of DEC's utter failure there, as Olsen himself described it. Analysts applauded this flexibility and acknowledgment of reality. For Olsen, it was the first time he shared the spotlight with another industry leader to admit that DEC could not go at it completely alone. Sculley characterized the DEC-Apple union as "a dream alliance."

The ascension of DEC to the top tier as IBM's chief rival caused rumblings within the Mill and other DEC facilities. Longtime employees worried about breaking ties to DEC's past. With more than 120,000 employees around the world, the DEC experience had changed irrevocably. Messages commenting on the new world of Digital appeared regularly on the vast electronic mail system.

One recently hired engineer complained that DEC felt like a company "split in half, fragmented and full of isolated individuals who missed out on the beginning, can't get connected, can't share the old stories about Ken walking the halls on Saturdays in the Mill."

A veteran employee calling himself a "1967 immigrant" took exception to this notion and keyed in a long reply on his view of the company. "Some of us, even in 1967 felt out of place, distant, unconnected," he wrote. "What was the culture and how could I fit into it? We were hiring about 25 to 30 people per week back then, and that seemed incredible.

"The average age was about 22 or 23, and it was the '60s, so the culture within DEC at the time was one of business and one of rebellion. We grew up together, fooled around together, got engaged, got married, got in trouble, as one big wave growing within DEC.

"We had windows for air conditioning, oil on the floors that many of us slipped and fell on, and spiders that fell on our heads when they sprayed the Mill. We fished out of the windows, made blow guns from conduit, rode around on fork lift trucks. I saw people come for interviews and leave saying that they would never work in a dump like this. It looked pretty good to us. This is where we worked and played. And built products. This is where we came back to after being in the hospital for exhaustion, after working till we dropped. This place is where we busted into the stockroom over the weekend because we needed the parts to put in a last-minute change. This is where we used heat guns to cook our suppers so we could keep on working.

"This was the place that when there wasn't any work, we sorted screws, swept parking lots, painted lines, read technical manuals, or were moved to other groups to help until things picked up.

"I talked to an individual a few weeks ago and he told me that DEC was out of control, that there was no way we could manage moving from 115,000 people to 150,000 without falling apart. I laughed and said that when I started, there were 2,000 of us and that now there are 115,000 and I was still here. That we were still making it and that we knew how to grow because we never stopped growing.

"When we were in trouble, we told someone. We didn't hide things. We asked for help and help would come. When we made mistakes, our mentors would pick us up, dust us off, smile and send us onward. Today, if someone fails, we put them out to pasture; some come back, some don't.

"DEC has a culture, but it didn't stop years ago like most people believe. If you stay around long enough you will understand it, not because you talked to a lot of the old folks, but because you became a part of it, lived it, slept it, loved it."

In most respects, DEC changed little in its concern for employees. DEC earned respect in the industry by spending several hundreds of thousands of dollars investigating an apparently high incidence of miscarriages among women employees in its Hudson, Massachusetts, semiconductor plant. The study became the largest examination of occupational effects on the health of production workers on semiconductor assembly lines. The results alerted an industry that continued exposure to semiconductor materials caused a higher rate of miscarriages. DEC was applauded for revealing the Hudson plant situation voluntarily despite the potentially negative publicity it could generate.

While offering a superior work environment, DEC didn't stray from Olsen's conservative views on paying people. Despite record revenues and profits, individual employees below managerial rank generally shared little in the financial rewards. Olsen's penchant for pressing harder during the good times showed up in his hard line on expenditures. Salaries did not go up hand in hand with profits, but rather, with the cost of living. Osterhoff's granite hand kept the pressure on for financial restraints.

To the rank and file, the lines of power and influence became more clearly marked than ever before. Though the matrix is very much intact despite the dismantling of the product lines, it is easier to see where direct actions will lead. Ideas continue to bubble up from anywhere in the company. A former twenty-year IBM veteran now at DEC points to a fundamental difference between the two companies. "Here I can pick up the phone and talk to anybody in this company," he says. "You don't do that at IBM." But gaining consensus through open debate became seriously threatened. "A lot has changed as the company has gotten bigger," says a former vice president. "Open debate just doesn't work very well when you've got 100 people in on it."

The strain is felt more intensely at the higher levels of the company. Political infighting doesn't focus on product lines as much as on marketing vs. technical issues. The company has divided up, some say, between Jack Smith and Jack Shields— engineering vs. marketing.

DEC is tilting toward marketing. "Now all the internal groups want to do their own marketing," says consultant Marty Gruhn. "But the last person in the world who should tell you about a product is the guy who invented it. He'll tell you everything you don't want to know about it."

DEC is still not the marketing juggernaut of its chief competitor. Despite the best intentions of the marketing proponents, DEC remains at its core an engineer's company. As long as Olsen is in charge, it will remain so. Shields's challenge is to convince Olsen that DEC must become more marketing driven rather than technology driven. Says one DEC watcher, "Engineers are still the pampered children; don't make them mad, let them play. It's very frustrating for the guys in the trenches."

Though DEC spends more than 10 percent of revenue on R&D, some analysts and employees believe the company is simply riding on Gordon Bell's strategy and that without him, there is no vision of the future. Smith is not generally viewed as the engineer who can lead Digital into the 1990s.

Bell watches closely, still bonded to DEC after being gone five years and immersed in his second start-up company. "Engineering cannot be run as a process," he says. "It has to be based on content, starting at the top. I'd like to hear about something interesting in development and am prepared to congratulate them when they do. They should be able to do something interesting with over $1 billion in R&D."

Digital now lacks a single engineering mastermind like Bell, though top VAX builders like Strecker and Demmer remain. Perhaps a company with more than $11 billion in annual revenue can no longer rely on one man, even if he is a visionary. The question DEC faces is: What should it do when the VAX architecture runs out of power? Writing for *Computerworld* in September 1987, Bell stressed that VAX/VMS has a

302 THE ULTIMATE ENTREPRENEUR

long life ahead of it, a life that should take DEC well into the next decade. But he pointed out that the hardware follow-on to VAX—VAX II—is already overdue. "I would have probably urged for greater innovation and carried on enough experiments to have selected a VAX II architecture by 1986 and delivery in 1988—a decade after the VAX-11/780."

No such follow-on is yet in sight. In the spring of 1988, DEC introduced version V of its VMS software and several new mid- to high-end VAX computers, effectively revamping most of the VAX line. Olsen said, "When we decided in 1975 or so on VAX/ VMS, we decided we would make an architecture that would last approximately forever. It's the same architecture and operating system now as thirteen years ago," he said. "The software written then still plays on it. Any careful observer will admit that VAX/VMS is the only modern architecture and operating system." Olsen then repeated a favorite joke to back up his point: "The reason the Russians want to steal VAXes all the time is because that's where the software is."

Bell cautions that DEC could run into trouble by "thinking VAX is the end, not simply the best thing around today. . . . While nothing is yet in the marketplace to challenge it, several new systems will. This thinking leads to arrogance."

DEC is searching for the answer to what is life after VAX. Smith says, "There may be other market opportunities that will require a different approach to computing than the VAX/ VMS architecture, and we have proponents out there every single day, banging away at that. We're constantly doing advanced development in those areas."

At DECworld, the company set up a "secret room" filled with next-generation products in prototype stages. The high-tech candy store displayed newly developed minicomputers, data storage devices, desktop computers, and other unannounced products. Executives from DEC's largest customer accounts had to sign nondisclosure agreements before being escorted around the room. "We had to sign in blood," one visitor joked to the *Boston Globe* before revealing what she had seen. Though the successor to VAX was not on hand, the new products demonstrated that engineering had not in fact closed its doors when Bell left.

The biggest challenge for DEC, analysts now believe, is strengthening itself to withstand IBM's inevitable technical and marketing reply. In early 1988, after two years of declining profits that rumbled through the computing industry like thunderclaps, IBM did what DEC has done so often: it reorganized. It is ironic that while DEC was consolidating, IBM followed the opposite course, restructuring into five highly autonomous organizations. As it instituted these changes, IBM furiously worked to overcome the tangle of incompatibility that Bell's VAX strategy had so aggressively exploited.

DEC is banking on its head start. About IBM, Jack Smith says, "They're good and they're big, but one has to realize that you don't do what we did overnight. It took us fifteen years. For them to convert (to our style of computing), if they should so decide, it's going to be extremely difficult. I would not like to have that problem."

Heading into his thirty-first year, Olsen was in firm control. But he would have to go on without his mentor, confidante and longtime friend, Georges Doriot. On June 2, 1987, the General died at age eighty-seven. "His influence and impact on Digital's culture and business philosophies are evident daily," Olsen said. "To us at Digital, the General's influence was cautious and indirect but effective. His analogies between business and cycles of life gave us a better perspective on the pressures that business organizations face. He taught us a sense of responsibility to the entire organization instead of for mere individual gain."

The General's death was not the only setback during 1987. On October 19, the business world reeled as the stock market crashed. DEC had traded as high as $199 per share in August. It skidded to $100 before leveling off. Always a volatile stock, DEC took a hit harder than most. The morning of the crash, Olsen sat down to breakfast worth $445 million; by dinnertime, his value fell to $336 million. But DEC was riding too high for him to worry about his personal finances. According to *Business Week*, Olsen called home to tell his wife the news of

DEC's forty-two-point drop that day. "Don't worry," she said. "We have one row of potatoes left, and we haven't touched the parsnips yet."

As 1988 unfolded, the company continued to roll out more powerful VAXes and flood business publications with press releases about million-dollar purchases by customers. But not surprisingly, the three-year roll suddenly got bumpy. Industry watchers questioned DEC's ability to fend off fast-growing companies such as Sun Microsystems, which was peppering the market with powerful workstations running the Unix operating system. These desktop systems, priced far below DEC's minicomputers, are capable of delivering great power to individual users. "Digital isn't getting weaker," says one Wall Street analyst. "Its competitors are getting stronger." IBM turned up the heat. On June 21, IBM brought together 170,000 people in 200 worldwide locations—its biggest product announcement since the original Personal Computer—to introduce the Application System/400. This long-awaited midrange system tied together two key IBM minicomputers and demonstrated IBM's commitment to correcting past mistakes. The machine's clear target: DEC.

In mid-July DEC countered, driving deeper into IBM's territory by announcing the long-awaited transaction-processing system. The target: airlines, banks, and retailers, which need to update data instantaneously. Though DEC chose New York's Plaza Hotel to launch its most important product of the year, the rollout paled before IBM's lavish AS/400 debut a month earlier. Acknowledging DEC's less flashy staging, Olsen said, "This is a dull announcement; we're not going to kill anybody." Industry watchers, however, insisted that transaction processing is a central weapon in DEC's war against IBM, and as one analyst said, "arguably one of the most significant announcements since the VAX."

Added to the market struggle is Unix, an operating system created, ironically, on a PDP-11 by Bell Labs engineers in the late 1960s. Could Unix, which boasts portability across different machines, be the long sought-after industry standard, and could it mean the end of proprietary operating systems such as

VMS? Olsen was dismayed at what he views as the hyping of Unix as a panacea. "Unix is not designed for general-purpose computing," he says. "It was specifically designed for one-person computing—therefore the name Unix."

When AT&T, Unix's creator and leading proponent, signed a deal with Sun, which urged that their version of the operating system be adopted by everyone as a standard, Olsen lashed out publicly, calling the proposed Unix solution "snake oil." In one of the year's great photo opportunities, Olsen joined IBM's Akers and several other industry leaders on a New York stage in May to announce the formation of a rival group dedicated to a different version of Unix. Thus the lines were drawn, and a long, potentially frustrating battle loomed ahead for disappointed customers hoping for some standard solution. But in one of his not-so-subtle turnabouts, Olsen expanded his "one message" (VAX/VMS) theme to include Unix as a DEC option. And he saw nothing hypocritical in his change of face. He was simply recognizing a key business shift and heading in that direction.

By the third fiscal quarter of 1988, the effects of the stock market crash finally took their toll, and DEC advised financial analysts to lower quarterly earnings estimates. The stock took another beating, dropping nine points in a week. Articles sprouted forecasting the impending decline of the minicomputer industry—the same dire warning repeated off and on for nearly a decade. Wall Street analysts generally maintained high ratings of DEC. "We still think Digital is a high quality growth company, and we recommend the stock," said John L. Rutledge of Dillon, Read & Company in the *New York Times*.

Nonetheless, with the announcement of third-quarter earnings in April 1988, DEC took its first blast from the media in several years. As anticipated, net income dropped from $307 million in the third fiscal quarter of 1987 to $305 million—the first actual dip in profit since 1985. DEC still outpaced most of the industry with a 17 percent increase in sales. But articles in the press started using words such as *poor showing* and *disappointing*. *Business Week* put Olsen on its cover and asked, "What Next for Digital? The Hot Computer Company has

Cooled Off. So Why Isn't DEC's Ken Olsen Worried?" Olsen argued for analysts to measure DEC's growth against any other mature company in any industry. Yet he knew that, as so often before, he would fail to get them to see it his way. Noting that he has been introducing Digital products for thirty years, Olsen said at an April product announcement, "I've never gotten the press at all to understand what I'm saying."

In fact, Olsen was worried. Coming off its industry-shaking year in 1987, DEC had budgeted far more aggressively than most companies for 1988. The stock market crash sent DEC's money managers back to the spread sheets. Budgets for 1989 were frozen, even after the fiscal year began, in order to reach tighter control on costs and spending. At the closed-to-the-press annual state of the company address in May, Jim Oster-hoff summed up Olsen's state of mind: "Ken said to me, 'If we're doing so well, why does it feel so bad?' "

Suddenly the Digital Express was slowing down, and the company faced another test of its mettle. Can quarterly earnings rebound? Can DEC survive Unix, IBM, and Sun? Can Olsen steer his now massive ship back into calm waters? For Olsen, such questions mean little. He knows the press and analysts love to make pronouncements about Digital's health as each quarter's results come in. He takes a far longer perspective. The day after the market crash, he spoke with his brother Stan and wasn't panicked that DEC's stock had plunged forty points. "You can't pay too much attention to that," Olsen said. He was more bothered by the ability of speculators and gamblers to so strongly influence the economy. Olsen had seen DEC's stock bounce crazily over the last five years and knew that his mission was not to watch the daily ticker but to keep the company strong for the long run. There was tomorrow and the next thirty years to worry about.

"The challenge I face today is to have more than 100,000 people working together in one direction and still maintain an entrepreneurial spirit."
                                                    —*Ken Olsen*

37
The Ultimate Entrepreneur

CHRISTMAS 1987. AT the passing of the three-decade mark, the personnel office reflected in a corporate memo on DEC past and future: "The thinking that accounted for our success in the past 30 years will not hold for the next 30. The center of gravity of the company has changed in fundamental and permanent ways. It can be seen everywhere you turn, in products, business, technology and workforce. If those areas are on the same wavelength, some real synergies and efficiencies could result."

The memo expressed the environment of DEC's future:

- In 1988, revenues from foreign operations will exceed those from the United States for the first time.
- By 1993, more employees will work outside the United States than inside.
- DEC has moved from being a hardware equipment company to an applications company, from being a computer company to an information technology company.

307

- Information is no longer hoarded, it is shared. Knowledge is not exclusive, it is inclusive. Expertise is not concentrated, it is dispersed.

- It is a new world with new realities and new rules that call for new thinking.

Digital today has 120,000 employees (the largest employer in Massachusetts and New Hampshire), 33.6 million square feet of space in sixty-two countries, a market value of $23.9 billion (10th among all U.S. companies), 475 sales offices, $11.4 billion in revenues, $1.3 billion in net profits, and is number thirty-eight in the Fortune 500.

Ken Olsen, the presider over all of Digital's past, still steers its future. "When I left MIT thirty years ago to start a business, I'm not sure I could pronounce the word *entrepreneur*," he told the 1987 graduating class at his alma mater. "Today, *entrepreneur* is a hot word. It's a challenging word, a fascinating word. The place of entrepreneurship in our society is obvious. The traditional enterprises do not or are reluctant to try new ideas and new approaches, and to gamble, to risk, to pay the price for competition. It is the place of the entrepreneur to introduce new ideas, new products, and new approaches. Few entrepreneurs survive very long, either because of success or because of failure. But out of many approaches comes good: as with evolution, improvements come with many attempts, better things arrive."

As he steps up the challenge to IBM, as he pushes DEC toward the 1990s, Olsen understands the tightrope that must be walked to stay his course. "The challenge I face today is to have more than 100,000 people working together in one direction and still maintain an entrepreneurial spirit," he said. "The challenge we as a society face is to accomplish that goal in all our organizations. Running a business is not the important thing, but making a commitment to do the whole job, making a commitment to improve things, to influence the world, is the important thing."

Olsen struggles to wear the mantle of achievement—one that he would as soon graciously shed. If he could run his company without the publicity, so much the better.

"Because he is physically a big guy," says Dick Berube, "because his image has grown as the size of the company has grown, some people who have worked closely with him have inadvertently seen him as larger than life. People tend to have very high expectations of him in their relationships. But that's unfair. The best and worst thing you can say about Ken is that he's a human being, like the rest of us."

Olsen still runs DEC through management by chaos, say his employees. Despite the greater focus on "one company, one strategy, one message," the culture of conflict, bargaining, and doing the right thing is still deeply embedded . The matrix lives.

"The problem with chaos is that 10 percent of the people are untrustworthy, evil, self-aggrandizing, ambitious at the expense of the company," says one longtime engineer. "So the question is, how do you keep the chaos from becoming anarchy?"

The singularities of Ken Olsen flare out under scrutiny. He has met every first Tuesday of the month for thirteen years with a group of local businessmen led by Thomas Phillips, president of Raytheon, for a prayer breakfast and spiritual discussions. He is a deacon at the Park Street Church in Boston.

"Ken always acted with moral certainty," observes a former marketing manager. "He knew why God put him here."

Still another ex-employee says, "Ken can represent both the New Testament and the Old Testament. He runs between the two, depending on his mood. Sometimes he's an 'eye for eye, tooth for a tooth' kind of guy, and sometimes he's a 'turn the other cheek' kind. He could rail against people and their lack of loyalty in a very unChristian way."

Those who get close enough to Ken and later leave the chaos that he stirs up at DEC begin to understand what motivates the anger, the table-pounding, the personal attacks. "What people are missing is that when you were in contact with the man and he was showing you that side of him, what he really was saying was, 'I have a problem. I'm trying to share it with you. Why don't you understand that? I'm really being open with you,'" says Julius Marcus. "If you could understand that he was a frustrated guy who was trying to let down his guard and share his innermost feelings, your attitude towards him would be somewhat different. It took me three years since I left there to understand that."

History, as Olsen sees it, is what he makes it. Loyalty is rewarded with a place in Digital's official record. Olsen's feelings about Gordon Bell, for example, reflect his attitude toward the corporate past. Like Ed de Castro and many others who have left, Bell has been relegated to small corners of DEC's history. After he departed, Olsen sent out a memo placing responsibility for the continued development of VAX with a committee headed by Bill Strecker. Thereafter, Strecker's name became publicly linked to the VAX strategy. Bell is described as a supporting player. In the thirtieth-anniversary issue of the company's internal newsletter in December 1987, a long review of the history of VAX mentioned Bell twice. The article credited him merely for setting up a meeting for the original VAX group.

There is kinship among those former executives whom DEC has forgotten. A few ex-vice presidents, including Ted Johnson, John Leng, and Nick Mazzarese, began to meet socially in the summer of 1987. At dinner in Boston's Algonquin Club, they reminisced about the good old days at DEC. It is, as Leng jokes, "an association of tired, fired, and retired executives from Digital."

Peter Kaufmann says that many of the company's current executives cut off relationships with these former vice presidents. "A company that kills off its mythology is doing itself and the people around them a disservice," Kaufmann says. "I don't want their jobs today, but I certainly have a love for the company and a love for Ken. They could have some respect for who I am and who I was, and what I did."

Olsen is undeterred by sentiment. DEC history for him is today and tomorrow. There is no time to place halos on departed heroes. IBM is out there working on its plan to beat DEC back. So he presses on.

"Success is probably the worst problem for an entrepreneur," he says. "As people get to be successful, they tend to stop learning. If you're too successful, you can delegate the learning to someone else, and suddenly you find you can't run the business." And therein lies the key to Olsen's longevity. Despite stubborn adherence to tradition or blind dismissal of an idea at times, he never stops learning. Despite occasional hard-hearted turns, he has remained humble enough to admit that others know more. He surrounds himself with these others, and together they drive DEC.

As he pushes further into his sixties, Olsen's energy level seems to increase. He is in firm control with no interest in retiring. He used to tell people that he would give up the reins of DEC at age sixty-five—in 1991. But that was when he was fifty. Now edging close to sixty-five, he simply says that he is too young and healthy to worry about such things as retirement or succession and then changes the subject. He confides to a few that he has planned for his succession, but that is all he says to even his top executives.

Who will take over from Olsen? Clearly, DEC's tradition—his tradition— requires that he choose a president from inside the company. Shields, Smith, and Hindle were promoted to senior vice presidents in the summer of 1986. Olsen played down the significance of this move. "Just overdue promotions," he said.

The threesome assumed similar stances. "We don't think about it that much," says Smith. "We have no mandatory retirement age, and Ken is going to be around for a while. It's never discussed at board meetings."

Hindle, quiet and efficient, is apparently out of the running since giving up much of his corporate responsibilities in mid-1987. He remains the consummate loyal right-hand man. About taking the top spot, he says, "I've never thought about it because Ken has always seemed like he's going to be going on here forever."

Smith certainly aspires to the job, but it is Shields, the youngest at forty-nine and the most aggressive, who has the inside track. "I keep my options open, as I'm sure Ken does," Shields says. "I've got plenty of time."

Most DEC watchers believe that if DEC is going to make its

next milestone—double in size to $20 billion in annual reve-
nues—it will take someone with Shields's marketing and sales
savvy to drive the company. "He's going to go a long way,"
says analyst Stephen Smith. "He's the logical choice."

Others who have climbed up to the rung below Olsen
believe that Shields's very success will be his undermining. He
may soon fall into the pattern of DEC history: Olsen does not
allow anyone to grow too strong or independent under him.

"It's interesting," says Kaufmann, "that neither of the top
two guys after Ken are college graduates. There's nothing
wrong with not having gone to college. But you wouldn't call
either of them real visionaries." That is a label that Olsen
shuns himself. "I like to think of myself as a professional
manager, quite different from a visionary. I was not a visionary," he says. "I was a leader who knows where people are
going and gets out in front of them."

As he has done in all other important matters at DEC, Olsen
will orchestrate his own succession. He will not place the seal
of command on anyone before he is ready to step aside.

DEC without Olsen is difficult to contemplate. Like the
Watsons at IBM, Olsen's spirit will pervade the company long
after he is gone. His presence is so dominating, so ubiquitous
that the question, What will it be like when Ken is gone?
seems to have no answer.

Ken is aka Digital. He is the roots of the company. Without
him, the very personality of DEC will have to change. DEC
will shift gradually to a more mainstream corporate attitude
and lose the folksiness and individuality that Olsen brings to
the Mill. Certainly his demanding presence and sharp engineer's eye on DEC's products will be missed. "If I ever wrote a
book," he recently told *Business Week*, "it would be a list of
things I said 'No' to."

"To say that a company won't be different after somebody
like that leaves doesn't make much sense," Shields says. "Of
course things will be different. Will they be a lot different? I
doubt it, because companies tend to take on a character, an
existence, and a culture that is very much reflected by its
leaders. A lot of the fundamentals will be the same."

Shields believes that Olsen will go down in American corporate history as the industrialist of the century. Unlike the laissez-faire environment that spawned the empires of Henry Ford and Tom Watson, Sr., Olsen created his entrepeneurial masterpiece in an age of heavy governmental regulation. But whatever he has built so far, he knows that the next Digital— the one without Ken Olsen—will be his true measure. "The final picture of success," he says, "is how well the company does after you're gone."

Appendix I
The People

Harlan Anderson   Cofounder of DEC. Came from Lincoln Lab with Ken Olsen to start DEC in 1957. Left in 1966. Was vice president at the time.

C. Gordon Bell   Joined DEC from MIT in 1960 as second computer engineer. Masterminded virtually all DEC computers including the PDP-4, PDP-5, PDP-6, and PDP-8 before leaving for sabbatical at Carnegie-Mellon in 1966. Returned as vice president of engineering in 1972 and oversaw the design of the PDP-11 and DEC's VAX line of computers. Left DEC in 1983.

Dick Berube   Joined DEC in 1973 from CBS. Served as Ken Olsen's public relations chief until 1987 when he left the company.

Dennis Burke   Joined DEC in 1969 to consult on personnel matters. Former priest, he became director of personnel until 1976 when he left the company. Member of the Operations Committee.

Henry Burkhardt   Joined DEC in 1965 at age nineteen. Was an engineer on the ill-fated PDP-X project. Left with Ed de Castro to start Data General.

Edson de Castro   Joined DEC in 1960 as employee number 100. Was the engineer who implemented design of PDP-5 and PDP-8. Left DEC in 1968 to cofound rival Data General.

General Georges Doriot   President of ARD. Associated with DEC as advisor to Olsen from 1957 to 1972. In 1972, joined DEC's board of directors until his death in 1987.

Barry James Folsom   Joined DEC in 1980 and headed the Rainbow effort, the back-up personal computer project. Left in 1985.

Jay Forrester   Dynamic scientist and engineer who led the Whirlwind and SAGE projects at MIT's Lincoln Lab in the 1950s. Joined DEC's board of directors in late 1950s and advised the company on business models for success. He left the board in 1966.

Ben Gurley   Joined DEC in 1959 as first computer engineer. Designed and built the company's first computer, the PDP-1. Left DEC in 1963.

Win Hindle   Joined DEC as assistant to Olsen in 1962. Ran PDP-10 product line and rose to position of senior vice president in 1986. Still with the company, he is Olsen's right hand man and member of the Executive Committee.

Ted Johnson   Joined DEC as first salesman in 1958. Head of worldwide sales and service until 1980. Left the company in 1982. Member of the Operations Committee.

Jeff Kalb   Joined DEC in 1981 to work in the semiconductor group. He moved into DEC's low-end development area in 1984 and tried to formulate the company's product development there. He left the company in 1987.

Peter Kaufmann   Joined DEC as head of manufacturing in 1966. Was vice president of manufacturing until he left in 1977. Member of the Operations Committee.

Andy Knowles   Joined DEC in 1969 to head the PDP-11 effort. A hard-driving veteran from RCA, Knowles was a vice president and member of the Operations Committee. He served in various high-level functions including head of the low end until he left in 1983.

John Leng   Joined DEC in 1963 and started DEC's overseas office in the United Kingdom. He later became a vice president and ran DEC's DEC10/20 large system line until he left the company in 1979.

Julius Marcus   Joined DEC in 1969 and helped build DEC's commercial markets working under Stan Olsen. Created DEC's office strategy that helped propel tremendous growth in the 1980s. Left in 1984.

Nick Mazzarese   Joined DEC in 1962. Became product-line manager of the PDP-5 and then vice president in charge of small systems. Left the company in 1972. Member of the Operations Committee.

Avram Miller   Joined DEC in 1979 and as a young and talented engineer, quickly took on the KO project, the company's primary personal computer effort. Left DEC in 1983.

Stanley Olsen   Ken Olsen's younger brother. Joined DEC as first employee in August 1957. Stayed until 1981. Was vice president in charge of DEC's commercial markets when he left. Member of the Operations Committee.

Edgar Schein   Sloan Fellows Professor of Management at the Sloan School of Management at MIT. He is also an organizational development consultant who has worked with Olsen and DEC since the early 1960s.

Jack Shields   Joined DEC in the fledgling service organization in 1961. Hard-driving and innovative, Shields rose through the ranks to senior vice president of sales and service in 1986. Still with company and considered the strongest of possible candidates to succeed Olsen. Member of the Executive Committee.

John Sims   Joined DEC from AT&T in 1974 as employee equal opportunity administrator and rose to his current position as vice president and member of the Executive Committee.

Jack Smith   Joined DEC as employee number twelve in 1958. Helped create the manufacturing function and rose through the ranks to senior vice president of engineering and manufacturing in 1986. Still with the company and considered one of the possible successors to Olsen. Member of the Executive Committee.

Appendix II
The Machines

Programmed Data Processor (PDP)-1 Unveiled in 1959 as DEC's first computer. It featured a cathode-ray tube and keyboard, making it the first commercially available, interactive, general-purpose computer. Priced at $120,000, fifty-three of these 18-bit computers were sold.

PDP-4 This 18-bit follow-on to the PDP-1 was released in 1962 at a price of $65,000. Bell, who designed the machine, felt that by offering a computer half the size of its forerunner, DEC would have a winner. The market didn't oblige and only forty-five PDP-4s were sold. DEC did go on to build several more 18-bit computers, including the PDP-7, PDP-9, and PDP-15.

PDP-5 Small, general-purpose 12-bit computer introduced in 1963. Created by Gordon Bell and designed by Edson de Castro as a front-end to a PDP-4 being used by Atomic Energy of Canada. DEC intended to build ten machines to cover the cost of engineering, but with a low price tag of $27,000, the PDP-5 was a surprise hit. The company eventually sold close to 1,000 machines.

PDP-6 DEC's first large system, this $300,000 computer was introduced in 1964 but led a short, troubled life. The lowest-selling of all DEC computers (only twenty-three were shipped), the PDP-6 introduced the concept of time-sharing but was simply too big a machine for the company to produce at the time. It was killed soon after its release. Based on a 36-bit architecture, the PDP-6 was created by Bell and given to Harlan Anderson, DEC's cofounder, to oversee. The machine was at the center of the controversy which resulted in Anderson leaving DEC in 1966.

PDP-8 The computer that triggered the minicomputer industry, the 12-bit PDP-8 was also created by Bell and designed by de Castro. Priced at an unheard-of $18,000 and introduced in 1965, the PDP-8 carried DEC from a small, unknown technical company into the ranks of the major computer makers. Eventually, more than 50,000 PDP-8s were sold and many are still in use today.

PDP-X Code name for follow-on machine to the PDP-8. This machine, intended to carry DEC into the emerging 16-bit world, was created by de Castro, Henry Burkhardt, and Dick Sogge in 1967. An overly ambitious and complex design, along with internal political problems, caused the demise of the PDP-X and the departure of de Castro while the machine was still on paper.

PDP-10 The 36-bit follow-on to the defunct PDP-6, the PDP-10 was introduced in 1967. The engineering group that had created the PDP-6 pushed hard to resurrect DEC's large-scale system. The PDP-10 went on to have a long life and was revered as the computer of choice by a small but dedicated group of users. The PDP-10 and its follow-ons Decsystem-10 (1970) and Decsystem-20 (1974), were phased out in 1983 despite the anguished pleas from DEC's user base to keep them alive.

PDP-11   Introduced in 1970, this 16-bit computer sold for $10,800 and reaffirmed DEC's status as the top minicomputer maker in the world. Bell had a major hand in conceptualizing the machine even though he was on sabbatical at Carnegie-Mellon University at the time. Andy Knowles was recruited from RCA to lead the PDP-11 project. This machine and its myriad follow-on models models sold 250,000 units.

VAX/VMS   Unveiled in 1977, DEC's 32-bit VAX line and its operating system were conceived by Bell and implemented by Bill Demmer, Larry Portner, and Bill Strecker. VAX (which stands for *Virtual Address Extension*), was a breakthrough architecture that allowed DEC to create a family of computers that could grow expansively into the 1990s. The machine became the cornerstone of Bell's VAX strategy, a combination of computers and networking that fueled tremendous growth for DEC in the 1980s.

VT100   A computer terminal introduced in 1978, the VT100's elegant styling and design drove it to become an industry standard. It was followed by VT200 and VT300 terminals.

Personal computers   Professional 325 and 350, Rainbow 100, and Decmate II. This trio of personal computers was introduced simultaneously in 1982 and created chaos and confusion at the low end for DEC. The Pro, which was code-named KO, was supposed to be the company's primary personal computer. But lateness to market and a dearth of application software caused it to sell far below expectations. The other two machines fared little better, and DEC was widely criticized for failing to provide a solution at the PC level.

Microvax   Introduced in 1983, this machine brought the VAX architecture down to the workstation level and created a wide ranging top-to-bottom line of VAX machines for DEC customers to build upon.

VAXmate Another attempt at a personal computer, the VAXmate was introduced quietly in 1986 and offered many networking features, plus IBM PC-compatibility—which DEC's first three PCs lacked. But DEC was unable to unseat the ubiquitous IBM PC in customer accounts and persuade new customers to buy this machine.

Index